Interactive Play for Children with Autism

Diana Seach

Routledge
Taylor & Francis Group

LONDON AND NEW YORK

First published 2007
by Routledge
2 Park Square, Milton Park, Abingdon, Oxon OX14 4RN

Simultaneously published in the USA and Canada
by Routledge
270 Madison Ave, New York, NY 10016

Routledge is an imprint of the Taylor & Francis Group, an informa business

© 2007 Diana Seach

Typeset in Garamond by
Prepress Projects Ltd, Perth
Printed and bound in Great Britain by
TJ International, Padstow, Cornwall

Every effort has been made to ensure that the advice and information
in this book is true and accurate at the time of going to press. However,
neither the publisher nor the authors can accept any legal responsibility
or liability for any errors or omissions that may be made. In the case
of drug administration, any medical procedure or the use of technical
equipment mentioned within this book, you are strongly advised to
consult the manufacturer's guidelines.

British Library Cataloguing in Publication Data
A catalogue record for this book is available from the British Library

Library of Congress Cataloging in Publication Data
A catalog record has been requested for this book

ISBN10: 0-415-35373-4 (hbk)
ISBN10: 0-415-33326-1 (pbk)
ISBN10: 0-203-41293-1 (ebk)
ISBN13: 978-0-415-35373-1 (hbk)
ISBN13: 978-0-415-33326-1 (pbk)
ISBN13: 978-0-203-41293-0 (ebk)

Interactive Play for Children with Autism

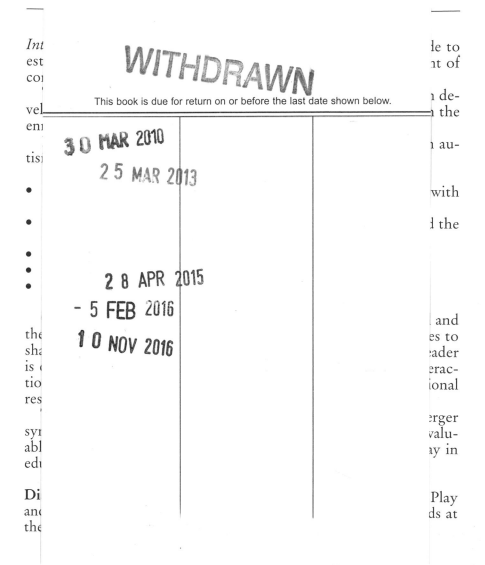

This book is dedicated to my family – my parents, Laura, Emma and Jasper. Thank you for being so special.

Contents

Figures

Acknowledgements

I am grateful to all the wonderful families and children with whom I have spent time over the years and who have inspired my work. My thanks also go to my friends and colleagues at the University of Chichester who have assisted with editing the chapters. My very special thanks go to Wendy Lawson for recognizing the value of my work and writing the Foreword, Tito Rajarshi Mukhopadhyay and his mother for kind permission to reprint one of his poems, to Carly Hatton (www.carlysart.com) for her cover artwork, and to the staff and pupils of Phoenix School for initiating the Interactive Play project.

Foreword

Play and children usually go together. The words 'play' and 'children with autism', however, may not. It is precisely for this reason that this book explores the role of interactive play especially for children with autism. It assists us in developing strategies for connecting with the child, sharing communication and exploring meanings through play and developing imagination. More than just explaining how play is a prelude to understanding, this book shows how to unlock the mysteries of the social world as adults interact with children through the medium of 'child-centred' play.

Shared understanding of the social world requires the following:

- awareness of others;
- a desire to belong, be part of, or to share with others;
- an understanding of how others are likely to behave or respond.

One of the ways children acquire the above is through the medium of play. For example, babies coo and smile when playing peek-a-boo and small children usually enjoy the attention of others who want to join in with their play. In a group of people, children often seek each other out and play together. Recently, in a doctor's waiting room, I noticed how a toddler sought out another child and together they seemed to engage in mutual admiration. They then joined one another at a kiddies' table and played with a toy bead counter. Although their shared play did not last long, it was a great attempt to get along.

When we understand that autism is a developmental delay and our children with autism often behave much younger than their chronological age, we may be part way to understanding the way in which they play. To be part of a game and play with other children is usually an exciting venture. Being able to share attention and focus upon a variety of things is something most individuals take for granted. For most children with autism play just moves too fast and their attention cannot keep up with it.

As a child growing up in a world that was full of confusion and sensory overload I, like many other children with autism, found playing with other children either boring, overdemanding or just plain terrifying! I did not understand most of the games that children played, nor did I see the reason behind them. Sand and water intrigued me but I only played with them as sand and water. They did not become roadways, castles, tunnels, rivers or volcanoes! I enjoyed solitary games that were under my control and I could play at a pace that suited me. Maybe if the rules of the game had been explained to me, maybe if the process of discovery had been presented in a non-threatening way, could I too have found other imagined roles for sand and water?

This book outlines how to get around those difficulties through interactive play. With a theoretical understanding of play and interaction, and with numerous examples, the author makes play available to our children. Children with autism need all the support they can get in understanding the world we are all part of and this includes the world of play. The author has taken the importance of interactive play and guides the parent and professional in strategies for setting up play sessions, the play environment both at home and in school, and activities to develop play. When we understand how crucial play is for developing an awareness of ourselves and interacting with others, we recognize how important this book is as another tool in our inventory of practical approaches.

The possibility of positive outcomes for children with autism will be enhanced as they develop their communication and social understanding. There is no better way to do this than by reducing fear, increasing fun and making interaction accessible through play. This book outlines clearly, effectively and systematically, how to do just that.

> My future may not depend on my stock,
> So much as it does upon sources.
> Sources of warmth, sources of care
> I depend on the nurture to be for me there.
> Then I can blossom and sing with the birds,
> Then I can grow my potential.
> So plant me in goodness and all that is fine,
> Please keep the intruders away.
> Give me a chance to develop, in time,
> To become who I am, in life's future, one day!
>   (Lawson 2003: reprinted by kind permission)

Wendy Lawson BSS BSW(Hons) GDip(PsychStud) GDip(Psych)

Preface

'Play develops creativity, intellectual competence, emotional strength and stability and feelings of joy and pleasure. The habit of being happy' (Piers and Landau 1980: 42–3). This quote comes for a book entitled *The Gift of Play and Why Children Cannot Thrive Without It*. It is a valuable reminder that play does not need to be defined as a set of behaviours but is linked to a process that captures the essence of a known experience. Play is a creative act that enables individuals to learn to think and behave with increasing complexity and flexibility, giving them confidence and a sense of achievement. Through their spontaneous interactions, children discover unique and innovative ways to respond to their environment, which need to be valued and understood by those who are nurturing and supporting their development. It is only when children begin to feel validated in their actions that they can begin to grow. All children need opportunities to explore and interact with their environment with enjoyment and playfulness, otherwise they will become limited in their ability to respond to the challenges and life experiences available to them. For children with autism it is vital that they are able to experience the joy of play that is not dependent on fixed activities but is about discovering new and exciting ways of being with others. By offering children the gift of play we too can discover how it can change our understanding of their inner life.

Most interactive approaches have tended to refer to joining in the child's world to gain an understanding of it from his or her perspective. Rather than emphasize different worlds, the focus of interactive play for children with autism is to discover how to create a world together. A world that firmly places play at the core of relationship-building and emotional well-being. For children to become more playful they need someone to play with, to develop empathy they need someone to empathize with them and to improve their communication skills they need someone who understands how to communicate with them. The establishment of these mutually enjoyable experiences leads to an 'openness to affective states' that will have a profound impact on the development of cognition and social interaction (Russ 1993).

This book provides much needed insight into the cognitive and affective processes that are embedded within an interactive play approach. Play is a dynamic experience that encourages resourcefulness, resilience and reciprocity, and parents and professionals need to recognize how essential these qualities are in helping children to gain knowledge and understanding of the world. Children rarely use play to consciously manifest a particular skill and therefore it is not always helpful to interpret their play purely in relation to their cognitive abilities.

For children who have autism, play is often presented as a skill to be learned rather than an experience to be shared and enjoyed. As a consequence they may not be given the same play opportunities that enable them to express themselves or gain mastery over their thoughts and experiences. One of the difficulties in determining the role that play has in children's development is that parents and professionals often see it as having a different purpose. Parents may want their children to find ways to occupy themselves or take part in play activities with their siblings and peers, whereas professionals tend to focus on the provision of play activities through which children can learn specific skills. Although both concepts are valid, they have created a dichotomy for some parents who may feel under pressure to play differently with their children at home, whereas those professionals wanting to use more playful and creative approaches to work with children might feel constrained by external requirements and attitudes towards the use of play in schools and the local community. Children, on the other hand, do not make these distinctions and therefore it is important to recognize that their reasons for using a certain type of play need to be understood in terms of its relevance to the individual.

A primary process in children's earliest play experiences is the playful way in which they establish interaction with objects and other people. This play involves the creation of a series of interconnecting actions and emotions, which, together, will impact on their learning potential. Playfulness describes the way in which children are able to make links between affect and creativity, giving meaning to their actions and allowing them to express their unique personalities in ways that are characteristic of all human behaviour. It also adds a dimension to the experience that can often be overlooked when functional play skills are deemed to be more relevant to children's cognitive development.

The natural approach to play discussed in this book is based on the central principle that playfulness and interaction will have a major influence on the development of communication, social competence and cognitive functioning. Although Chapter 1 begins with a focus on the developmental need for play, there is also an acknowledgement of how the child's perspective determines the value of the play experience, particularly if he or she has autism. Rather than discuss differences in play, this chapter ensures that play is regarded as the primary method through which all children spontaneously learn about themselves and their surroundings.

The cognitive and affective processes that underpin the development of social communication are described in Chapter 2 within a model of interactive play. This model offers an integrated approach to the developmental needs of children and firmly identifies the adult's role within this process. It is a model that can be applied to a range of psychological, therapeutic and educational practices, particularly those that recognize how the establishment of positive interactive states will have a core influence on children's cognitive and emotional growth. The model also acts as the foundation for the interactive play strategies that are described in the remaining chapters of the book. The key principles and practices are characterized by the presence of a loving and supportive relationship that is based on the need to:

- establish an emotional connection;
- enhance the flow of communication;
- create meaning from the experience;
- discover imaginative and creative potential.

Establishing a connection, enabling communication, creating meaning and developing imagination are discussed separately but each of these chapters interrelates to provide a holistic perspective on children's developmental play needs. Through the examples presented they identify strategies that focus on the repair and development of and emotional responsiveness and how this will impact on children's learning and cognition. When children are able to internalize these experiences, the capacity for symbolic communication and representational thought is enhanced.

It is through a commitment to these developmental principles that those who live and work with children who have autism come to recognize how such experiences will help to 'transform the child's availability to human companionship and shared experience' (Trevarthen *et al.* 1998). Chapter 7 focuses specifically on working with families. Interactive play is used within the home-based s m i l e programme to assist in the establishment of mutually enjoyable activities that are based on patterns of early attachment within family. Unlike many interventions that focus on the child with autism, the s m i l e programme is a family-focused intervention that takes account of the system in which the child with autism is nurtured and cared for. The need for sensitivity, empathy and positive regard towards the family is key to how the strategies for developing interactive play are implemented. Parents and carers are seen as major contributors in planning and maintaining the activities that are devised to empower and enrich the relationships that exist within a loving and supportive family context.

Having been a teacher for many years it is appropriate that I acknowledge the importance of learning through play and show how an interactive play approach can be used in different educational settings to support children's access to the curriculum. In maintaining the discussion on the principles of interactive play, the focus in this final chapter is not on learning play skills but how the experience of play enables children to gain increasing confidence in, and understanding of, the skills that will aid their learning. This ensures that playfulness, developing an awareness of self and others, and discovering new ways of thinking and behaving remain at the core of educational and therapeutic practices. It is through the use of play and the creative arts in schools that children with autism will have greater opportunities to participate in, and contribute to, their wider social community; a community where people are able to acknowledge their shared interests and develop an understanding of the different ways in which the world can be perceived.

I would not like the reader to think that this book is only about working with children within a certain age range, in other words young children who we typically assume will spend most of their time engaged in playful exploration before more formal learning experiences are introduced. For many individuals with autism who do not have the independence to create their own leisure time it will always be important that they have people around them who want to share their interests, give them new experiences and enjoy their company. This is the way in which relationships develop, alter and grow and are an essential feature of our lives. In addition to the many descriptions of playing with children, there are several examples of my work with older children, teenagers and young adults that reinforce the value of having fun and the enjoyment of being with others.

This interactive play approach follows a developmental social–pragmatic model of intervention that bridges the gap between educational and therapeutic practices by emphasizing the growth of social communication through mediated learning. This model recognizes how the motivation for social exchange is developed via the establishment of a warm interactive relationship, the responsiveness of the play partner and increased engagement by the individual (Mahoney and Powell 1988). *Interactive Play for Children with Autism* should be seen as one among many approaches that offer an unconditional valuing of the child and ways to support his or her developmental and psychological needs. If there is an innate drive to unify experiences through play then it must be regarded as one of the most potent of behaviours to influence patterns of human development.

Chapter 1

Valuing play

For children, play is an expression of their unique interaction with the world. Their playful engagement with objects and activities enables them to establish a dialogue with all that they encounter, creating experiences that promote their emotional well-being, transforming their knowledge and establishing a sense of belonging to a particular social and cultural group. Play emerges through a vast array of relationships and experiences that are defined by the quality of the interactions with significant people and places in the child's life. This is because play development for all children relies on others to both facilitate and support their play experiences. In these defining attributes are the foundations of human development.

Cognitive developmental theories have dominated much of the literature on play and as such they have considerably influenced attitudes towards the value of play in children's development (Wood and Attfield 1996; Sutton-Smith 1997; Wolfberg 1999). This perspective has also influenced interpretations of play and its functions and has tended to ignore some of the intrinsic elements of human adaptability and emotional dependency that the act of playing provides. An inevitable consequence of this is the notion of play deficits in children with impaired cognitive development. This can undermine the quality of the experience for the individual and result in further deprivations in both play and development. By removing the concept of a deficit in play, it becomes easier to identify how and why the individual uses play to seek out ways to interact with his or her environment. Play should not only be defined in terms of its extrinsic functions and the effects on knowledge acquisition and socialization as this does not fully support a discussion on the benefits of play. A more detailed perspective is one that incorporates and gives as much importance to the intrinsic functions that focus on the development of the self, identity and emotion through the individualization of the experience.

Whether a child is playing alone or with others, with or without objects, play represents an attempt to gain mastery over an experience that has particular significance to him or her. Even if a child is not playing with an object representationally, it remains true that it provides a symbolic function. This occurs because the child is absorbed in a playful activity that is pleasurable, engaging, motivating and active. It is through the manipulation and use of objects and the way in which this allows for shifts between reality and fantasy that children will transfer their feelings and symbolize how they want to respond to their environment. For the child, the content and outcome of play is always based on the intrinsic value of the experience and the way in which it is interpreted and processed. This is particularly relevant in terms of how others interpret and assess children's play potential.

When implementing play approaches for children with autism it is vital to consider why they need to play, and how their play is regarded developmentally as being both intentional and purposeful as they actively explore ways to learn about the world. By looking into the play of children with autism, rather than just at it, it is possible to recognize the immense value and effect that playing has on their lives.

The role of play in development

Most literature on the subject of play concludes that it is impossible to identify how play can have discrete influences on children's emotional, cognitive and social development and that what is required is a holistic approach to play and development. Jennings (1999) expresses some concern over particular theoretical orientations towards the role of play in children's development. She emphasizes that much scientific research and interpretation can in fact limit our understanding and views of play. As much of the literature and research on play in children with autism has focused on the deficits in play behaviours, this perspective can be supported to some extent; rather than view the play of children with autism from a developmental paradigm, its use has often been limited to the teaching of specific social or cognitive skills. However, one of the possible outcomes of teaching social skills through play training is that social development may continue to be impeded because of the lack of spontaneity and affective engagement. More importantly, children need to satisfy their own drive to explore the world through play supported by a wide variety of play experiences made available to them by their main carers. It therefore becomes more beneficial to focus on the observable progression within a play activity to identify its effects on development.

Vygotsky (1978) believed that play is not only significant in reflecting development but also in leading it and his theories have been influential in promoting the importance of play as a vehicle for social interaction. Vygotsky's view was that play was vital in mediating cognitive growth but the potential for this only occurs when there is an adult facilitating the child's learning experience. It is the interplay of the contextual nature of the play, the child's disposition and the role of the play partner that will significantly affect the development of social understanding and social behaviour. Thus a child who remains isolated from such experiences will not gain the knowledge required for establishing social relationships. In order to acquire these social competencies, children need play experiences that take place within a social context. Children do not develop in isolation, nor through manipulation, but through interaction. 'Play is in advance of development, for in this manner children begin to acquire the motivation, skills and attitudes necessary for their social participation, which can be fully achieved only with the assistance of their peers and elders' (John-Steiner and Souberman, cited in Vygotsky 1978: 129).

For the young infant, interaction with a primary caregiver is their first experience of social play. Throughout these exchanges there is constant encouragement for the child to develop independent actions and thoughts. The caregiver provides assistance as and when it seems appropriate so that the child is gradually being prepared psychologically and socially for their future independence. Vygotsky's developmental model of play recognized that such play is also vital in helping children to self-regulate their emotions. Children learn to remain a part of the play scenario because it appears intrinsically motivating to do so. He observed that children's ability for self-regulation and their social behaviour during play is frequently more evident than in other socially demanding or non-play situations. I have often observed that when the focus of the play between the child and a play partner is one of mutual engagement, such as 'rough and tumble' play, chasing or bouncing on a trampoline, the child with autism displays significantly more skills in social interaction and emotional reciprocity than at other times. As Jordan (2003: 351) writes: 'Such play is the context for learning about intimacy, trust, negotiation and compromise, concepts and skills that are vital to forming and maintaining friendships.'

The origins of self and identity are also rooted in the emotional states that are created by the young infant's innate ability and his or her interaction with people and the environment. When they are playing with another person, children are involved in an activity in which they learn to experience a wide range of emotions that help in regulating both social and cognitive behaviour. According to Thompson (1991) it is the child's emotion that guides and motivates the adaptive mental processes. It is important to make a distinction between the emotions that a child might be experiencing as a result of playing and what he or she understands as an emotion. Play for the child can be an exciting, absorbing experience or it can become frustrating and challenging, but within the context of play, the child is learning to develop an awareness of his or her own emotional competence. It is through the interaction with a caregiver that the child's emotional expressions are not only supported but also mirrored, and this is a vital component in the development of social understanding. In the same way, the development of an empathetic relationship is crucial in helping the child to feel secure and develop confidence. The child can then make use of past experiences to accommodate incoming information more effectively.

Cognitive theories have emphasized that human developmental potential involves a much more complex interplay of experiences, which may or may not occur through play but nonetheless will have a profound effect at critical periods in a child's life. Piaget (1962) attempted to link his developmental stages of early childhood and brain maturation to developments in play. He saw play as a behaviour that emerges as a result of combining skills, knowledge and understanding to create a learning experience, and this perspective has come to influence much of the practice in current early childhood education. It is, however, an oversimplification to link play and cognitive development as Piaget did, particularly in relation to the identification of types of play. Many of these stages of play exist through to adulthood and can occur at different levels of complexity across the lifespan. Because play is predominantly social in origin, the infant can be observed engaging in rule-governed play at a much younger age than was previously assumed. Even with a game of peek-a-boo the child soon learns that there is a rule to the play with another person. Whatever the nature of the play, it should not be dependent upon a set of age-related criteria, as what may be considered as appropriate play for a young child may still be an enjoyable activity for an adult; for example, building sandcastles on the beach. Play is not a stage that we have to go through to reach adulthood, but is a continuing feature of how we have fun, make discoveries, take risks and accept challenges throughout our lives.

The notion of developmental stages in play can also affect interpretations of what is or is not play behaviour and can result in some play being disregarded as lacking in quality and purpose. Observations of children with autism playing frequently reveal skills in perseveration, experimentation, memory and concept formation, which are all aspects of cognitive development. Variations in perceptual understanding, motor control and pro-active responses have as much to do with individual differences in development as the extent to which relevant experiences are presented to the child to practise these skills.

Piaget's theory of play development linked to cognitive growth only relates to skill acquisition and takes little account of the creative and affective nature of the play. It is inappropriate to regard children's play merely in terms of a behaviour linked to a set of intellectual competencies when what is being communicated at an emotional level may give us more of a clue to the progress a child is making. For children with autism, and indeed adults, it is crucial to interpret play in terms of its relevance for the individual, how it is sustaining his or her interest, what emotions are being expressed and whether it is process led or goal directed.

Play potential

Landreth (2001) emphasizes the fundamental qualities that exist when children engage in activities that support their developmental needs. In recognizing the importance of play in development this implies that all children, regardless of their abilities, need to play.

> Play is an integral part of childhood, a unique medium that facilitates development, social skills, decision making skills and cognitive development in children. Play is also a medium for exploration and discovery of interpersonal relationships, experimentation with adult roles, and understanding of one's own feelings. Play is the most complete form of self expression developed by the human organism.
>
> (Landreth 2001: 4)

Children's potential in play has to be recognized and encouraged by those adults who have a responsibility for their well-being and development. Young infants show a strong desire to be active and explore the environment and will make use of whatever means are available to them. Although play becomes the most effective method by which to achieve this, there may be difficulties in defining what that play is. Some children will resort to engaging in activities in ways that others may consider inappropriate or have little value, whereas some children do not necessarily seek out others to play with them. Children who are given limited access to toys, objects or physical contact, or who do not receive sufficient attention from others, will find ways to occupy themselves that are frequently referred to as self-stimulating or reactive behaviours, such as rocking, screaming, tearing, emptying and destroying. Similarly, some children may be so overwhelmed with too many toys and from not knowing what to do that they withdraw and then appear not to be able to play. This may lead some to suggest that children either cannot or will not play.

As Greenspan and Wieder (1998) state, so often children with special needs are not given appropriate opportunities to play because more functional activities are deemed more relevant for the child to learn. Consequently, they can miss out on play experiences, particularly those that form the basis for developing communication and establishing relationships. Educational establishments and some early intervention programmes for children with autism need to be particularly sensitive to placing too many expectations on a child who, developmentally, is not ready for a more formal approach to learning. When learning is predominantly controlled by adults there is a risk that opportunities for self-directed learning are limited to those times when the child is left alone to 'occupy herself'. In these circumstances the child is less likely to engage in spontaneous interaction and may show only a limited response to new and stimulating experiences. To bring about changes in the child's functioning and behaviour it is important to establish more opportunities for interaction that are child led and match the level at which he or she is functioning. It is essential for growth that children:

- gain *experience* that is relevant to them;
- learn through activities that *challenge* them;
- develop *skills* that support their development;
- are given an opportunity to have a *choice*;
- recognize how to manage *change*.

While it is important to acknowledge that children should be given a variety of experiences which enable them to respond in ways that are uniquely individual, play also provides a highly supportive framework in which this can be achieved. Sutton-Smith (1997: 225) describes play as having a role in the 'actualization of brain potential'. For many children with autism, their potential for play is contingent upon the extent to which adults provide the appropriate opportunities and resources to enhance their play experiences. The role of the adult in schools and at home is vital not only in planning and resourcing opportunities for play, but also in the active engagement that they have with the child in their play. The adult needs to take on the role of being not only a play provider, but also a play partner so that when the child's play is spontaneous and engaging, it provides an opportunity for the adult to interact with the child, to create meaning and support both learning and development. It is through a more dynamic approach to children's learning and play that their potential can be realized.

Learning through play

In 2002, the National Foundation for Educational Research (NFER) commissioned research on international perspectives in Early Years Education. All of the twenty countries involved in the study acknowledged that play has a major role in the holistic development and wellbeing of children and, as it is the most significant occupation of early childhood, undoubtedly, all children will learn through it. One of the outcomes of the study was the recognition that there needs to be an important balance between learning through child-initiated play activities and play that is directed by adults.

Too much emphasis on adult-directed approaches to learning may limit children's opportunities to be more spontaneous and explore their own learning potential through play. As shown in Figure 1.1, for effective learning to take place a balance between adult-led teaching and child-initiated activities is paramount. Although this is not likely to be achieved solely through play, it does, however, provide a framework for planning quality learning experiences. The components identified in both child-initiated and adult-led activities are not exclusive. They are interchangeable and, to some extent, interdependent, as it is ultimately the responsibility of the adult to ensure that children have access to a variety of learning experiences. Moyles (1989) describes this as a 'play spiral' in which directed play by the adult is channelled through children's spontaneous or free play. The potential for learning is thus more effective than when it is based solely on structured teaching. Bruner (1966) refers to the adult's role as one of scaffolding children's learning and development, thus ensuring greater potential in the child's ability to engage in social learning.

Structuring children's play has become an essential aspect of early childhood education. It has also led to much debate about what constitutes an effective intervention for the delivery and content of children's learning experiences and the assumption that children are only learning through play when it is structured. Within an educational

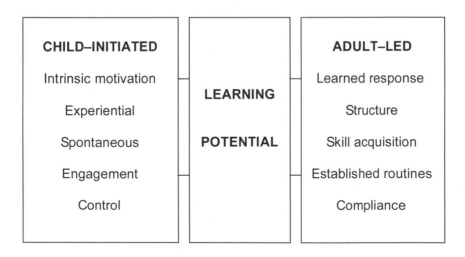

CHILD–INITIATED		ADULT–LED
Intrinsic motivation	**LEARNING**	Learned response
Experiential		Structure
Spontaneous	**POTENTIAL**	Skill acquisition
Engagement		Established routines
Control		Compliance

Figure 1.1 Effective learning.

context, play is always seen as structured as it is dependent upon the adults and the resources they provide to facilitate what takes place in the learning environment. Integral to this, however, is the notion that children will be given opportunities to initiate choices about what they want to play with, to make their own discoveries and to respond to a variety of play materials in ways that are uniquely relevant to them. Sadly, such opportunities are not always available to children with autism especially if their behaviour and poor skills in social interaction are deemed to limit their access to such experiences. The adult-directed tasks that are put in place may conversely determine what the child can learn through play. This has the effect of reducing opportunities for the child to develop knowledge through creative discovery, which is the precursor for developing flexible and symbolic thinking. If play for children with autism is only regarded in the context of what can be taught, this could affect not only their educational experiences but also their developmental potential.

It is the provision of motivating and stimulating play that gives it educational value. Children are naturally curious and can be frequently observed experimenting with all that they encounter. In the early developmental stages of play it is important that children have access to a variety of sensory experiences that they can explore spontaneously. By allowing the child to initiate and express his or her preferences for objects and giving them time to discover the qualities of the objects, the child's capacity for learning and adaptation is greatly increased. They will be learning skills such as how to discriminate, understand causal relationships, acquire new information, solve problems and develop motor control. With an interactive approach, the adult interacts in so far as they share the experience with the child, to mediate how to extend the play to support their learning. Unlike a structured play training approach, the emotional and social connection between the play partners may well be the catalyst for helping a child to move forward in his or her knowledge and understanding.

Wolfberg (1999: 30) states that 'When provided opportunities to explore and create, children will experiment with new and unusual combinations of behaviour that might not occur in externally structured situations.'

Although a structured approach should not be applied to the spontaneous exploration of objects, it can be relevant for developing a role play or drama sequence using 'play scripts'. This may be helpful to the child with autism in offering a particular theme to the play, but it is also important that the child is given opportunities to incorporate their own creative response to the drama or activity.

Whether a child is engaged in structured or spontaneous play experiences, play in a safe environment should provide an opportunity for children to:

- explore, develop and represent learning experiences that help them make sense of the world;
- practise and build up ideas, concepts and skills;
- learn how to control impulses and understand the need for rules;
- be alone, alongside others or cooperate as they talk or rehearse their feelings;
- take risks and make mistakes;
- think creatively and imaginatively;
- communicate with others as they investigate or solve problems;
- express fears or relive anxious experiences in controlled and safe situations.

(DfEE 2000: 25)

For play to be considered as a relevant tool through which children can learn, it is important that it is defined in terms of both a *process* and a *product*. This ensures that the functions of play, whether directed or spontaneous, will be relevant to the development of children's learning attitudes as well as skills. The product-led description of play implies that children can develop their thinking, increase motor activity, learn to respond to particular stimuli and become more adaptable. The process-led view identifies play as providing motivation, enjoyment and opportunities for learning and interaction. Moyles (1989) believes that defining play in this way assists the child in the creation of a learning ethos. The dilemma for the adults might be in attempting to categorize types of play in order to achieve this, or making too rigid a distinction between work and play. Bennett *et al.* (1997) suggest that it may be more useful to conceptualize work and play as a continuum in which children can move between activities that offer intrinsic value and opportunities to extend and formulate new ideas. This ensures that whether the play activity is skill based or has a playful orientation, the child's increasing engagement in play and learning will bring about significant changes in all areas of development.

Play assessments can be a valuable tool for identifying how a child is playing but should not be used to determine deficits in play or learning. This may undermine the value of the experience for the child and lead practitioners to use play in ways that do not spontaneously correspond to the child's abilities and motivation. A child who is spinning the wheels of a car rather than pushing it along the floor is still discovering how it moves but will need acknowledgement that this is meaningful, before learning from someone else how to play with it in a different way. Assessments also need to consider how the adult's involvement contributes to a child's play and learning potential. This will be discussed further in Chapter 8.

The therapeutic nature of play

The value of play for children lies not only in its influences on learning but the process through which children can use play to express their emotions and establish new or improved relationships. Children's emotional development is inextricably linked to these changing relationships within the play process, from the infant stage of playing with and exploring oneself, to establishing interaction with one other person and then as part of a group. Furthermore, the connection between emotion, thinking and experience is the basis upon which all learning exists.

When children are absorbed in a play activity their levels of concentration and relaxation are heightened. Similarly, when children's play is self-generated and spontaneous it can provide them with a sense of control over the experience. It can also be used to reflect their feelings about their interactions with objects and people.

Landreth (2001) describes play as 'a complex multidimensional series of behaviours' (p. 4) that are engaged in by the child at both conscious and unconscious levels. Thus play does not have to be goal directed but can be engaged in simply for the fun and enjoyment of it. It is also possible that many of the emotions expressed when playing alone are heightened when there is a supportive adult facilitating the play.

Any play can have therapeutic value when:

- it is self-directed and spontaneous;
- it is a vehicle for communication;
- it facilitates self-expression of emotions;
- it is intrinsically motivating;
- it enables discovery of one's capabilities;
- it allows for growth;
- it creates a sense of being in control;
- it gives pleasure.

One of the difficulties with any subjective interpretation of the play experience is that it can make it much harder to assess the benefits. However, when the emphasis is on both the intrinsic and extrinsic value of the play this ensures that it rests firmly within a framework that is child focused, that is not just what the adult wants the child to learn through play, but the experience that the child is gaining when playing.

Axline (1969) developed a set of principles for establishing an effective relationship with a child in a therapeutic context that can equally be applied to the relationship between a child and a supportive adult who is facilitating play. She emphasized that in a therapeutic relationship the child is able to utilize his or her own capacities for growth; the adult does not control but, through permissiveness, helps the child discover their own potentialities. It is crucial that within any structured or non-directive play activity the relationship does not in any way attempt to make the child conform to a different way of being but should remain one of warm acceptance. As the child develops trust and confidence in the relationship so they learn to make their own decisions about how they want to change. It is important that the child's capacity to alter his or her way of being is never overlooked. When given the freedom to express their own creative inner self, children with autism can and do respond in remarkable ways, often beyond their assumed capabilities.

The principles of interactive play were being implemented with a class of pupils aged thirteen to fifteen who had autism and moderate learning difficulties. Rather than play, we were focusing on developing their personal awareness and social understanding through creative exploration. A behaviour displayed by one of the male pupils was his difficulty remaining in class for any length of time and he frequently withdrew himself to the outside area but was able to return when he felt comfortable enough to do so. After a period of preparation and discussion, the class were asked the question, 'If you were an animal what would you be?' They then had the opportunity to draw or paint this animal. Each pupil worked in their own space but returned to the circle with their pictures to share them with everyone. David, the pupil mentioned above, described the black and brown dog that he had painted. He said, 'This is Fang, he spends a lot of time outside, he makes a mess and people get cross with him. When he comes in the house he can be very friendly. He's a nice dog really.'

Describing play and the creative arts as therapy or therapeutic gives it an added dimension that some professionals and parents may be wary of. Landreth (2002) recognizes that attitudes towards the therapeutic value of play can be overlooked because it is being viewed in terms of what the play is, rather than how it is being used by the child. Although there are some significant overlapping ideologies about the function of play, play and the creative arts are not used in the same way as play therapy, which requires practitioners to have a specialized training and qualification. Play therapy that comes from the psychoanalytic tradition has not been widely used as a treatment for children with autism, except when additional psychological traumas or disturbances have been identified. To a large extent this relates to the way in which views about the aetiology of autism have changed from its original diagnosis as a psychogenic disorder to being more physiological in nature. However, as Alvarez (1992) points out, although it is important that there is this recognition, there is a need to look beyond causation and the behavioural descriptors of autism and extend awareness of the psychological needs of the individual within a therapeutic context. Some play therapists may also be uncertain about working with children who have autism because of the need to draw on the symbolic meaning of their actions, and as such may feel unable to help in bringing about changes in the child's emotional states and social relationships.

A broader range of therapeutic interventions and creative arts therapies has emerged from the traditional view of play therapy. Jennings (1999) suggests that this has created a move towards a new philosophy in the therapeutic use of play and therefore one that educational and childcare establishments can work with. Interventions can be seen as therapeutic when they involve the adult working with the child's motivations to establish a positive and trusting relationship. Music interaction, Intensive Interaction (Nind and Hewett 1994), art, drama and movement focus on the core need to support the child's emotional well-being to help bring about changes in thinking and behaviour. Like interactive play, they all work towards the enhancement of children's play, communication and social interaction in meaningful, creative and enjoyable ways.

By acknowledging the therapeutic benefits of play it is possible to recognize how it can be defined through the value of the experience and not just as a set of observable behaviours that determine levels of skill. The following sections place play firmly within a developmental framework that is essential to understanding how children with autism are learning to interact and make sense of the world around them. The key to reducing children's sense of isolation and gaining knowledge of the self and others is in the establishment of a therapeutic alliance between playful exploration, emotional well-being and social interaction.

Sensory play

Exploration begins with the infant developing an awareness of his or her own body and the body in relation to another. At this stage the infant is unaware of the separateness of 'other' and links all awareness to the bodily sensations that are being experienced. Jennings (1999) describes this as the *embodiment* stage, when all the child's early experiences are being expressed through bodily stimuli and the senses. It is these physical experiences that enable the child to develop the 'body-self' that is essential for the development of identity.

In normal patterns of development, this stage is passed through quite rapidly as the infant increasingly engages with objects that are in close proximity. The child comes to recognize the object as separate from 'self' and other people in relation to 'self'. For the person with autism, this state of awareness may be one that is either not well developed or constantly fluctuating, and can remain through to adulthood. Williams (1998) describes how, in her early childhood, she experienced a lack of separateness between herself, objects and people, which made it difficult for her to understand the nature of 'things'. Consequently she learnt to develop concepts about the physical properties of objects through the emotional sensitivities that she assigned to them. 'We require concepts in order to interpret and understand but we do not require concepts in order to sense or experience. It is through interpretation of what we sense or experience that concepts evolve' (Williams 1998: 57).

Children's exploration of objects is a sensory experience whether or not they have sensory perceptual difficulties. Exploration involves using all the senses and it is the imprinting of this information on the neural pathways that enables the child to respond to objects in increasingly complex ways. Sutton-Smith (1986) suggests that 'Exploration tends to precede mastery which tends to precede play and they are not always easily distinguishable' (p. 145).

Thus children can be said to be playing with objects that they are exploring by licking, biting, sniffing or flapping. Similarly, the physical manipulation of an object, the way it is held or dropped repeatedly continues to be part of the exploratory process. In one of my workshops I was asked to suggest a strategy for a child who it was felt never played with anything because he would always throw whatever was given to him. For this child his exploration of objects was not determined by holding on to them but the sensory experience he received by throwing them. As he was interested in exploring objects in this way, he needed to be given things that he could safely throw, such as a koosh ball or a feather. To develop this into an interactive game the carer had no difficulty in realizing that throwing the ball back would let the child know that his actions were meaningful and that the flow of interaction could be maintained through the activity. 'If we ignore the child's needs and the incentives which are effective in getting him to act, we will never be able to understand his advance from one developmental stage to the next, because every advance is connected with a marked change in motives, inclinations and incentives' (Vygotsky 1978: 92).

It is the link between emotion and self-initiated exploration that provides the foundation for increased engagement and concept formation. An object draws the child's attention and what takes place is a spontaneous discovery of its qualities, which can be reassuring or create uncertainty, leading to a response of the child's own choice. It is through the manipulation of the object that the child becomes dependent upon it as a source of sensory and affective stimulation. This behaviour is often observed in children with autism as being 'obsessional' and 'stimming' (stimulating) and can result in the object being removed so that a more functional activity can be presented in its place. In the absence of objects that were previously stimulating, the child may well revert to the previous stage of exploratory play, that of bodily stimulation or an inappropriate physical reaction towards another person. Hence the child comes to learn about the world by being reactive rather than pro-active in his or her explorations.

It is the sharing of the experience with the child that will most effectively alter how the child is playing with an object. First, by mirroring how the child is playing with it, it gains their attention and acknowledges their play as meaningful. When the object is moved or played with differently by the supportive play partner, this enables the child to discover other qualities that the object has. Once the child gains a different concept of the object, that information, presented kinaesthetically, will come to impact on the child's learning and play experience.

A further perspective on exploratory and sensory play is that of attachment to objects; Wing (1986) suggests that this relates to the knowledge of objects as first experienced. I taught a teenage boy with autism who loved to hold on to a handful of string and leather. His earliest experience of this came from the riding stables that his parents owned, where, as a young child, he had been allowed to explore, and had gained a lot of pleasure from the sensory experience of handling string and leather straps. The feeling a child receives by being held or from the comfort of a particular object will strengthen the emotion the child has about the experience and this will determine how often he or she will want to repeat the experience. Many parents express concern that their child with autism prefers to focus on a favourite toy or object rather than seek comfort from them. This attachment to the object does not symbolize the rejection of the affection of the parents in favour of the object but the object is being used for security in a place of uncertainty. This is similar to the use of a transitional object that a young child requires as they learn to experience separation from their main carers. Winnicott (1971) described this not as the first object of attachment but the first 'not me' possession. In other words, in the process of separation, the child finds a preferred object with which they can continue to feel safe. The bundle of string and leather helped the child to make a connection with his parents so that in their absence he could still experience the same feelings of comfort and security. Once again it is the attachment to objects in early infancy that may continue to support the child emotionally at specific times of anxiety or stress. In the same way as the removal of a child's 'security blanket', the object of attachment cannot suddenly be removed but rather replaced with activities and experiences that will continue to engage the child's interests and aid their development.

The manipulation and sensory exploration of toys and objects is vital within early play as it is forms the basis for the development of symbolic play. Toys and objects can become representations through the meanings that children place on them. Adults need to be wary of placing their values on how children are playing. By rationalizing what children need to do they may miss what are fundamentally their own efforts to interact with the world in ways that make sense to them. It is how the adult learns to share the child's explorations, toys and objects that will help to extend their representations and build knowledge and understanding.

Play as a repetitive experience

Another important developmental aspect of play in children is the need to establish cohesion through repetition. It is a significant feature of their development and learning that children will seek ways to create order and consistency in their efforts to learn about the world. The establishment of rituals and routines begins with the deep significance of early sensory experiences and movements that occur first at an unconscious level and then emerge into consciousness as the child's language and thinking develop. According to Piaget's cognitive theory, children develop schemas (or ways of thinking) that are a means of unifying and creating general principles. Schemas are established through repeated experiences, which then operate to provide a basic underlying structure to learning and behaviour. 'A schema is a repeatable pattern of organisational behaviour which the child generalises' (Bruce 1991: 136). But as Nutbrown (1999) points out, some children get 'stuck' in their development, which results in apparent 'aimless repetition' of the schema content. What is required is an adult to intervene by tuning into the child's existing schema so that different experiences and actions can be introduced.

Within any forms of ritualized or repetitive play, there is an underlying emotional experience that is linked to how children manage their own levels of frustration tolerance and take risks by experimenting with unusual ways of manipulating the objects. In addition to this, repetitive behaviours help in establishing a knowledge base from which the child can extend their understanding. It is through their perseveration and concentration that they will be able to grasp concepts such as pattern, shape and spatial awareness. The predictability of an activity within the context of what is known needs to be fully established with the help of an adult or older peer, before the child decides how to change it so that it remains 'safe'. 'Too much newness in the experiences we offer can lead to children becoming anxious as they are unable to link the new experience to their existing frameworks' (Duffy 1998: 85).

Lining up objects is also an activity that can become very ritualized for children with autism. However, through observation, it is possible to see how this play represents an established schema that relates to a child's own unique exploration and interpretation of an experience worth having and for no other reward. Csikszentmihalyi (1990) refers to this as *flow*. Flow experiences give immediate feedback as a result of the deep concentration and lack of questioning about the goals, hence the levels of self-absorption and pleasure that the activity provides. 'Flow is the essence of experienced creativity: deep concentration, problems forgotten, lack of self-consciousness, time forgotten and an experience that is worth having simply for its own sake and no other reward'(Wentworth 2001: 53).

I arrived at the home of a six-year-old boy with autism to be informed by his mother that he was spending a lot of time lining up his cars. As we commenced our play session in the sitting room, every vehicle that he possessed covered the carpet. He began to line them up in rows and I asked if I could join in. This was acceptable but he would occasionally check that I had got them perfectly straight, and if there were some vehicles that he did not want me to put together he moved them. We eventually covered the carpet with rows of cars, lorries, bikes and trucks and when stopping to look at what we had done together he told me 'that's Sainsbury's car park'. He was able to relate his play to his experience of going to the supermarket and for the rest of the session we moved the cars in and out of the car park, and although it was repetitious, it was also typical of what would be happening at the supermarket! Having established the familiar play he was able to extend it by using Lego™ bricks to build a supermarket with me.

It is important that the child is given support to find different ways to play otherwise they do not develop the flexibility to extend their learning in increasingly complex and creative ways. Wentworth (2001) believes that any experience that enables a person to become deeply involved, and has an intentional goal that involves the merging of action and awareness, provides the foundations for creativity. The ritualized and repetitive play of children with autism can equally be regarded as a highly creative act because it is a representation of their unique perspective, thoughts and feelings about their world.

Social play

Early play with caregivers provides the foundation for understanding the nature of social relationships and it is the quality of this interaction that will influence all future relationships with others. It is often overlooked that children are engaging in social play during those early interactions and that it is the process of social engagement with one other person that will lead to the emergence of social play with others. It is clear that the child's main carers have a considerable responsibility in establishing opportunities for mutual play that build on skills in cooperation, empathy and enjoyment. It is a key aspect of my work with families in the smile programme that parents and carers establish a special playtime with the child on a daily basis. As the child with autism may not spontaneously engage with others in a play activity it is therefore important to create this experience for him or her. Once established as a regular activity, the parents and carers may then begin to notice the child's spontaneous interest in sharing play. This is most effective when the play activity matches the child's level of interest and engagement.

Jordan and Libby (2000) point out that sensory and physical play tends to dominate the play interests of children with autism, but rather than a deficit, it should be seen as an opportunity for increasing joint attention and mutual enjoyment. Sensory and physical play is often viewed as an experience only for very young children but it can also help in bridging the changes in social play development. It also remains evident in the way that adults play or use their leisure time (Figure 1.2). Skills such as taking turns, waiting, imitating and cooperating may be more easily established as a result of the child's motivation to take part in an activity. This is because the skills are being learnt more spontaneously than in other formally structured situations. On a recent family visit to Disneyland in Paris, the parents told me how they were amazed at the way in which their five-year-old son with autism was able to queue for fifty minutes to have another go on his favourite ride!

There has been a considerable amount of research evidence identifying the social delay in the play of children with autism but it remains unclear to what extent this is due to their difficulties in social

Playing alone	bodily movements, sounds, tastes, touching, visual stimulation
Playing with one person	physical play, music and singing, play with objects and toys
Playing with a small group	sand and water play, outdoor play, soft play, music and movement
Playing in a large group	swimming, horseriding, walking, cycling, parachute games, music, drama

Figure 1.2 Sensory play and the development of social interaction.

interaction or the frequency and type of playful interactions that are made available to them. In schools, the demands of the curriculum are often considered to outweigh the potential gains from more interactive approaches or the creative arts. The TEACCH approach used in the majority of educational settings for children with autism emphasizes individual programmes of learning that can reduce opportunities for learning and playing through peer interaction. As Jordan *et al.* (1998) concluded in their research into different educational and therapeutic interventions, the most effective programmes were those that had a more eclectic approach and made use of a range of different interventions to aid children's learning. Developing a programme of interactive play in which the child is supported by an adult or older peer increases opportunities to gain mastery of social situations. It is the powerful influence of the empathetic relationship that is occurring during these playful dyadic interactions that is most likely to bring about changes in the child's social competence.

If children show a preference for observing their peers at play or playing alongside them, it is important to recognize this as a key strategy in learning about social play. Observing others playing and even solitary play are not only developmentally significant but also provide time for the child to absorb the details of what is involved in playing socially. Often demands are placed on children to take part in social activities in ways that even adults would find uncomfortable. Just because I like physical activity does not mean I would want to play international rugby! The child is assimilating a vast amount of information about not only the play, but also its social dynamics. It is only when an adult mediates for the child that there is greater potential for the play to become a positive social experience. When play is a mutually enjoyable activity rather than a socially demanding one, the interrelation between play and children's social competency is unequivocal. The outcome is due to the nature of the activity that is providing the motivation for the child to take part and the feelings of safety and enjoyment this provides that leads to increased confidence in participating.

Imaginative play

There is now a considerable body of research that has identified that children with autism are capable of symbolic and pretend play but that it may not occur spontaneously or within the typically expected developmental stage of play. It is through the manipulation of objects that children begin to use toys to represent or 'play out' certain scenarios, for example picking up a doll and cuddling it instead of holding onto its hair or putting bricks on top of one another rather than banging them together. The interpretation of the way objects are perceived leads to the child developing increasingly different ways to play with them and gain knowledge about them. It does not have to be a toy but any object that interests the child.

> A mother described how her four-year-old daughter with autism showed an ability to use symbolic thought through her interest in trees. Whenever they went for a walk her daughter would always ask numerous questions about the trees they passed. She also had favourite trees and did not like the ones with large growths on them because they reminded her of 'tummy buttons'. Often it became quite difficult to change the subject so one day her mother asked her why she was 'so obsessed' with trees, to which her daughter replied, 'because they are beautiful'.

Because the development of imaginative or pretend play involves the child being able to think in increasingly more flexible ways, the capacity for symbolic thought is regarded as a central feature of cognitive development. The use of a transitional object or object of attachment is the child's first symbolic creation. For the child, the symbolic use of this object is one that can be understood in terms of its external qualities and in what it intrinsically represents.

Children with autism may well need to be tutored into using objects differently but the difficulty might arise that the child is only responding to a learned behaviour rather than demonstrating spontaneous pretend play. Providing a simple narrative or label to an action helps to draw the child gradually into thinking about an object or experience differently. I have used this technique where instead of just tickling a child I would call my fingers 'spiders'. Eventually when the child wanted to be tickled he would come and ask me for 'spiders'. Another child I worked with was fascinated by her collection of plastic dinosaurs, which she liked to line up. During a session where we were using play dough she made a 'figure' that I called a dinosaur. Interestingly, she was happy to include the play dough dinosaur in the line of her plastic ones!

Jennings (1999) suggests that to bridge the gap between sensory and symbolic play, it helps if the sensory materials can be used in imaginative ways. The use of sand to build castles or tunnels or a roadway can guide the child into representing a familiar story or event that is significant to them. In Chapter 6, I discuss the use of Sand Play with a child who has Asperger's syndrome. Similarly clay, water or collected natural objects can be used along with a variety of other manufactured objects to create a familiar story or make models and pictures with a child.

Sherratt's (2002) research showed how children with autism and severe learning difficulties were able to extend the symbolic use of objects. Initially they were guided to use non-specific objects and shown how to represent them in a pretend play sequence. Although this occurred within a structured programme, a significant factor that influenced their spontaneous pretend play was the modelling of additional affective gestures and responses by the adults. From this research, Sherratt concluded that the symbolic mechanism, the ability to pretend play, occurred more rapidly because of the combination of structure, affect and repetition. This further implies that the development of pretend or imaginative play is not fully dependent on increased cognition and that socio-affective aspects of play are a significant factor in the development of imaginative play.

The development of role or dramatic play is a further development in imaginative play, which, again, researchers have noted is particularly difficult for many with autism. This is not necessarily due to difficulties in being able to symbolically represent an object as something else but because it involves a level of social understanding to interpret the intentions and emotional states of others. Drama sequences and the use of narratives provide children who have autism with a structure for understanding 'role'. Taking on a role helps them to develop an awareness of how others might be feeling and at the same time it develops skills in communication, decision-making and cooperation.

With a group of six boys with autism, aged five to six years old, I worked on a drama piece based on the book *The Enormous Turnip*. The children were all of different abilities and not all of them were verbal communicators. The children chose which characters they wanted to be and chose the props to fit the characters and retell the story. Through their engagement in the drama they were unaware how their physical contact, negotiations and shared enjoyment were teaching them about social interaction.

Children become active learners through play and it is through playing that the skills they need to become socially competent are more attainable and meaningful. There is no mystery to children's play and this is because it represents themes in their lives that are highly significant. It is in these experiences that adults should find ways to engage with children as this will help to extend the socio-affective bond between them.

Toys and activities

Sometimes it is necessary to help parents and professionals choose appropriate toys and activities that will interest and motivate the child, particularly if these are not already well established. Often homes and educational settings can be overwhelmed with toys that the parents or professionals hope will be stimulating when in fact the child shows a preference for objects not usually considered toys in the conventional sense, such as twigs and leaves. On the other hand, limiting access to toys and activities can result in a much narrower range of interests becoming established. According to Dixon (1990) the marketing of toys has significantly influenced what children are given to play with and he expresses some concern about how this has influenced notions of play. Sutton-Smith (1994) reiterates this when he discusses the sanitization and domestication of play. He believes that there is a danger that the overtly Western perspective of what constitutes play and the toys and activities that adults provide may in fact be limiting rather than promoting children's development. Children do need a range of playthings to occupy them but, as Dixon suggests, it is important to guard against the use of the terms 'educational' and 'non-educational' toys, as any object can embody ideas and develop conceptual awareness. Although societies accept these changes and deem certain toys and play activities appropriate or inappropriate, it is still important to consider how they are being used and the relevance they have in terms of the child's social participation.

Television can be used as medium for learning and relaxing or giving children a break from formal activities, and at home it can be a useful way to entertain them while other family matters are more important, such as preparing a meal. When the television becomes an occupier for visual and auditory stimulation rather than a source of knowledge and inspirational ideas, other activities that interest the child will need to be introduced. The use of character toys has shown how videos and children's programmes can be incorporated into play but, as Kline (1993, cited in Belton 2001) points out, these may still restrict imaginative play by the need to follow the script. Adult involvement will be essential if more spontaneous imaginative play is to be encouraged. Older children may be interested in factual as well as entertaining programmes from which they can redirect their interests by creating models or stories, but having someone to share in their creative ideas will help to motivate and support new ways of thinking.

The use of computers as toys has had a considerable influence on the ways in which children spend much of their leisure time. For many people with autism they can be an enjoyable source of visual stimulation and help to develop skills and interests as well as provide a safe way to interact with others. Although computers may been seen to encourage isolating behaviour, computer games can also enhance interaction with a peer, sibling or family member, developing cooperation, concentration, turn-taking and shared enjoyment. Like the television, computers are one medium of entertainment that should be used in conjunction with other activities to broaden interests and engagement with other aspects of their environment.

The play space should not be restricted to the indoors as it cannot provide the child with all the elements that he or she needs to feel part of a wider social experience. An essential part of children's life is their local community and sharing aspects of it with others increases their knowledge that they are connected to a society that can offer them support and understanding. I also advocate the need for children to experience their natural environment, to find a connection with what is essentially a vital element of healthy living. Moving around in awe and wonder with the wind on their faces or jumping with excitement in the snow, splashing in puddles or walking through piles of autumn leaves is how they learn that they are connected to the world around them. Societal attitudes and circumstances have resulted in much greater fear of the outside, and less time in more natural environments reduces children's opportunities to playfully explore their wider world. Safety is of course paramount and considerations that carers give to this will influence where they go with the child. As children become absorbed in the natural discovery and exploration of different sensory experiences, such as the beach, the woods and parks, it can both relax and rejuvenate them, making it easier to engage with others who want to find positive ways to interact with them.

One of my visits to a family coincided with the child's regular visit to the go-kart track. Initially I could not be sure that this was going to help us to play interactively but I followed both the child's and the parent's enthusiasm for the activity and so joined him on the track in my own go-kart! He raced on ahead of me, clearly indicating his skill while I was still getting used to my machine. Eventually he came up behind me and tried to push me out of his way and then we became involved in a game of 'chase'. He effectively established our pattern of interaction, reacting by going fast and slow, moving away and then moving alongside me. Although he had not previously made any attempt to interact spontaneously with me at school or at home, he was clearly confident about doing so on the go-kart track.

Seeing a child respond in this way helps parents and carers to recognize the child-like qualities and enthusiasm for engaging in pleasurable activities that are a vital part of growth and development in all children. It is when opportunities for exploration and play are limited that children have greater difficulty adapting to different life experiences or learning new skills.

There has not been an attempt within this chapter to provide a broad definition of play but to create an awareness of the playful ways in which all children explore the world and create their own meanings from these experiences.

Understanding the play of children with autism comes not through objective analysis but through the subjective experience of being a play partner.

> Children do not passively take in information from the world around them and learn from it; rather, they actively transform it into something that is unique and personally meaningful. They use their experience as the context for building new meaning and skills onto what they have already learnt.
>
> (Levin 1996, cited in Dau 1999: 7)

A model of interactive play is described in the next chapter. It focuses on identifying the core competencies that enable the development of a mutually regulated relationship and how interactive play assists in achieving these. Play with a supportive partner is the foremost activity that enables the child to discover his or her own potentialities and motivations for social communication. The power of interaction lies in seeking out relationships with others that help the child to become a creative, adaptive and autonomous person. When an adult and child discover how to play and have fun together there is greater potential for personal and social development that can affect every aspect of their daily lives.

Chapter 2

A model of interactive play

A developmentally based model of interactive play identifies the process of mutual engagement as having a positive influence on cognition, communication, socio-affective functioning and motivation. The foundations for establishing sociocommunicative behaviour are embedded within an interactive play approach that is based on the early reciprocal interactions between the parent and the child. As play becomes an integral part of a child's world, it is the most effective medium through which the child and carer can communicate and establish a meaningful interpersonal relationship.

Where there has been a breakdown in interaction or a difficulty in forming the relationship owing to a child having a neurological developmental disability, interactive play has a therapeutic role in mediating for the establishment of interpersonal connectedness. Regardless of the type of attachment relationship, interactive play enhances the parent–child relationship and provides a framework for interacting positively with others. The primary goal of interactive play is to create a mutually enjoyable experience that opens the pathway for increased spontaneous interaction by the child and flexibility in his or her thinking and behaviour.

A developmental perspective indicates that interventions based on early parenting models of interaction have been effective in the socio-affective and cognitive development of children with autism. An increasing awareness of the benefits of an interactive approach has led to numerous studies being carried out (Christie *et al.* 1992; Tannock *et al.* 1992; Nind and Hewett 1994; Sussman 1999; Jernberg and Booth, 2001; Mahoney and Perales 2003; van Berckelaer-Onnes 2003; Wieder and Greenspan 2003; Webster *et al.* 2004). What most of these studies identify is that there are significant benefits to the development of interpersonal relationships when the interaction is child led and not based solely on adult-directed interventions. Webster *et al.* (2003) point out that the range of therapeutic interventions available for families and children with autism has resulted in a variety of assumptions being made about their validity owing to the lack of empirical evidence. Neisser's point (1976) that 'A psychology that cannot interpret ordinary experience is ignoring almost the whole range of its natural subject matter' (p. 4) is a relevant response to this.

Child-led interactive approaches focus on the developmental needs of the child with the major emphasis on communication and social and emotional growth. The child's repertoire of behaviours is seen as having a specific function in terms of what is being communicated, and through appropriately cued responses by the adult these behaviours are supported and adapted. As the child initiates an interaction with an object, activity or person so the play partner responds by sharing or following the child's focus of attention. When the adult is supportive rather than directive within the play situation, interactions become reciprocal and the level of engagement in the activity is increased. This follows the same pattern of interaction that is a feature of early development where the child, recognizing that they have some control over their learning and play experiences, gains more confidence in maintaining the social interaction.

It is important that a distinction is made between interactive play and play development. The primary role of interactive play is in the development of reciprocal communication and socio-affective relationships rather than the improvement in play skills. However, changes in play behaviour and symbolic understanding are more likely to occur as a consequence of the child's altered perspective of playing within an interactive sequence that is providing the motivation to explore the environment in more complex and enjoyable ways. As Rogers (1980) points out, having openness to an experience in new and different ways is dependent upon the fostering of meaningful social relationships and the individual's responses to stimuli that are made available.

Interactive play, like the creative arts therapies, emphasizes the role of non-verbal communication in supporting the development of socio-affective functioning. In the same way that music, movement and art function as a catalyst for creative expression so play also stimulates and supports impulses and feelings in the child that are not dependent on verbal communication. The model in Figure 2.1 shows that interaction is at the core of the development of communication and social understanding. The experience of interacting in positive and meaningful ways leads to a range of competencies that impact on motivation, thinking and behaviour, that will bring about significant changes in children's emotional and cognitive growth. However, the extent to which these competencies are utilized will depend on the child's individual abilities, the responsiveness of the caregivers to the interests and feelings of the child, and the way in which the relationship between them is established.

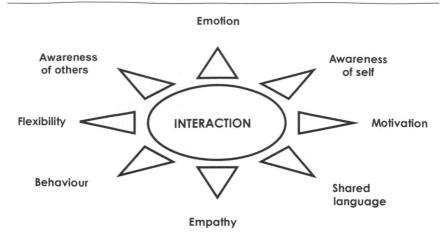

Figure 2.1 The foundation of social, emotional and cognitive development.

In autism, the recognition of a cognitive impairment affecting the development of communication and imaginative thinking is seen as impacting on the establishment of reciprocal interaction and the quality of the relationships. In infancy, developing an awareness of self and others and understanding emotions is influenced by the interpersonal nature of shared language and the motivation to communicate. Furthermore, the ability to represent thought with language aids the development of symbolism and the ability to think with flexibility. Any delay or disturbance in the development of symbolic thought will undoubtedly affect perception and the ability to interpret and predict what is happening. As a consequence individuals use their behaviour to deal with their anxiety of confusing and unknown situations.

Many interventions for children with autism focus on strategies to manage these behaviours so that their skills in social interaction will be improved. Working from a deficit model, however, undermines the developmental base from which social and communication skills emerge. The establishment of positive interactive states is seen as essential in strengthening the core competencies, giving meaning to communication and the development of relationships that are empathetic and rewarding. Hobson (1989) believes that autism is a core difficulty in emotional interaction. This viewpoint supports the use of interventions and approaches that emphasize the establishment of reciprocal, affectively attuned interactions that are more likely to increase the potential to develop sociocommunicative understanding and flexible thinking than those which sustain the view that externally structured methods are required to provide the coping mechanisms needed to adapt to the environment. Some of the methodologies applied in the more deficit-focused interventions may also imply that individuals with autism do not benefit from or have the same emotional needs that are essential for the physical, social and cognitive development of all individuals, regardless of any circumstances that might affect their lives.

Interactive approaches focus on the fundamental premise that the establishment of mutually rewarding experiences mediates in children's social and emotional development. Interactive play provides opportunities for self-initiated behaviour, spontaneity and flexibility – helping to bring about significant neurological changes in the child's cognitive–affective states.

Depending on the child's developmental level there may be significant variations in the acquisition of these core competencies. As Green (2003) suggests, development is not a one-directional process. It is the dynamic interplay of relationships between the child, the caregiver and the environment that will influence the process of development and how the child comes to perceive other people and objects that they interact with. Having a positive regard and an acceptance of the child's motives, communications and feelings will increase the child's awareness of his or her own sense of autonomy and interdependence. As Axline (1982) suggests, the main objective of therapeutic play is to provide a relationship that will enable the child to 'utilise the capacities that are within him or her for a more constructive and happier life as an individual and as a member of society' (p. 121).

Awareness of self

What takes place during interaction, particularly when it involves shared play experiences, has a dynamic effect on the emergence of the self. It is the coregulation of the interaction that leads to an increase in the child's capacity to develop a conscious awareness of self. The creation of a nurturing atmosphere during interactive play enables children to explore and experiment with a range of different realities through which they can express emotions, experience control and construct knowledge about the world around them. 'An individual who is successfully accepted into an interaction acquires an increment of positive emotional energy. This energy is manifested in what we commonly call confidence, warmth and enthusiasm' (Collins 1981, cited in Schore 1994: 106).

The developing child is dependent upon the continuity of the experience that a secure attachment gives, to maintain patterns of behaviour and affect regulation that will help in the establishment of the core self. Cognitive theorists do not necessarily take account of variations in knowledge about the self, seeking instead to identify the mechanisms that will bring about changes in awareness and behaviour. Stern (1985) points out that having a concept of self is not a cognitive construct, but an experiential integration of sensation, affect and time.

> Ryan and I were playing together with a blanket. First it was a parachute that we waved up and down together and then he wanted me to roll him in it. When he stopped for a rest he was calm and lay quietly on the floor. I gently stroked his forehead and then he said 'tummy' so I tickled him on his tummy. I continued by tickling him on his knee but again he asked for 'tummy'. I built in some anticipation of this and he became very excited. I tickled his ear and again he said 'tummy' so I repeated this pattern of interaction several times by tickling his foot and his head after tickling his tummy as he requested. He stopped again to relax and to my surprise he did not then ask me to tickle his tummy but his back. Playing together was not only increasing his knowledge about his body but through the anticipation and excitement of being tickled he was building more understanding of positive interaction. His repeated requests gave him the security to alter what he wanted, giving him an opportunity to feel more confident about how he wanted to communicate with me.

For many children with autism the reliance upon sensory stimulation is a significant aspect of their interactions and requires a careful assessment of their preferences and sensitivities if they are to be shared in interactive play. Parents tend to do this intuitively as they nurture and are sensitive to their child's affective states. The quality of the stimulation that individuals receive, particularly from their main carers, enables them to establish preferences for the sensations they seek to engage in with others. Developmental research is now showing that through the integration of physical and sensory experiences, newborn infants are learning to regulate their physiological needs and are equipped with social sensitivities to influence the actions of others (Damon and Hart 1992). Children learn about themselves through play when they are given opportunities to:

- make decisions;
- experience control;
- internalize experiences;
- experiment with the environment;
- express emotions;
- concentrate on a chosen activity.

An increase in the child's sense of agency draws them into more a subjective awareness of self. Providing a non-threatening environment, in which play is self-directed and supported, lets the child know that they are accepted and valued. Interactive play assumes that a subjective view of self is enhanced by the recognition of emotional states during these mutual exchanges. An objective view of self evolves from the knowledge that children gain about themselves as they interact more with others and find effective ways to express their thoughts and actions (Figure 2.2).

Knowing the self is a complex anomaly of thoughts and facts that can be presented in conjoined, separated or isolated states. What most individuals do, including those with autism, is build up a self-image based on how others perceive and behave towards them. Children who remain isolated from social experiences will not develop an awareness of themselves or an understanding of how they think about themselves. How a child is playing and interacting provides an insight into his or her perception of self. Helping a child to become more self-aware involves the sensitive integration of affective, carefully timed interactions that specifically focus on the child's actions and behaviour.

The mirroring of emotions or verbalizing them for the child during the interactive process heightens awareness of what they are feeling and brings the emotions into increasing consciousness. As a result of these experiences the child learns to organize his or her thoughts that provide a perspective about the self, resulting in more self-directed behaviour. Bruner (1986) believes that play gives children their first and most crucial opportunity to have the courage to think, to talk and to be themselves.

Singer and Salovey (1993) recognize that how individuals see themselves has considerable significance in understanding the biological underpinnings of the conscious self and the capacity to perceive, learn to communicate and adapt to the environment. Through the process of interaction there is greater potential for the development of these intellectual competencies. Having an awareness of self is the precursor to thinking about oneself, in other words, the ability to symbolize and have a self-concept. 'I am self in the becoming' (Williams 1998: 19).

Self as subject	Self as object
What I feel	Who I am
What I like	What I am
What I don't like	What I can do
What I want	What I know

Figure 2.2 The view of self.

Burns (1982) states that having a self-concept provides an inner consistency and a set of expectations and beliefs that individuals hold about themselves as a result of their experiences. As children strengthen the knowledge they have about themselves so they also learn to evaluate and organize their behaviour towards others. It is the nature of social interactions that leads to a positive or negative view of the self and, in turn, it is the self-concept that enables the child to mediate their social experiences. The internalizing of these experiences and the child's predisposition are at the core of the development of personality.

Awareness of others

According to Harter (1998) developing a sense of self is central to the process of developing social cognition. Frith (1989) states that the ability to make sense of other people is also the ability to make sense of oneself. It would appear therefore that awareness of self and others tends to occur simultaneously through shared social interactions. In early development there is considerable variation in a child's ability to recognize a familiar person and the ability to emotionally differentiate between him- or herself and the person. As Schaffer (1996) points out, this is a process that occupies much of childhood. The ability to identify those who are significant in one's life, such as the family, and to recognize differences between people, is a significant aspect of the socialization experience. This presupposes that overcoming the difficulties that children with autism have in developing knowledge about people occurs most effectively through the dyadic interactions that are maintained within the process of relationship-building. Gaining knowledge of others as social beings includes:

- the need to be in close proximity;
- a sense of feeling 'safe' in the company of another;
- gaining a response to one's efforts to interact;
- being able to predict another's behaviour;
- recognizing the other person not just as an object;
- activities that provide the experience of cooperating.

Each one of these factors, however, is dependent upon the vast array of emotional sensitivities that the child receives during positively charged interactions with his or her main caregiver. Depending on how a person makes them feel will influence the extent to which they seek out opportunities to learn about them.

The regulation of emotional states during these experiences helps the child to establishing an internal working model of the self as separate from an 'other' and how they relate within the dyad. Aitken and Trevarthen (1997) describe this as the Self–Other system. It is during this vital stage when the intersubjective relationship is being established that concepts about others as social beings are formulated. Intersubjectivity occurs when both partners engaged in an interactive dyad are able to perceive each other's subjective experience and match their behaviour to influence the other. The absence of this knowledge about the self as separate from objects or people will make it difficult for children to interpret the social actions of others. Likewise, if children have not yet reached the developmental stage of being able to emotionally differentiate between themselves and their carer, they will find it difficult to understand that someone can have a different emotion from themselves.

Although having an emotional awareness is a social dimension that is essential for the growth of the relationship, it is the nature of the interaction that will assist in the development of social knowledge about others. The re-introduction of the patterns of social behaviour that are established in early infancy, such as reciprocal play, is essential, particularly for children who have a developmental delay. Rather than adopt an approach that may be inconsistent with the child's developmental level, the maintenance of the reciprocal relationship will lead to greater opportunities to generalize learning about the self and others. The consistent rhythm and flow of the interaction assists the child in organizing knowledge about the social behaviour of the carer and the emotional regulation of the mutual exchanges provides a more cohesive understanding of what it means to be with another person.

Creating an interactive sequence does not mean doing the same activity each time or responding in the same way, nor does it necessarily occur at the first attempt. Variation is a significant feature of close relationships and it is within the security of the established relationship that the child learns to predict the behaviour of others. Play that is child led rather than adult directed is more likely to help children to manage variations in others' behaviour because they are creating their own internal models to help them understand what is involved in social interaction. The variations in the reactions received from different people when playing will help to generalize more social life experiences, as well as enable the child to establish preferences for doing particular activities with them.

Neema was playing with dolls in the sand, engrossed in her own narrative about what they were doing. Her mother introduced another doll, as if introducing herself, and placed it near to the others. Neema picked up the new doll, examined it and then picked up another doll and 'danced' them together. Her mother sang a familiar tune as Neema continued the 'dance' action with the dolls. This scenario symbolized a social act of engagement and showed her how interaction can be non-threatening and enjoyable.

It was the child's predisposition to act and the responsiveness of the caregiver that provided a unique pattern of interaction and influenced the development of her social understanding. The adult's role in facilitating the experience involves:

- expressing a desire to be with the child;
- showing pleasure and enjoyment in his or her company;
- creating opportunities for spontaneous reactions to stimuli;
- encouraging different responses to stimuli;
- synchronizing with the child's behaviour;
- allowing for a sense of agency in the interaction.

These principles of interactive play enable the child to make the necessary distinctions between the self and other, while at the same time they establish a core relatedness that is essential for the continuity of shared experiences. Engaging in playful interactions that involve the ability to react naturally to expressions and gestures is the key to building up knowledge about the self and the other person. The extension of interactive experiences beyond the primary caregiver will provide the child with an increasing awareness of more complex forms of social behaviour. Barnes (2004) believes that an important social experience for children is the need to develop the skill of togetherness. The extent to which this is achieved will be dependent upon the socially sensitive signals that are being transmitted by the carers during those interactions so that the child comes to understand what this means within the relationship. The emotional communication that is shared between them strengthens the child's capacity to understand the motives and behaviours of the person they are with.

Empathy

The capacity for the development of empathy is a vital part of the process of socialization that adds a fundamental ingredient to the maintenance of relationships. Psychologists also recognize the links with emotional and moral development, as empathy involves the capacity to relate to one's own and another's emotions and respond in a way that facilitates prosocial behaviour. Empathy is more closely associated with the affective processes that are occurring during the dyadic interactions when the child and caregiver discover how to synchronize their behaviour and emotions. This emotional synchronicity is vital in developing an understanding of another person's feelings.

Peeters and Gillberg (1999) identify several neuropsychological tests that consistently show that individuals with autism have significant difficulties in empathizing when it involves the ability to mentalize the thinking and feeling states of other people. The theory of mind experiments are regarded as being at the forefront of psychological investigation into the difficulties that individuals with autism have in understanding others' mental and emotional states (Baron-Cohen *et al*. 1985). The problem with this theory is that understanding how another person is thinking does not just involve the ability to mentalize, which is a complex cognitive function, but it also has an emotional component. Although this can occur at both conscious and unconscious levels, it is not possible to separate cognition from emotion, as they are both regarded as integrating mental functions that guide actions and thoughts. Hobson (1993) also regards the reciprocal, affectively patterned reactions of others as essential in developing an understanding of others' minds, leading to an increase in social competence, emotion regulation, and symbolic awareness.

The creation of an appropriate environment that fosters empathy is one that:

- satisfies the child's own emotional needs but discourages excessive self-concern;
- encourages the child to identify, experience and express a broad range of emotions; and
- provides numerous opportunities for the child to observe other people's emotional responses.

(Barnett 1987)

During one of my visits to a school for children with autism, a child came to the playroom in a very distressed state. He was uncertain about the room and was possibly unsure about what was going to happen while he was there. He was crying and asked for his bag because he wanted to go home. We acknowledged his distress and made no attempt to impose on him something with which he would not feel comfortable doing. As he had requested a bag, although not his own, I offered him a bag of toys. He stopped crying when he found the bubbles and, using another bottle, I began to blow some towards him. He reached out to pop them and gradually I could move around the room with them as

> he popped them. He began dancing and singing and requesting
> more, to which I responded. His altered state meant that he was
> able to interact with me, to express himself in a different way and
> share the delight of the activity with his human bubble machine!

Acknowledging the child's emotions and actions in the play situation
helped him to feel understood but, as the play partner, I had a responsibility additionally to establish interaction in a way that promoted the
development of empathy with the child. It is through a process of self-
discovery that there is an increase in the child's capacity to consider
others' feelings and understand their actions. This also makes it easier
for the carer to empathize with the child. Playful interactions that are
not directed by the adult but involve mutual engagement in the activity, create a resonance with the child's experience and strengthen the
capacity for empathetic understanding.

Emotion

In the same way that humans cannot live without breathing, so they
cannot exist without emotion. Having emotions is fundamental to survival and is dependent upon the relationship that a person creates with
other people and his or her environment to regulate and alter them.
The emotional foundations established through parent–child bonding
experiences are based on the unconscious awareness of sensations that
feed the autonomic nervous system. 'Emotions evolved not as conscious feelings, linguistically differentiated or otherwise, but as brain
states and bodily responses' (LeDoux 1996: 302).

The emotional regulation of these sensory experiences by the primary caregiver helps the child to create a flow of energy between the
emotional areas of the brain and the rational, thinking brain that brings
these states into more conscious awareness. Both the physiological
processes of emotion and the cognitive systems of arousal and appraisal lead to an increase in the expression and organization of emotional
information about the self and others' emotional states.

Research into the brain development of individuals with autism has
identified weak executive functioning in the frontal lobes that are the
core regulators of emotion and motivation and any disruption in this
development will result in profound changes in the formation of social
bonds and emotionality (Gillberg and Coleman 1992; Trevarthen et
al. 1998; Flavell and Miller 1998; Brisch 2004). Schore (2001) believes
that during infancy there is a critical growth period that takes place in
the connectivity between the limbic system and the prefrontal cortex,
combining emotional activity with cognitive formation. Courchesne

et al. (2001) have identified that brain growth, particularly in the prefrontal cortex, takes place in individuals with autism more rapidly than in the normally developing population. One suggestion is that such rapid growth occurring during the critical attachment phase may be exacerbated by difficulties that children with autism have in establishing emotional and reciprocal relationships with their primary caregivers, leading to an impairment in the pruning of the neural connections that are the core regulators of emotion and social reciprocity (Brisch, personal communication). Rapid brain growth may also imply that, if developments in emotional and social processing are interrupted or are not sufficiently established during the critical attachment phase, it will impact on all aspects of cognitive functioning. Trevarthen (1989) believes that brain growth is dependent upon the brain–brain interaction that occurs in the context of positive affective states between the child and main carers. Given the dependency of brain development on interpersonal transmissions and the maintenance of mutually affective experiences, this provides strong evidence for any changes that might occur in the development of emotional awareness, social understanding and cognitive growth.

The interactive process provides an opportunity to rebuild the neural connections between the emotional brain, the amygdala and the rational brain in the frontal cortex. According to Panskepp (1998), in early development the feedback from the amygdala to the prefrontal cortex is stronger than that from the cortex to the amygdala. This suggests that, in the early stages of development, emotional responses are more likely to result from unconscious than conscious feelings. That a child has not shown an appropriate emotional response does not mean that they do not have that emotion but, rather, they have not yet developed the capacity to interpret its function in response to a particular situation. Extreme expressions of anxiety, fear, sadness and happiness originate from deep within the emotional brain and are common to all mammals. Such emotions are indicative of a personal response to stimuli and are therefore more easily identifiable in the individual than those that might have a social dimension, such as embarrassment. Individuals with autism do not lack an awareness of others' emotions but they may have difficulties with the conceptual understanding of what another person is feeling. Given the emotional connectedness that naturally exists between people, emotions will always be recognized and acted upon but how they are evaluated will depend on the relevance that an individual places on them, whom it relates to and the context in which it occurs. A mother told me that she had had to spend some time in hospital away from her three-year-old daughter who has autism. At that time her daughter used very few words to communicate but on the mother's return from hospital she announced, 'I've really missed you.'

Emotions are powerful communicators of internal states. This is because the non-verbal representation of an emotion impacts more strongly on the neuro-affective states of others. In the context of shared play, emotions are regulated through the synchronizing of action and affect between the child and the adult. Play that engages the child in both affect and cognition is more likely to increase perceptual understanding and intentionality in their own and others' emotional states. Interactive play assists, therefore, in changing the child's emotional structures; whether from passivity to activity or from sadness to joy, it involves a process of change that allows the child time to adapt to a different way of being. For children who developmentally have difficulties with emotional connectedness, interactive play can provide a therapeutic role in both supporting emotional development and facilitating the regulation of emotions to create more opportunity for interaction.

Emotional stability is not a human characteristic and children, like adults, will respond differently even if situations and environments stay the same. Through their interactions, children come to develop their own internal representations of emotion and their actions and behaviour are a response to their need for self-expression. This is a significant feature of emotional development. 'There is a frankness and honesty and a vividness in the way children state themselves in a play situation. Their feelings, attitudes and thoughts emerge, unfold themselves, twist and turn and lose their sharp edges' (Axline 1969: 1).

Interactive play provides an environment that is non-judgemental, does not seek to correct, but guides the child to broaden their understanding of interpersonal relationships. This enables the child to feel comfortable in the company of others and creates a feeling of competence in the activity that will give rise to certain affective states. When playing children tend to express a wide range of emotions and they can vary between frustration, annoyance, excitement and contentment. In the absence of play or positive interactions a child might remain in a state of permanent arousal or constant distress that limits the experience of understanding one's own emotions or recognizing the emotional states of others. Denham (1998) provides a useful developmental model for the socialization of emotional competence that fits well into an interactive framework. She cites the socializing, or learning about emotion, as reliant upon both the inter- and intrapersonal contributions of the child and the carer. The child's ability to understand and express emotions is dependent upon the modelling and the giving of reactions by the adult during the interactive exchanges. When an adult reciprocates or exaggerates emotions during play the child is provided with more clues as to what they, and the person they are with, are experiencing. Tustin (1981) recognizes that the link between emotional development and the establishment of relationships is undeniable but she guards against educational approaches and therapies that are aimed at 'socializing' the child. 'It is important that we do not bombard the child with crude, simplistic attempts to make him become a social being. Other work has to be done on a level of sensuous integration before he is ready for that' (p. 162).

She also cites the interactive process of early bonding as vital to the knowledge of the 'experienced' self and others. It is the emotional experience of interacting that will lead to the development of thinking about one's own and others feelings. As Keenan (2002) points out, this emotional coding of experience guides all learning. In the same way that emotions contribute to the understanding of certain concepts, the ability to link feelings with communication is an additional aspect of social competence. Although emotional communication is not fully dependent upon language, the sharing of ideas and feelings acknowledges the value of the experience for the child, building confidence, self-esteem and the discovery of oneself as a communicating individual.

Shared language

The development of language and social relationships originates from the dyadic interactions that involve the sensitive responsiveness and non-verbal gestures of communication that occur before the emergence of speech. To develop communication and language, children need a reason to communicate and a context that determines the purpose for which language will be used. When a child is playing alone they have no need to share the experience and therefore no motivation to communicate what they are doing to someone else. The context for the development of communication and language is one that fosters the child's interests, involves joint activities and seeks to create a sense of partnership in the patterning of the interaction. Becoming a play partner facilitates the experience of shared intentions and shared meanings, allowing the child to discover the pragmatic basis for communication. Facilitating joint interactive exchanges enables the child to develop an understanding of what communication is and how it can be achieved. Developmentally, the acquisition of speech and language skills depends upon the establishment of reciprocal activities that involve anticipation, joint attention, and the gentle to and fro of the interactive exchanges. These preverbal proto-conversations are a significant feature of early interactions and are essential for children's language development. As Griffiths (2002) suggests, it is in realizing the value of what comes naturally to parents that will help communication and language make sense to the child. Parents naturally attune to their child's level of communication and carefully time their own interactions to ensure maximum response. Parents also make more use of non-verbal gestures of communication to ascertain their child's level of interest and carefully regulate their own language to match the child's understanding.

For children who do not develop language and communication skills at the same rate as others with typical development, there has been a tendency to teach them by breaking it down into small tasks, using artificial constructs that can become devoid of meaning for the child. Anderson-Wood and Smith (1997) found that when children were taught fixed meanings and syntactical structures prior to the pragmatics of communication, speech and language skills continued to be impaired. Farmer (2002) also recognizes that the development of communication and language is less effective when taught through strict reinforcement and that what is more relevant is the maintenance of the 'sensitive scaffolding of interactive encounters' to promote the generalization of skills (p. 137).

A parent told me how he had been trying to help his three-year-old son who has autism to follow the instructions 'stand up', 'sit down' and 'stop' using discrete training but his son had failed to comprehend what was required. One day when they were running around the lounge together, he said 'stop', and as he stopped running so did his son. He said 'sit down' and they both sat down, then he said 'stand up' and as he did so, so did his son. They continued the 'game' with great excitement as he recognized that learning in this way had greater meaning for his son.

As Prevezer (1998) suggests,

> Teaching spoken language, or indeed alternatives such as signs and symbols, is not enough for those with autism. We also need to help them engage in frequent positive interactions with familiar people as a context for learning so that they realise that they not only have to communicate but that it is a worthwhile and enjoyable thing to do.

(p. 7)

In typical development the ability to express communicative intent precedes the use of spoken language and symbolic representation. This occurs as a result of the mutual understanding that is taking place during reciprocal interactions. It is therefore crucial that strategies for developing playful interaction are applied before the implementation of rigorously structured language programmes. For children with autism, the establishment of communicative understanding and shared meanings is vital if they are to develop spoken language. Making a specific time to be with the child in playful exchanges helps in providing a structure to the interaction and focuses the experience of using non-verbal and verbal communication that will aid linguistic development. This is supported in research by Girolametto *et al.* (1994), who found that joint engagement during parent–child interactions was made possible by the responsiveness of the parents to the child's focus of attention. This is because, for the child, the object or activity they are focusing on is 'known'; it has qualities that the child understands both at a level of affect and cognition. An introduced toy or an expectation to react in a certain way might be confusing and therefore harder to comprehend until the child can relate to the relevance of the experience. Expectations for the child to achieve something may override the need to spend time assimilating what is taking place and can influence the extent to which he or she learns to communicate spontaneously. Being over enthusiastic or demanding when it does not match the child's reactions to an experience might have the effect of reducing the child's motivation to share in the activity.

For many children with autism, difficulties in verbally expressing their personal preferences and beliefs can affect their behaviour and interactions with others and it is questionable whether discrete language teaching can compensate for what is, more fundamentally, the need to acquire knowledge of linguistic structures through a more naturalistic approach. This process is likely to achieve more shared understanding of communication, whereas encouraging a child to talk using controlled responses and enforced repetition does little to help the child sustain any interest in communicating.

Sussman (1999) also advocates using more naturalistic approaches to enable children with autism to develop communication skills. Ensuring a natural response through play and interaction increases opportunities for the child to participate in and initiate interaction whether preverbally or through spoken language. Regardless of whether a child can respond verbally it is important to create a sense of mutual understanding through the verbal responses that are given by the play partner. Being responsive to the child's utterances and communicative gestures acknowledges his or her efforts to interact. This occurs more readily because the playful exchanges in themselves are following a narrative structure. In the early stages of development, children are also experimenting with different ways of communicating and this is often more evident in their actions rather than their vocalizations.

In one play session, a child began eating the play dough and his co-worker attempted to stop this by taking it away. Rather than remove it, I suggested that she tried to show him why it was not nice to eat and so every time he picked up some play dough to eat, she told him it was 'disgusting' in a voice that made him laugh. He soon realized what was happening and to our surprise he began teasing her by holding the play dough near his mouth and looking at her before she got the chance to tell him again. His ability to tease represented a more complex communication skill that otherwise might not have occurred had the play dough been removed.

Language becomes more meaningful when it is linked to experiences and activities that are relevant to children rather than taught in isolated contexts. Every context in which children find themselves is an opportunity to learn about language. As the child is playing, so the play partner is imbuing the experience with language that is describing, labelling, and building conceptual understanding. The aim of interactive play is to reduce the complexities of communication and language and increase the understanding that social interaction is a means to gaining more knowledge.

Communication and language skills are reliant upon the adult's role to facilitate development and there is a need to adopt an approach to being with the child that is appropriate to his or her level of communicative competence. Within the narrative structure of the interactive play it is important to ensure that the child does not have too much information to process, in terms of both the language and the activity, as this can limit both verbal and non-verbal responses. The extended use of gestures, facial expressions and imitation that are indicative of early interactions with infants provides a much more comprehensive system for establishing mutual engagement and communicative exchanges. In addition to facilitating these interactive experiences, other studies have looked at interactive styles of early intervention for children with autism (Chandler *et al.* 2002; Bernard-Opitz *et al.* 2004). They indicated that it was the parents' training and their ability to maintain the strategies suggested in the programmes that most significantly affected the children's potential communicative and linguistic abilities.

Motivation

Motivation is a key factor in directing behaviour. It also influences the intensity and persistence of goal-oriented behaviours that ultimately affect all interactions. Consequently, behaviour has tended to be used as a measure of the levels of motivation that pertain to an individual. The difficulty with this perspective is that it may not always be possible to ascertain the links between an individual's strengths and interests and their subjective well-being, which are key elements of self-motivation. This implies that there is a need to look at what is implicit in the behaviour to ascertain the reasons for differences in motivational states.

Play occupies children in such a way that absorption in the activity and the focus of attention leads to a qualitative experience that is defined by the individual. Chazan (2002) emphasizes that it is the child's attentive state during play that provides a framework for the development of competence and confidence in coping with the world: 'The attentive state seems to arise from the child and transport him to a different sphere – a place of possibilities' (p. 19).

Motivation occurs as a result of the internalization of the experience, based on the individual's own response to the stimuli. The sharing of the focus of interest during interactive play heightens the feelings of competence and the desire to express this to others. Schore (1994) suggests that it is during the formation of early social relationships that the brain develops the capacity towards both intrinsic and extrinsic motivation. Relationships that provide individuals with an awareness of their own social competence are more likely to result in the development of intrinsic motivation. The orbitofrontal area of the brain most responsible for motivation is also critical in the formation of selective attention towards specific stimuli. This area has been found to be significantly impaired in individuals with autism and would therefore account for the difficulties in the appraisal and significance of socially motivated behaviour (Waterhouse et al. 1996). Developing the motivation to relate to others is dependent upon the environmental stimuli and the nature of the dyadic interactions that inform the child's sense of autonomy and self-worth.

Temperament can be regarded as secondary factor in motivation. As with tolerance, temperament plays a significant role in the formation, maintenance and repair of relationships. Although it will be constitutional, the child's temperament will also be influenced by early bonding experiences, owing to the frequent changes in emotion that occur during the gaining and withdrawal of interaction. They constantly shift between negative and positive states that enable them to regulate their behaviour. It is the consistency in the ways that these states are responded to by the carers that will enable the child to regulate emotions and establish a particular temperament. Through interactive play the child is provided with opportunities for spontaneous arousal, the exploration and mastery of new experiences (Peeters and Gillberg 1999), persistence and creativity. It is these principles that are embedded within the play experience that will qualitatively influence the development of motivation and the child's personality.

Research suggests that individuals with autism lack the motivation to take an interest in developing social interaction and this impinges significantly on their learning and experiences (Peeters and Gillberg 1999). This is not to say that they do not possess their own internal motivations for specific activities, but that they limit the extent to which they seek out others to share in those experiences that are intrinsically motivating for them. However, to date there have been few studies carried out that indicate how to bring about more socially motivated behaviours in individuals with autism with the exception of those strategies that make use of external motivators and reward systems. Although there is evidence to suggest that external rewards can assist in gaining a response that will lead to more self-determining behaviour, there is a distinct difference between rewards that are given as a recognition of achievement and those which are used for controlling behaviour. Whether it is a play- or task-based activity, it is crucial that children are not taught that they are only valued when they conform. Individuals are less likely to develop intrinsic motivation as a result of compliance because the action is based upon the external validation of others.

Play is usually intrinsically motivating for children except when they have to play in a way that someone else wants them to. This has a tendency to reduce the incentive to perform or complete a task because it is being controlled by external factors rather than internal motivation. Teaching play routines through structured teaching methods lessens opportunities for the spontaneous use of toys or objects and the ability for the child to make preferences or choices in their interactions. Activities that children come to associate with success will stimulate interest and lead to increased motivation, whereas activities that they do not understand will result in avoidance behaviours. In the study by Koegel *et al.* (1987) they also found that children with autism would engage in social avoidance behaviour to terminate interactions that were non-reinforcing. This would suggest that children benefit from both structured and spontaneous opportunities to increase their motivationally responsive behaviour.

Regardless of the level of the child's intellectual functioning, it is his or her interest and engagement in the experience with another person that will determine the extent to which it is motivating.

When the play partner comes to regard everything the child does as purposeful, this gives meaning to the experience and opens up the capacity for the recognition of self-efficacy. Ryan and Deci (2000) suggest that intrinsic motivation is strengthened when individuals are offered choices about how to complete tasks and when positive feedback is received this increases the levels of competence. The immediacy of the feedback provided during interactive play and the use of naturally reinforcing consequences increase the child's interest and confidence in communicating a response. By valuing the child's actions, this builds self-esteem and gives him or her the ability to regulate interactions that become intrinsically motivating.

Behaviour

Interactive play experiences that are meaningful and positive and provide children with a sense of their own agency are paramount in extending the social experience. This includes the conscious development of socially motivated behaviour as well as engagement in those activities that are specifically ego related. As Sherratt (2001) points out, when a child's play has personal relevance it will also have communicative relevance. This includes a strong desire by the child to respond in ways that reflect the emotional experience that is offered during the play. As the child determines the relevance of what is being achieved, the pattern of the interaction becomes more goal directed. This is influenced by the way in which the child uses emotions to assist in the regulation and modulation of behaviour.

Frequently, in play sessions, I have observed the child's gradual realization of their own ability to be more self-assured about their actions. This occurs for two reasons: first, that the approach to play is not directed at what the child should be doing; second, because the process of change is being positively supported through mutually affective interaction. Any acting-out behaviour that takes place during the play is a response by the child to gain control of their feelings.

I had been playing hide-and-seek with a child in her playroom where she had spent three years following a structured learning programme. As she became more familiar with the game and we took turns to hide her favourite objects, she became very excited each time she rediscovered them and this resulted in her pulling my hair and then her mother's and sister's hair. Her mother was clearly distressed at this response and felt that perhaps this activity had not been appropriate because it had resulted in some challenging behaviour. However, what is often regarded as regressive or 'acting-out' behaviour is instead an act of self-discovery. The interactive nature of the activity had heightened her reactions and as the play continued she realised that she could have some control of the experience.

Clements and Zarkowska (2001) argue that once judgements about a particular behaviour are removed it makes it easier to enter into a shared dialogue and focus on the underlying emotional needs to help maintain an individual's sense of self-worth. Behaviour is a representation of thoughts and actions and how a toy or object is being played with communicates its relevance for the child. In educational terms 'relevance' is often confused with 'competence', and children's behaviour is often referred to as 'good' or 'bad' depending on how appropriate it appears to be. Such judgements are frequently placed on the ways that children with autism might be playing with an object or toy; for example, if they are mouthing or flicking objects and whether it is considered age-appropriate.

It is the nature of the play experience and the establishment of meaningful interaction that will have the most significant effect on how a child responds to new challenges and different experiences. During interactive play, the supportive play partner seeks to maintain an atmosphere that provides the child with a sense of achievement and enjoyment. This has the potential to alter the ways that a child might behave to get his or her needs met, increasing the possibility for more socially responsive behaviour. These changes also occur because the motivational basis for the interaction has changed.

> I observed a child who frequently took her parents by the hand and led them to the kitchen to open the door so that she could go in the garden and play with the water hose. As this was where she liked to be, I encouraged her parents to think of ways that they could join her in a variety of other outdoor activities. This would provide her with a range of new experiences that would motivate her to play and interact with them.

Interactions that involve high levels of arousal, interest and pleasure are more likely to influence motivational states than those activities that are demanding or of low interest. As children play, so their absorption in the activity, their ability to accept the challenges they impose on themselves and the satisfaction that is inherent in what is achieved all impact on their sense of well-being and behaviour. The development of motivation increases competence in the activity and the desire to communicate with others. It is this emotional engagement in meaningful experiences and the child's recognition of their own autonomous behaviour that leads to the construction of more complex ways of thinking.

Flexibility

In all its diverse forms, play is a valuable occupation that enables children to adapt their thinking and behaviour, especially when they can have some mastery and control over what is happening. Whether it is through play that is provided for them or created by themselves, children can learn to develop more flexible thinking when they are given different ways to explore and represent those experiences that are meaningful to them. Flexibility in thinking involves the capability for self-reflectiveness, hypothetical thinking and symbolic functioning, and this relates to the socio-affective influences that are involved in all interactions. The role of play in cognitive processing is synonymous with the influence of interpersonal relationships on the development of mind. Interactive play impacts on the development of cognition in the same way by placing value on the dynamic process of self-discovery, the manipulation and symbolic use of objects, and the interpersonal connectedness that is essential for learning.

Theories that link play and cognitive development are now well established. From a historical perspective, Froebel (1792–1852) believed in the benefits of play in providing a holistic approach to learning as an alternative to the compartmentalization of chunks of knowledge and experience. Montessori (1869–1952) saw play as instrumental in furthering cognitive development through children's recognition of their own independence and autonomy in the learning experience, in much the same way as Piaget. On the other hand, Vygotsky considered the actions of children, and the knowledge they gain from their interactions with others and the world around them, as the major influence on cognitive development. Sutton-Smith (1997) takes a more philosophical view of play in that he regards it as the actualization of 'potential brain and behaviour connections' (p. 229). Whether from a biological, psychological or philosophical perspective, play is invariably considered in terms of its function and influence on cognitive processes. As such, play provides:

- new and different possibilities for action;
- a means to acquire and organize knowledge about the world;
- the ability to develop transferable skills;
- an opportunity to take risks and be challenged within a safe context;
- the stimulation for the development of perception;
- access to representational thinking;
- a forum for processing language;
- experiences that involve planning, sequencing and memory.

Play is not the only context in which these skills can emerge but it is relevant to this discussion that it is regarded as an essential medium for their acquisition. The development of flexibility in thinking is dependent upon experiences that children are given to build a conceptual framework for furthering knowledge and understanding. Early exploration, in which sensory play predominates, provides the basis for concrete thinking. Time has to be given to enable children to process new information so that the ability to represent an experience or object differently reflects the growing awareness of their own mind. Introducing new and different concepts in a way that focuses the child's attention – for example with an element of fun, enjoyment and mutual interest – increases the capacity for altering how an object or activity is represented (Figure 2.3).

Whether it is the action of the play or what it represents, it is the experience of playing that aids children's thinking and perception. For individuals with autism, the nature of their perceptual differences has compounded views about their perceptual competencies. Often others do not recognize that underlying these differences, particularly in relation to sensory perception, are the same emotional and cognitive structures that are common to everyone. The extent to which the mind has the capacity to create representations or imagined thought is linked to emotion. Emotional states significantly affect the way in which individuals respond to specific stimuli and this accounts for the unique ways in which they perceive and understand the world.

A further key feature in the development of flexible thinking is the extent to which actions, experiences and emotions demonstrate causal relationships. Ozonoff's theory (1995) that individuals with autism have a weak central coherence of executive function implies that much of their thinking occurs in a more detached form. Frontal lobe functions that are involved in the regulation of social behaviour, emotional

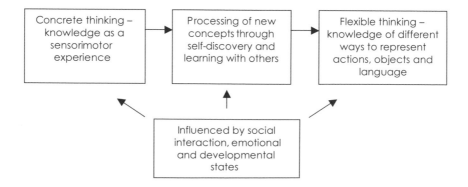

Figure 2.3 The development of flexible thinking.

reactions and the maintenance of internal representations are identified in the difficulties that individuals with autism have in integrating ideas and experiences. The need for coherence is a significant feature of life, not just for individuals with autism. As such, the search for coherence is highly individual and what becomes a relevant way of thinking and behaving for one person may be very different for another. A child may become mesmerized when playing with spittle and even quite creative with it by observing the colours and shapes and visual distortions it makes, but for someone else this activity might be considered quite unpleasant. That children with autism do not develop imaginative ways of thinking is a misconception. The internalizing of early sensory perceptual experiences underpinned with the emotions is represented as images in the memory. At some point in the child's development they begin to use objects to project those same feelings. At any time while children are playing they have the capacity to use an object and represent it symbolically. It is through their creative use of objects that children have an opportunity to comprehend and explore their world in new and different ways, to make new connections and develop new understandings.

During a literacy session, six boys in the class were given an opportunity to choose five objects and, using an individual tray containing sand or rice, they had to make up their own stories. Connor chose his five objects and a tray of rice and sat by himself exploring the objects and moving his hands around in the rice. In addition to his autism, Connor also has verbal and motor dyspraxia. This meant that his exploration of his objects and the rice involved him in making several uncoordinated movements and making repeated sounds. When I asked him to tell me his story he placed the animals he had chosen in the rice. He repeatedly picked up handfuls of rice and said, 'It's raining on the giraffe, it's raining on the elephant.' I joined in with his narrative and our shared focus on his story was maintained as I imitated his actions. This encouraged him to use more sentences to describe how the rain was falling, spreading and wetting the animals.

Symbolic acts occur as children engage in play activities, particularly if they have had a choice about what to play with. What the child perceives as an appropriate way to play with an object must be reflected in the reactions of the play partner. This communicates to the child that his or her intentional behaviour has meaning and therefore symbolic relevance. Werner and Kaplan, cited in Hobson (1993), also recognize that symbol formation is inextricably linked to the interpersonal domain. They identified that when children are given opportunities to contemplate objects as part of the shared experience, they develop the capacity to alter the sense of the object 'as it is' to what it can become. The teaching of functional play to children with autism may conversely affect the potential for using objects creatively and imaginatively. There are limitations in predicting and structuring a play sequence, in that the controlled expectations for interacting and playing are more likely to maintain inflexible thought processes. Wolfberg's study (1999) found that children's capacity to establish joint action, role enactment and role playing corresponded to an increased sense of social awareness and shared understanding. Similarly, the development of imagination lies in the opportunities children are given to represent their experiences, feelings and ideas and to share them with others.

As a result of the interpersonal connectedness that is occurring during interactive play, the capacity to recognize symbolic acts has greater potential. Hobson (1993) emphasizes that the child's experience of being with others is in fact a prerequisite for, rather than a precursor to, the development of creative symbolic functioning. Shared experiences increase opportunities for developing an understanding of others as having separate minds and therefore the capacity to represent thoughts and actions differently. Children are more likely to hold onto the thought that an object can be represented as something else when they understand the other person's intentional use of it, for example using a plastic bottle as a rocket. The capacity to understand pretence does not come just from the use of an object, but also through the actions and responses of the play partner, who might, for example, exaggerate pretending to cry when the child is reluctant to share a toy.

According to Duffy (1998), once children have the opportunity to separate objects and actions from their meaning in the real world and give them a new meaning they are no longer bound to concrete ways of understanding the world and can start thinking in more abstract ways. The impact of more flexible ways of thinking will also be significant in the creation of a more coherent construction of reality. However, ensuring that an understanding of 'reality' remains firmly with the individual will be essential for ascertaining any potential development. When given opportunities to engage in interpersonal communication and autonomous behaviour, the capacity for the development of social cognition and flexible thinking is consolidated. As a range of skills can occur simultaneously during play, any progress can be regarded as congruent with the availability of the shared experience.

The identification of these competencies establishes this model of interactive play as a theory of interconnectivity in that it provides a more holistic view of children's potential development. Examples of interactive play are used in the following chapters to show how children with autism have developed competencies in interpersonal connectedness and communication, playing with toys and objects in ways that are both purposeful and meaningful and using their imagination. In particular they focus on how to foster their motivation to interact and how this can lead to an increased capacity for social understanding, adapting to new experiences and shared learning. The next chapter considers the physiological, emotional and developmental needs for interaction and positive relationship building. It specifically focuses on the importance of establishing the kind of relationships that promote playful interactions.

Chapter 3

Establishing connection

> We need to realise that one of the most powerful influences on development is what happens *between* people.
>
> (Hobson 2002: 7)

As a social being, the young infant strives to create relationships with others that are essential for survival. This innate need to establish connectedness with significant people in the child's life provides the foundations for social development and emotional well-being. Psychologists have always been interested in the inter- and intrapersonal influences on children's development, acknowledging that there is a fundamental biological and emotional drive to interact with others. It is not only the experience of relating to another person to have one's needs met that is regarded as having a significant influence on emotional and intellectual growth, but also the quality of relationships.

Unlike other disabilities or deprivations in childhood, autism is unique in that there is a significant neurological dysfunction that results in the poor development of relatedness to another that is compounded by impairments in the emotional and communication aspects of interpersonal relationships. Where there has been a disruption in the development of affectional bonds this will undoubtedly influence the extent to which a reciprocal relationship can be established by the main carers (Bowlby 1979). Interaction is a two-way process, which not only involves the personal capabilities of the individual but is influenced by the specific social context in which those interactions take place. As a consequence of this it is impossible to refer to the difficulties that people with autism have in social interaction as a one-person condition. Hence an interactive model that focuses on the development of a positive social dyad becomes more salient.

Rather than focus on a deficit-based model of interaction, this chapter relates theories of social and emotional development to current research on the neurobiological and psychopathological effects of interaction on both the child and the caregiver. Any changes in the social and emotional functions are viewed as resulting from the interplay between the child's neurophysiology and the establishment of positive relationships with the primary caregivers.

Establishing a connectedness to others always involves sharing in sensoriaffective experiences and the significance attached to these is the basis upon which all encounters are made. The embodiment of sensory play within a nurturing relationship will have a profound influence on the child's development and, in discovering another way of being with a child it becomes a new encounter that can significantly alter previously held opinions about his or her difficulties and potentialities. Through engagement in shared play, more secure bonds between the child and the play partner can be established so that as the child gains in confidence, together they seek out more elaborate ways of interacting and connecting. It is through this process of interdependence that there is greater potential for the enrichment of the relationship.

Fraser was ten years old and had Asperger's syndrome. I had spent a few sessions with him and his brother to help them to develop more cooperative and positive ways of interacting. Towards the end of one of our sessions, Fraser picked up two very strong magnets that were in a tray of other magnetic shapes that I use for story-making. He held a magnet in each hand and as he brought them close together his hands were moving about as he tried to keep them apart. 'This is like brothers fighting,' he told me. Then he put the magnets together and said, 'And now they're hugging and they can't let go.'

Although playing with these magnets symbolized Fraser's ability to recognize how the work we had been doing together had become very meaningful to him, the magnets also provide a useful analogy for describing the power of human connection. Connectivity demands an energy flow that links mind and emotion with experience. Positively charged interactions are indicative of our need as social beings to find ways to reach out to one another that can bring about a transformation in the relationship. For children with autism, establishing connectedness through interactive play creates a new therapeutic alliance that can become the catalyst for personal and emotional growth. By looking at normal developmental patterns of interaction it is possible to identify the individual's cognitive and affective capacities for developing meaningful relationships. The maintenance of any relationship is regarded positively as being experience dependent and based on the personal strengths, emotional well-being and motivational states of both people within the dyad. Shared play experiences that are influenced by the psychobiological attunement between the child and the play partner are implicit in the establishment of mutually affective relationships. Both Tronick (1998) and Fosha (2001) recognize that secure relationships play a major role in the child's ability to manage emotions to bring about more adaptive behaviour.

The dyadic emotional communication is maintained for the self-needs of the individuals as well as the relational experience of connecting and feeling close to each other. It is through these core states that changes in the relationship are more likely to happen – not only in the child, but also in the parent or carer. For those children who appear unavailable or unresponsive to mutually affective experiences, the potential to transform the relationship is most likely to be achieved therapeutically via the empathetic responsiveness of meaningful interactive exchanges.

The need for touch

Having a dialogue of touch is not only necessary for physical protection and survival; it also provides an emotional need for comfort and security. This is not just a feature of child dependency but is also a significant aspect of the emotional lives of adults. Establishing connectedness through the experience of touch helps children to be more available to the development of the relationship. Emotional reactions towards others may appear distorted in children with autism and this can often be manifest in an emotional sensitivity towards touch. For the child who is withdrawing from touch it is essential that the play partner begins by offering a warm presence towards him or her in the play space. If the child is uncertain of physical contact, synchronizing and mirroring the child's movements will help to increase an awareness of that presence. Essentially, the child's recognition that touch is not something to be feared enables them to equate a comforting experience with feelings of being nurtured. Field *et al.* (1997) found that when children with autism experienced a programme of touch therapy there was a decrease in touch aversion and improvements in social relating. Although there are many different cultural attitudes towards touch, it remains true that it is an essential component for the maintenance of mutually supportive relationships.

It is by acknowledging the child's motives to interact and the emotions that accompany them that the play partner can engage in activities and games that can help to reduce any sensitivities towards different types of touch. Through the use of safe, caring touch children's knowledge and understanding of different sensations emerges into consciousness with increasing awareness. Gentle touch with light objects such as feathers and other soft materials mimics the arousal and comfort experiences of the young baby. Similarly, deep pressure touch, which can also be offered through massage, stimulates the chemicals in the brain that increase the capacity to feel pleasure and happiness. Grandin (1992) describes how, for many individuals with autism, deep pressure touch can be more energizing and comforting than light touch and therefore massage and being rolled in a blanket may be preferable to being stroked. Massage is a valuable tool for establishing connectedness. Not only does it provide an opportunity to be in close proximity, but it also helps in shaping experiences that form the emotional self. It has also been found to be beneficial for parents who have had difficulty bonding with their child and can assist in reducing levels of stress and improving sleep habits in young infants. Many children with autism respond to and gain a lot of enjoyment from tickle games, rough and tumble and gross motor physical activities, and while these can always be included in a play session it is important that they match the child's levels of sensitivity towards touch.

Movement and touch are the primary means of non-verbal communication between two individuals whereby the pattern and sequence of interactions are essential for establishing a dialogue of attunement and reciprocity. Through the playful interactions of 'peek-a-boo' and 'tickle' games that are typical of early lap play, the adult and the child are constantly striving to create a pattern of movement between them that is synchronized by their emotional states. Trevarthen (2004) acknowledges that there is a deep need for individuals to make contact with one another through the rhythm and power of moving. With the impulse to move, the child is communicating a desire to connect with his or her surroundings, which results in a greater awareness of the self outside the body and the self in relation to others.

Experiencing the presence of another who is providing sensitive responses enhances the likelihood of the child initiating contact towards that person because it is based on the recognition of trust. Touch communicates at a preverbal level, intensifying how attuned individuals can become towards one another. It literally is about *getting in touch*.

Aishah was a fourteen-year-old teenager with autism who I met in a school for children with autism. She was non-verbal and had severe learning difficulties. When not involved in a task, Aishah would spend most of her time seeking out food. She was overweight and sometimes it resulted in three members of staff trying to prevent her from moving around the school looking for something to eat.

We set up some time for me to work with Aishah to see whether we could begin to engage her in other interests. In a very plain room there was a table, on which I had put some play dough, and a mat on the floor. The play dough had been made with flour and water and I was interested to see whether she regarded it as food. She briefly explored the play dough by rubbing it between her fingers. Although it was home-made she made no attempt to eat it. I imitated how she was manipulating the play dough and together we made a pattern of small shapes on the table. She then indicated by holding my hand that she wanted us to sit on the floor together. As she became more comfortable with my presence she put my hand on her head and her arm. I used this spontaneous action as an opportunity to massage her head and stroke her arms, which calmed and relaxed her. I was pleased that she had taken such an interest in wanting me to be with her and it was essential for future work that I did with her that we were able to establish our relationship in a way that gave her more confidence in relating.

Creating a dialogue of touch that is mutually acceptable and establishes feelings of safety and trust will develop the child's capacity to relate more effectively across different emotional, physical and cognitive modalities. The responsiveness of the child to the touch helps to stimulate pleasurable states between individuals and increases the availability to mutually enjoyable experiences. Interactive games that are matched to the child's sensory preferences, such as swinging, rocking or chasing, will help in maintaining proximity and enjoyment. It is through such experiences that children are more likely to develop sensitivity to the affective states of others; this is not only because they are discovering how to create a dialogue through the physical contact, but because they are mirroring the same pleasure chemical response in the brain as their play partner.

Smiling

It is a feature of relationships that intense emotions will arise during their formation, maintenance, disruption and renewal. This is particularly the case with an infant's first smile that has a profound effect on furthering the bond between the child and main carer. In the first few weeks of life a physical bond is being established, which is predominantly based on the physiological needs of the child. The first smile is an external gesture that signifies the desire to interact, while at the same time it internalizes feelings of pleasure and comfort that will impact on emotional development. It is the first true social interaction. The mirroring of the gesture by the carer also marks a primary phase in the infant's conscious recognition of self as separate from 'other'.

A smile is the most powerful and rewarding act of communication initiated by the child that psychologically impacts on the carer's desire to attune more with the infant. Through this system of non-verbal communication the child and the carer co-create a context that allows for the outward expression of internal affective states. Trevarthen (1993) describes this emotional connection as one that is based on the coordination of eye-to-eye messages, vocalizations, tactile stimuli and body gestures that produce positive effects of excitement and pleasure between the child and the parent.

> The transfer of emotional information is thus intensified in resonant contexts. The phenomena of resonant, rhythmic matching and affect synchrony thus underlie the maximization of the communication of emotional states within an intimate dyad, and represent the psychobiological underpinning of empathy.
>
> (Schore 2003: 32)

Once established as a gesture of positive social engagement, opportunities to repeat the experience are sought as much as possible, initially by the child and then by the parent who uses increasingly more playful ways to ensure the maintenance of the interaction. In conversations with many parents about their child's early development, they frequently refer to sharing smiles in mutual engagement as very much in evidence prior to the onset or awareness of autism. This would appear to be significant, in that, although the child may not fully develop a conscious recognition of emotional connectedness to another, there is an unconscious awareness of those emotional states which help to maintain the parent–child bond. It further implies that the re-establishment of early bonding experiences can be used as the catalyst for enhancing children's emotional awareness.

Smiles also become the catalyst for extending pleasure into laughter. Playful interactions that result in laughter become powerful communicators of emotional connectedness. Laughter is a contagious emotion and provides a natural diversion to dealing with stressful situations.

Miya enjoyed her trips to the park with her parents but they were concerned that she seemed to prefer playing by herself on the swings, slide and roundabout while they watched her. There was also very little interaction between Miya and the other children and this was because she was unable to respond verbally when they spoke to her. During one of our sessions I went with them to the park and observed how she was playing. While she was playing on the slide I suggested to her father that he went and stood at the bottom to catch her. As she came down the slide she was surprised to see him there and smiled. She went up the slide again but this time I suggested to her father that he exaggerate his reaction towards her as she came down. He caught her and gave her a big hug and this made her laugh. They did this a few more times but when Miya wanted to change the activity she ran off onto the grass area of the park. Her father chased her and Miya was laughing and smiling. As he caught her they shared their laughter and smiles. Occasionally she would fall over as she ran so he tickled her before she could run off again. Her mother and I had sat watching this and when I turned to comment on the fun they were having she had tears in eyes. It had a been a while, she told me, since she had seen them playing so happily together and it was very moving for her to see them enjoying themselves.

It is always interesting to observe that when children with autism are sharing playful interactions that are bound by laughter and fun their capacity for social interaction increases. Through laughter children express greater confidence physically and mentally and this triggers the release of endorphins, providing a sense of well-being. Neurobiological studies have shown that the chemicals that run the body and the brain are the same chemicals that are involved in emotion (Pert 1999). When interactions are based on positive arousal factors the brain produces more of an energy flow, which has been found to significantly impact on the development of the right hemisphere of the brain that is responsible for socio-emotional functioning.

Schore's studies (2003) suggest that it is the socio-emotional experiences established through emotional synchronicity with a significant adult that are responsible for the maturation of the amygdala during infancy. In particular, the amygdala has been found to influence emotional learning, social behaviour and social cognition, and it has a significant role in linking social stimuli with social meaning. It mediates both inborn and acquired emotional states that are then brought into conscious awareness.

In young children who are still preverbal, smiling and laughing occurs predominantly during face-to-face interactions with a parent rather than when they are left alone to occupy themselves. This signifies the importance of the face in facilitating the socio-emotional connection between them. Research into facial recognition in autism has added to the discussion that difficulties with eye contact are the result of problems that individuals with autism have in social and affective functioning (Hobson et al. 1988; Boucher et al. 1998; Marcus and Nelson 2001) and research into the neurological base for the development of face recognition has identified that it is the amygdala dysfunction in individuals with autism that accounts for the lack of social interest in faces (Adolphs et al. 2001; Grelotti et al. 2002).

During interactive play the potential for increases in smiles and eye contact is heightened because there is a greater emphasis on the amplification of positive states that stimulate the child's responsiveness (Schore 2001). I have frequently observed that when the play partner mutually engages with the child in a way that promotes vocalizations, smiles and laughter, there is a significant increase in the use of eye contact. Tickling, bouncing and exaggerated facial expressions also provide opportunities for spontaneous communication and the motivation for social and emotional engagement.

Identifying the deficits that individuals with autism have in understanding and using facial expressions to denote specific emotions might contribute to a better understanding of a developmental pathology, but it would appear to be more relevant to consider the impact that positive relationships have on brain development and how an increase in playful interactions can bring about potential changes in brain function. Numerous studies are now focusing on the neurobiological influences of attachment and bonding on the child and parent (Insel 1997; Carter 1998; Modahl et al. 1998; Uvas-Moberg 1998). Their findings suggest a strong correlation between positive states of social arousal and emotional regulation and the release of neural endorphins such as oxytocin and vasopressin. A study by Hollander et al. (2003) suggested that raising oxytocin levels in individuals with autism led to a reduction in repetitive behaviours and an increase in social processing and feelings of trust and security that are a feature of social bonding. Panskepp (1997) has highlighted the relevance of identifying those treatments and interventions that may assist some individuals with autism to develop more social awareness by raising oxytocin levels, particularly via the establishment of positive models of interaction such as play. The experience of fun and enjoyment between the child and the play partner is heightened during interactive play and becomes enmeshed with the giving and receiving of smiles that unifies the relationship and stimulates the desire to maintain the dyadic interaction. Trevarthen and Aitken (2001) refer to this as proto-conversational play, which is based on the rhythmic patterning and repetitive expressions that the parent offers the child and in which the child responds with increasing interest. This mutual regulation of emotions has both a psychobiological function and neurobiological consequences and, as such, is fundamental to how relationships develop.

Encounter

In order to experience connectedness there has to be an encounter that is based on unconditionally valuing the child as he or she is. An acceptance of the child becomes an unconscious communication that enables him or her to develop a greater understanding of the nature of relationships.

> an encounter
> is a strange
> and wonderful thing
> presence one person to another
> present
> one to another
> life flowing
> one to another
>
> (Vanier 1973: 76)

Responding to the play encounter in the present also acknowledges the relationship without preconditions or expectations. Sometimes what is known about the child's behaviour affects how the play partner will respond to attempts by the child to interact. Being attentive to the child enables the play partner to gain insight into the child's emotional world and provides the child with a sense of adequacy and worthiness.

In a school for children with severe learning difficulties I had been asked to work with Ali, whose behavioural outbursts in the classroom had become a concern to his teacher. Ali's frustrations and anxieties often presented themselves by throwing objects or physically attacking staff. I had been informed that when confronted Ali would respond by attempting to bite the other person. At the beginning of my first session with Ali I did not attempt to interact with him but let him explore some of the objects that were in the room for him to play with. He stood in a corner of the room and covered himself with a piece of bubble wrap. I moved towards him and lifted up the bubble wrap and then moved away from him. After doing this a few times he realized this as a game that he could be in control of and he started to move around the room. I responded to his game of 'peek-a-boo' by imitating him and covering my head with a piece of bubble wrap. He accepted my presence and, as he gained more confidence in my being in the room with him, he moved towards me and removed the bubble wrap that was over my head.

When play becomes an interactive experience, both partners are encouraged to enter into a dyadic relationship that immediately engages both emotion and cognition. Such immediacy offers a containing and congruent presence that has the potential to provide empathetic contact. For encounters to be meaningful, children need a safe environment in which to explore different stimuli and a sense of agency towards the experience. Other key influences that will affect the most profound of all social learning experiences are as follows.

The motivation to participate

This is reliant upon others acknowledging the need to establish more mutual ways of being together. Because some children withdraw from knowing why interaction is relevant it becomes the responsibility of the adults to consciously become involved in making playful encounters available. The child is invited, but not coerced, into play by making available activities that interest the child. Children need the reassurance that such encounters will encompass their sense of emotional well-being in order for them to make a judgement about whether they want to repeat the shared experience.

Mohammed had been described by his teacher as a child with profound learning difficulties and poor communication skills. He took very little interest in what his peers were doing and only related to staff when they initiated contact with him. He found it difficult to engage in activities independently and frequently occupied himself by flicking his fingers and spitting on objects around the room. This pattern of behaviour was evident as Mohammed explored the playroom. He took no interest in the objects that were there for him to explore but rather he explored the room by moving around it and tapping on the walls, the chair, the door, sometimes adding spittle to what he was touching. When he tapped on the wall I copied him and moved around the room like him. I altered my tapping with my hands to tapping on two sticks and he continued to tap around the room and flick his fingers. He seemed for some time not to be aware of my imitating him and became fixated with tapping on the door handle, which I took to indicate that he had perhaps had enough of being in the room. However, his teacher who was observing felt that he was beginning to gain an understanding that I was copying him and suggested that I continue. This certainly was the case. Mohammed had begun to anticipate that I would tap after he had tapped and started to use eye contact to await my response. He moved across the room and with his back to me he tapped on the wall. He turned and smiled and then looked at me to respond to his tapping. It had taken most of the session for him to gain an understanding of my presence but there was clear evidence that this had impacted on his awareness of how another person could respond to him.

The following week I observed his teacher with him in the playroom. He began with the same behaviour as in the previous session but this time it did not take long for him to realize that she was following his actions by tapping the sticks together. He reached out and took the sticks from her and tapped these instead. This was an indication of a development in his understanding, not only about his own behaviour but also how he could extend his interactive skills.

The availability to the play experience

This is not only based on external factors such as when and how it will take place, but also on what is happening to entice the child to express a willingness to be part of the play experience. In order to create an empathetic presence, the play partner has to take into account the child's way of seeing the world. It is important to remember the unique ways in which this occurs for individual children and to acknowledge that their interactions with objects and people have specific meaning to them. In those initial encounters, how the child wants to play will have a significant influence on developing the interaction.

Clara was standing on the stairs, holding on to a 'Thomas the Tank Engine' comic, as I was welcomed into the family home. She looked at me and in response to my 'hello' walked past me into another room. I was taken into the main living room but it was clear that Clara did not want to join us. Her parents explained that in the past few weeks she had become very anxious about being in that room and preferred to spend most of her time in the garden or her bedroom. We discussed some of the ways that Clara would engage with them and her sister through play. She would bring them a toy (usually a train) and push it along the floor for a few minutes and then go away again. Her sister wanted to be able to play more with Clara but expressed how she often got upset because Clara did not understand what she wanted her to do. As we made a list of the activities that Clara liked we noticed that they mostly involved water, shiny objects, trains and physical activities such as the slide, the trampoline and her bike. Clara's play was a significant part of her multisensory world.

For the next session her parents had collected a variety of shiny objects that included scarves, Christmas decorations, spinning tops and hats and we put them in the living room. Clara was delighted as she explored these objects with her parents for thirty minutes. There was an incentive for her to be in the living room and her parents were pleased that they had found a way to be together as a family. Her sister realized that she also liked being outside and the garden provided an opportunity for them to discover how to play together. In future sessions we observed them holding hands on the trampoline and taking turns on the slide. Clara would copy her sister walking up the slide and they would follow each other around the garden on their bikes.

Making a special time

Planning a special time to be playfully engaged with the child is crucial. The child needs to recognize that time has been made available for him or her that focuses on developing trust, empathy and openness. Without a clearly defined time, the effectiveness of the interaction will not be recognized, activities may not be fully explored and there may be pressure on the child to achieve something through the play, rather than engage in the process of mutual enjoyment with a play partner. Once the child has established some knowledge of this pattern of communication then any situation, however brief, can become a playful response to his or her spontaneous interactions.

Using the play space

This should always create an atmosphere that promotes warmth and acceptance. The child should have the opportunity to explore objects in ways that are both supportive and reassuring, and this does not need to take place in a specific room. Teachers will often comment that children will become more playful and interactive when they are in the swimming pool or outside than when they are in the classroom. Encountering others is easier when the child feels emotionally safe. It harmonizes the child's feelings about the interaction and helps in regulating levels of arousal. In assessing the child's preferences for different sensory experiences and environments, it is important that he or she recognizes how those environments that give pleasure can also be shared with others. During one family session a father asked me if it was alright to go outside in the garden and play football with his son because he was often at a loss to know how to engage him with his toys in the playroom!

Being together in a play space enables both the child and play partner to become more aware of each other through the rhythm and movement of their actions. The synchronizing of these thoughts and actions helps to create a resonance between the child and the play partner. It mobilizes the brain to become more attuned to the other's emotions and increases the capacity for mutual engagement in an activity.

> Expressions of the self 'invade' the mind of the other, making the moving body of the self resonant with the impulses that can move the Others body too.
>
> (Trevarthen *et al.* 1998: 60)

The experience of resonating

This draws upon the sensory, emotional world of the unconscious and brings an awareness of the nature of 'self' and 'other' into consciousness. Once a positive emotional connection is found it lessens the child's need for withdrawal from social interactions and changes passive reactions into active ones. To resonate with another person does not mean being like them but understanding how to be with them so that a shared experience can be maintained.

Liam has autism with severe learning difficulties and ADHD. At home he constantly moved around the house, investigating many things that would be a danger to him without his mother's watchful eye on him constantly. Her desire to find a way to play with Liam was paramount in wanting to spend time with him in a positive way. I began by asking her to find an activity that she could play with him and she found a toy garage and several cars. Liam sat on the sofa having a drink as his mother sat on the floor encouraging him to join in with the activity. Liam showed little reaction to this; he wandered around the room and appeared uninterested in playing with the cars. After a few attempts to leave the room his mother decided to stop the activity. We discussed how to focus on activities that Liam preferred as his lack of interest in the garage and cars resulted in him paying little attention to his mother. In another session I provided a few sensory toys in a box for him. He began to explore these by emptying them on to the floor and then he picked up the tube of bubbles and handed them to me. As I was blowing the bubbles he joined me on the carpet. He did not stay there long and then found a white cloth that he wanted to be covered in. I was able to roll him on it and made a game of saying 'hello' and making funny faces when he reappeared. Throughout the session, which lasted an hour, he repeatedly changed his interest between the bubbles, the cloth and being 'chased' and tickled. It was an opportunity for me to connect with Liam and it enabled him to experience the fun and pleasure of being with another person.

The next time his mother played with him she started by using the cloth as I had done and then she found a large physio ball that became the focus for developing their interaction. Their play became transformed, as his mother was able to be in close proximity to him and support him as he bounced on the ball. She matched the level he was sitting at so that they were able to make eye contact. In his enjoyment of the activity he began to vocalize and his mother copied the sounds that he was making. By attuning to his interests and responding to his vocalizations there was an increase in the positive reactions he gave her that included smiles and hugs. He did not stop being hyperactive in his explorations but he showed greater pleasure in being with his mother in ways that she was also able to enjoy.

Encountering others always involves an awareness of their emotional and perceptual sensitivities. The quality of the connection lies in recognizing how to *be* with the other person and not to seek or demand what has to be done. By intuitively following the child's responses and reactions, the play partner remains positively engaged in the interaction. Pearmain (2001) describes this as the 'art of attending to the other's preverbal self' (p. 58). When interactions are contained within the availability of mutually enjoyable experiences they heighten the motivation to explore a different way of being.

Exploration

Because children's early experiences are predominantly physical, their multisensory world becomes the tool for relating to others. Their sensory preferences and dislikes become linked to experiences and environments that have significant meaning for them and include the unconscious communication that they receive from others. Longhorn's (2002) Sensory Happiness Profile can be used as an effective method for identifying a child's sensory preferences (Figure 3.1). The Profile helps to identify specific schemas in the child's play that enables the play partner to attune to the child's explorations, making it easier to create a feeling of connectedness and increase the child's interest in sharing the play experience.

Experience	Examples
The touch I like from humans	Tickles, hugs, kisses
The tastes I like	Jam tarts, bananas, yoghurt
Smells that make me happy	Plastic, Mum's hair
Sounds I like to hear	Soft music
What I like to see	Bubble tubes
Vibrations I like to feel	Swinging, water splashing
Touches from the world around me	Silky cloths, the wind, cats
Movements that stimulate me	Spinning, rocking
Multisensory environments that please me	Sensory rooms, woods, swimming pool

Figure 3.1 Sensory happiness (Longhorn 2002).

In Chapter 1, schemas were described as consistent patterns of behaviour that relate to a series of actions and stimulations which are dominant in the child's repertoire of activities. In the example provided (see Figure 3.1), the child's sensory preferences indicate a connection with gentle continuous movements. Matching the child's play to these preferences provides consistency for the child and an opportunity for the play partner to recognize how the learning experience can be extended. Establishing a connection with the child by rocking him on a large ball provides a link between the internal and external representation of a preferred experience; the ball could be used in the swimming pool to encourage an interactive game of throwing and catching. Experiences that engage the child will help in constructing different realities that can bring about a change in behaviour so that he might then want to take the ball to the woods or the park to kick it around.

According to research by Libby *et al.* (1998), sensory play tends to predominate in the play behaviours of children with autism. As the spontaneous exploration of objects is a significant feature of play development it is relevant to the establishment of interactive play that children are able to make use of their sensory preferences and interests. Rather than see these as something the child has become fixated on or is using as an object of stimulation they can be included in a session to extend and develop the child's play. The reaction of the play partner to the child's explorations is more likely to encourage the child to respond interactively and develop the way they think about the object.

> Carly was a very physically able child with autism who loved to climb. She also liked to dance to music and go for long walks. When she got excited she would flap her arms, jump up and down, spin and run around the room. One of her favourite objects was string, which she liked to flap and twirl. As I observed her doing this I noticed how she would move the string in ways that very much matched her own physical movements. When I joined her in moving a piece of string in the same way that she was doing, she began to take more notice of me. She looked up at me and gave me a wonderfully big smile. Together we discovered how to move and respond to one another and had found a rhythm that helped us to share her movement experience.

Van Dyk and Wiedis (2001) have noted in their work with preschool children that empathically mirroring back to the child positive feelings about their interactions with objects or people helps to repattern the child's Self–Object experience. The level of stimulation will depend on the child's response to the opportunities given to explore these sensory experiences and take part in activities with a play partner that match his or her sensory threshold. It may be relevant to begin by using only one activity that matches the child's sensory preference as this can help to maintain his or her focus and create an understanding of the reciprocal nature of the interaction, through the object that both play partners are attending to.

In another session with Carly I wanted to help her find a more relaxed way of being following a period when she had become very distressed and had been throwing objects around the room. To help her transfer her interest in throwing to an activity that was less harmful I used a balloon which I knew she liked and threw one up in the air. She immediately responded by hitting it up as well. As we took turns in hitting the balloon, this gentler form of play helped to relax her. The action of the balloon floating up and down and our shared smiles eased her frustration and made the environment safe for her once again.

Through the self-discovery of objects or toys the child remained in control of what she was learning because the exploration was matched by the emotional response to the activity. Having a few toys or activities available is preferable to putting them out of reach as this limits the child's opportunity for self-initiated exploration. Being able to make choices and decisions about what to play with, the child has the opportunity to discover more of the person they want to be.

Carly was becoming increasingly receptive to new experiences once she recognized how she was being supported in activities that she enjoyed. She sat for fifteen minutes in another session smearing glue on to some brightly coloured paper and then sprinkling sparkly shapes on to it. When she had finished she went back into the room where we had been playing, found the balloon and handed it to me to play with her again. Initiating play with someone else instead of the self-stimulatory activities that she had engaged in previously displayed a significant change in her communicative behaviour.

Finding out what stimulates and interests the child can also be observed when they are presented with baskets of objects to explore. The child is immediately engaged in his or her own exploration and discovery and is making choices and expressing preferences for certain textures, smells and sounds. Curiosity may involve licking, dropping or handling the objects but these are relevant to what the child needs to understand about the object. The role of the play partner is to be both supportive and attentive to what the child is playing with, only responding playfully when the child initiates an action or comment rather than offering an object to be played with.

> Visiting Aaron for the first time I took my basket of toys and objects, which immediately took his attention. He politely asked me if he could play with my toys and I let him explore what was in the basket. His parents and I were able to observe what he did with each object that he took out of the basket. He wanted to manipulate each one, explore its shape and any sound it made and discard ones that he was not interested in. Only after he had spent about ten minutes doing this did he start to comment on them and want to share them with us. My observation of him with the basket of toys and objects helped to establish how he liked to play and interact and the strategies we could work on to help him to develop his language and social play.

The establishment of interactive play through sensory exploration enables the child to value the experience of play and to make connections between the object and play partner. Joining the child in their play does not just involve being there with them but attending to his or her interests and offering new and exciting ways to continue to enjoy the activity.

> Rosie is an identical twin and her sister also has autism. Rosie rarely showed any change in her facial expressions, even when looking at herself in a mirror. She had several preferred activities and toys she liked to play with but had never been observed laughing or smiling when she held these. I wanted to establish a comfortable presence with her in the playroom and offered her a choice of hand cream, talcum powder or bubbles. She was happy for me to rub cream on her hands and arms and then on her cheeks and

occasionally she was able to give me eye contact but in that first session I also observed how she did not alter her passive mood or her facial expression.

In our next session she chose the cream and talcum powder but seemed more confident in letting me use the powder to tickle her hands and feet. She would look at me to anticipate when the next 'shower' of powder was going to come. As we were lying on a large cushion on the floor she rolled away from me and when I touched her to roll her back she giggled and smiled. For her teacher who was observing this, it was the first time she had observed Rosie react in this way to someone else.

Another way to ensure that the shared play becomes a meaningful experience is to consider the types of toys and activities that will encourage interaction. If for example, the child is skilled in completing complex puzzles it may be harder to engage with him or her than when playing together on a see-saw. In considering how toys can be used interactively it is always important to ensure that they do not lead to frustration or interfere with the child's free expression or creativity. This might lessen the child's interest in sharing the activity and result in the adult feeling uncertain about the benefits of the play experience. Likewise, play at a sensory level of exploration can become messy and it will be necessary to match the activities to the appropriate environment and an understanding of the safe use of materials by the child and the adult. Landreth (2002) highlights that the use of toys and materials should be based on:

- facilitating a broad range of creative and emotional expression;
- how interesting they are for the child;
- the extent to which they allow for verbal and non-verbal exploration and expression;
- providing experiences for the child in which they feel successful without having to follow pre-ordained procedures;
- ensuring they are well made and durable.

Within the play space in which appropriate toys and materials have been provided, the child needs to recognize that they have the freedom to explore them in ways that represent his or her interests. This might mean that a child will play continuously with one activity or they may explore several within a session. I have worked with a child who wanted to spend all his time at the sand tray and with other children who have moved within a range of different activities. The focus is always on what the child is doing so that, by not imposing what else should be happening, the play has its own evolutionary dimension.

I was playing with Jake in the garden with some water and each time he squeezed the water out of the sponge I used the word that accompanied his actions. He thought the word 'squeeze' was a very funny sound and would laugh each time I said it. Then he started running around the garden so that I would chase him. When I caught him I held him and asked him if he wanted a squeeze or a tickle. Of course his reply each time was a squeeze. His father informed me that prior to this activity the word 'squeeze' had not been part of his spoken vocabulary.

Sensory exploration provides children with the means for creative expression and comes to determine how the play will develop. If children's need for early exploratory play is overlooked in favour of teaching them more functional ways to play, this could limit the extent to which they might use their natural curiosity not only to investigate materials and objects around them, but also to discover different ways to think creatively and imaginatively about what they are playing with.

Engagement

One of the most profound influences on social and emotional development is the capacity to engage with another person. Engagement provides a connection with the world that optimizes children's knowledge about relationships and builds their competence, trust and self-esteem. The adult's role in ensuring quality in the interactive experiences they provide for children is therefore considerable. Engaging with another person occurs through a process of mutual discovery that is constantly being fine tuned to maximize the psychological and physiological attachment between the two individuals. The rhythmic patterns of interaction that take place during the early developmental phase of parent–child bonding are the same as those which will increase the capacity for the child with autism to develop a relational sense of others. The consistency of this focused attention creates a rhythm of interaction that will entice the child to enjoy new experiences.

Hobson (1993) describes this recognition of connectedness as 'The domain in which bodily inter co-ordination between people is also mental co-ordination, in which the intra-individual configurations of bodily expressed feelings are potential sources of inter-individual patterns of social experience' (p. 195). This highlights that levels of attentiveness and engagement are more likely to be achieved through the responsiveness of the play partner to the child's emotional and physical sensitivities. By playfully mirroring the movements of the child it deepens his or her concentration, reduces self-consciousness and becomes an experience worth having for its own sake.

I had been invited to observe Aishah's behaviour at home and it was an opportunity to meet her mother and talk about a programme of activities that she might like to share with Aishah. Aishah spent most of her time alone in her room either resting or listening to music on a personal CD player. Her interactions were limited to making requests for food and when these demands were not met she would become very distressed. Her mother was understandably quite concerned about these times as she found it difficult to manage her behaviour. A way of calming Aishah was to let her listen to her music. For Aishah to build up an understanding of how to relate to others, we needed to help her feel comfortable in our presence and show her that being with her was as important as doing things for her. We were able to transfer her music to a portable player so that we could all dance and move around together. Her room was soon filled with music, singing and dancing. Aishah's mother held her hands and they danced, sharing smiles and eye contact. Her mother's ability to relax and enjoy this time with Aishah helped her to recognize the potential for Aishah to interact in positive ways that did not always involve getting a reward of something to eat.

Embedded within this pattern of interaction is a process of creativity that is fundamental to relationship-based play. As the supportive play partner finds ways to engage the child, so the interaction becomes enshrined with new possibilities for flexible thinking and behaviour. Wimpory *et al.* (1995) identified the extent to which music interaction therapy facilitates social and symbolic development through joint playful activities. Music interaction is geared towards developing the same dyadic responsiveness through musical activities that encourage shared attention and mutual engagement.

Kamilah was a young woman in her early twenties, whom I met at a post-school training centre. The staff expressed some concerns that she was very prompt dependent in managing both her personal needs and in taking part in any activity. They explained that, because of a difficult time of war in the country, attending to her needs had been a priority as the family tried to keep safe. As she had grown up so this pattern of behaviour had remained. The staff felt that to increase her independence Kamilah needed opportunities to initiate what she wanted and to experience being able to make decisions for herself. Kamilah used streams of words not to communicate to others but to occupy herself and she would wave her fingers in front of her face and make lots of pleasurable sounds. English was not her first language but as a child she had learnt some nursery rhymes and could count to ten in English.

As she stood next to me waving her fingers in front of her face and vocalizing, I began to sing 'Ten Green Bottles' while pointing to her fingers. I noticed a box of skittles on the floor in the room where we were standing so I lined ten of these up and began to sing the song again. Kamilah had not given me any eye contact but she had watched what I had done and joined me on the floor. At the end of each verse she counted the skittles and then chose which one she wanted to put back in the box (not necessarily in the order in which they were lined up). In this way she was leading the song and I was following. She initiated her own actions when all the skittles were back in the box by deciding that her time with me was finished and she left the room.

Providing a playful presence that is continuously responsive to the spontaneous reactions of the child is the key to establishing engagement, focused attention and communication. Becoming a good companion enables the child to discover the capacity for intentional behaviour and encourages the expansion and exploration of different ways to relate.

Elaboration

An increased capacity to be receptive to a different kind of presence with another person allows for more elaborate communications. Giving attention to whatever arises during the special playtime provides a mirror-like space that is always open for the child to respond to. With this sensitivity the flow of interaction invites the child to create something new in the relationship.

When Rafiq and his father played together they always did activities that had specific rules, such as card games. This was because Rafiq understood what was expected and could anticipate his father's response. Although the games enabled them to engage in a shared activity together, his father felt that his son rarely expressed enjoyment or surprise and was no longer challenged by this way of playing. Rafiq nervously began to play a game of 'snap' with me that was more physical and involved following instructions to jump on a circle that was the same colour as the one that I was standing on. Rafiq knew the rules of 'snap' and soon became excited about jumping on the circles to 'win' the game. When his father joined in, their shared enjoyment became very evident. Sometimes when his father made a planned mistake, Rafiq would tell him which colour circle he should be on. Rafiq was discovering a new way of playing and interacting that remained within the safe boundaries that he already understood.

When play together becomes more dynamic it invites the child to explore further possibilities that are vital for the maintenance of the interaction, namely intention. In establishing an intention towards a particular behaviour the child develops the capacity to integrate more complex ideas and ways of being that affect not only their spontaneity but also their relational flexibility. By attuning to the child's intentional behaviour when they are playing, the play partner can build on what the child is doing in a way that increases awareness of their own and their partner's behaviour. The quality of the presence not only elaborates understanding about relationships, it also allows the child to think about the self more intuitively. The supportive play partner facilitates conditions for the child whereby there is a greater opportunity to experience:

- the reflective self;
- the responsive self;
- the knowledgeable self;
- the relational self;
- the enabling self; and
- the integrated self.

The more conditional the relationship, the less opportunity there is for the child to learn about the real self. It is also possible that in recognizing more of the real self the child reacts to this as a new experience full of uncertainties. By sensitively maintaining the shared play experience, the interactive process can help in supporting the child through this transitional phase.

In his play Aaron showed a preference for playing imaginatively with his toys and would frequently use them to act out situations he had been in or did not want to experience. He found this much easier than taking part in activities that were based on him socially interacting with others. He seemed to be uncertain about the expectations for social engagement and therefore found it easier to play imaginatively with objects. For example he would play 'hide-and-seek' with his toys but did not like to be the one to hide or seek. In trying to engage him in play with activities that did not involve his toys he would often decide he could not do it and would leave the room. He would return, however, without being prompted because he had a genuine interest in playing. For Aaron I established a programme of short activities that involved us playing a game together and then I would let him choose the next activity, which invariably became something involving imaginative play. When playing with me he would often say he did not like what we were doing even though he clearly indicated that he wanted to display his ability at playing the games. He would also try to sabotage the activity, on occasions, by doing something he knew he was not allowed to do, such as throw the sand. However, as I maintained this pattern of activities with him he began to increase his knowledge of what he could achieve when interacting positively with another person. It enabled him to develop more awareness of how to respond in social situations and helped him to reflect on and regulate his own behaviour.

Maintaining a consistent approach to the interactive play by providing opportunities for initiating positive experiences helped him to recognize his connection to others and assisted in heightening his awareness of being a participant in a wider social context. According to McGee et al. (1987), therapeutic interventions that are relationship based will involve the sensitive adaptation of the environment and an unconditional valuing of the individual that enables him or her to achieve greater independence and autonomy.

At a deeper level the emotional and physical well-being of both the child and the play partner underpins the need to widen their exploration of different relationships and establish empathetic understanding. Hughes (2006) recognizes that establishing playfulness, acceptance, curiosity and empathy are key to understanding the other person and being understood by them. These enjoyable experiences amplify the child's feeling of safety in the relationship and allow the other person to create an emotionally supportive presence. Natiello (2001) describes empathetic understanding as the bridge to connectedness. She further states that such relationships generate an increase in energy, empowerment and creativity and become open to change. In essence it is the authenticity of the empathetic relationship that is continuously being co-created through the playful interaction.

When two individuals are able to sustain the connectedness between them it expands the circle of communication and facilitates an increasing array of possible ways to express what that relationship means. This may require considerable patience on the part of the supportive play partner who must carefully create an environment in which the child gradually comes to understand what communication is. How interactive play assists in the emergence of this new dialogue is considered in the next chapter. The core conditions that have been described as assisting in creating or re-establishing a sense of connectedness can also become powerful motivators for the child, influencing their own communications and those of others.

Chapter 4

Enabling communication

Participation in playful encounters that establish feelings of connectedness has the potential for developing more elaborate ways of communicating. It is also essential that any situation that involves positive engagement with a significant person is seen as supporting the foundations for meaningful communication. The previous chapter highlighted that there are specific interactional patterns that aid children's communication development. It emphasized that the key to developing communication is to be attentive to situations that will be intrinsically motivating for the child and this is heightened when both partners in the social dyad are able to communicate the same pleasurable response to the play experience. To further exploit this discussion there is the need to focus on how both partners are communicating during the interaction and to acknowledge how playful encounters will support the child's development of social communication.

According to Bruner (1983) positive social engagement through play also provides the foundations for language as well as the development of understanding about the rules of interaction, turn-taking and behaviour. Brazelton *et al.* (1974) noted that it is the prespeech and proto-conversational activities that occur during playful interactions in infancy that provide the opportunities for increased participation in the social world and thus the extent to which children effectively communicate with others. Augmented communication systems that have been devised for children with social communication difficulties often inappropriately emphasize the development of speech and language that has not been underpinned with the pragmatics of communication. Visual representations of language using signing and symbols may be effective in supporting and increasing children's awareness of a language system but without the establishment of the natural patterns of social engagement, the use of language is likely to remain impaired. They may also inadvertently teach the child the functional use of communication rather than the value of relating to others through mutual enjoyment and reciprocal interaction. As Griffiths (2002) points out playful exchanges have within them their own narrative qualities, whereas interactions that are not emotionally engaging will limit the child's understanding of the linguistic structures required for meaningful communication. For children with delayed speech any reparative work is achieved through the increasing responsiveness of the adult to:

- engage with the child at his or her developmental level;
- react positively by mirroring the child's actions and vocalizations;
- provide opportunities for the child's self-expression and self-evaluation;
- link the child's utterances to meaningful experiences; and
- assist the child in developing intentional communication.

Playful interactions provide a meaningful context for observing the qualities inherent in how children are communicating. Using an interactive play approach that offers an empathetic and positive presence, the child's capacity to extend and participate in communicating increasingly rests within the child. As Rhode (cited in Alvarez and Reid 1999) suggests, the therapeutic role of play and interaction for children with autism is to help them to 'find a voice of their own'.

Play as a narrative

One of the fundamental functions of play is the way in which it unconsciously provides a narrative that consciously transforms thoughts and actions. This is because play contains within it the same elements of timing, role and emotion that form any narrative structure. Play takes place within a context that is always linked to the present experience, in much the same way that a conversation is specific to the individuals involved. The way in which play repeatedly creates interactions between the object and the action reinforces its function, which then becomes synchronized with the internal thought processes. Because play is an external expression of the child's inner mind it follows a natural sequence of events and actions that is then communicated to others. The difficulty here is that if only the external play behaviour is interpreted it can undermine what the child's intentions or personal narrative might have been for the specific play content. A parent told me that during one of her child's assessments, her daughter had been asked to draw a picture of a person. Instead of drawing a person she drew a face with a beard on it and it was therefore assumed that she had difficulty carrying out the task and following the instruction. Taking her cue from a comment her daughter had made after a previous visit to this setting, the parent realized that the reason her child had drawn this picture was because the word 'beard' was very similar to the name of the doctor who was in the room with her at the time. Although the child had been able to internalize the experience and make the connection, those assessing her were unaware of it until her mother gave meaning to her child's actions. Difficulties in the interpretation of the play content can arise if the child is unable to verbally express what is taking place but it is equally dependent upon how the play is viewed by an observer.

Faaris had been brought to the playroom at his school but he was very unhappy about being in a place that he did not understand. Beginning to share play with him was problematic as he was determined to try and leave the room with his teacher. On another occasion he was becoming used to the new environment but wanted to remain near to his teacher. I moved closer to him and putting a cloth over my head I started to play peek-a-boo. As I emerged slowly from the cloth so as not to alarm him, he clapped his hands and smiled when I appeared and then he ran across the room. I went after him and picked him up and then he ran back to his safe place by the door. We repeated this several times and each time my appearance from under the cloth and his being caught increased his excitement. As his first language was Arabic and mine was English I had not used a narrative during our play. However, we had learnt to communicate through our playful reactions towards one another. His smiles and response towards me had helped to establish some trust in the activity and I had wanted to find a way to maintain our interaction that was positive for him. I needed to extend his play and I wanted to see what Faaris' reaction would be to my changing of the pattern of play. The next time he ran across the room I did not go towards him. Instead, I remained near the door and he waited across the room. Without using words, he turned his head to look at me and gestured with his head for me to come to him. His pleasure at my picking him up again completed this play narrative. It was a profound realization that the language we had shared was not with words but play.

Creating narratives between play partners will become a predominant theme in this chapter as they are not always dependent upon spoken language but on the mode of interaction and play. Narratives in play are created through a dynamic pattern of action between the players. Play assists in rebuilding narratives as well as creating new ones and this is most likely to occur when the child is given the security to express his or her own view of the experience. Play is not a static experience but reflects the flow and rhythm of narrative that matches the child's level of communicative competence. The addition of a play partner in this narrative sequence supports how the child will develop more complex ideas about representing him or herself through the play.

According to Bruce (1991) play is implicated in all forms of representation. Play is a symbolic act regardless of whether children are playing alone or communicating with others in shared play activities. The child's ability to make shifts between fantasy and reality is also indicative of the internal narrative that is taking place. This perspective can be applied to play at a sensory level of exploration, playing with toys or engaging in pretend or imaginative play. For example, lining up play people might be described as a repetitive action or rigid play sequence, whereas for the child it could represent an internal narrative that relates to an aspect of his or her knowledge and experience. The use of toys and activities for self-expression, creative expression and emotional release enables children to engage in establishing different narratives that can be represented through their play. These include drawings and paintings, sand play, using puppets and drama sequences as well as representational toys. As each of these activities involves different levels of social contact so this in turn will increase their communicative competence.

I began working in a school for children with autism with a class of boys aged between eleven and twelve years old. The boys wanted to use the puppets during their literacy session and having chosen a puppet they wanted to work with they got into either groups or pairs to create a story with their puppets. Three of the boys immediately started 'play fighting' with their puppets but then one of them stopped and watched the other two continue. Then one of the boys stopped fighting and moved his puppet towards the boy who had stopped first. He introduced his puppet by saying, 'I'm shy, I just want to stay here quietly.' To which the boy replied, 'What's your name?' 'My name is Freddy, what's your name?' 'My name is Freddy too, come and meet my friend.' 'Hello, what's your name?' 'My name is Freddy, let's all play a game together.'

This simple narrative grew from their interactions with the puppets. They had at first seemed unable to decide what to do with the puppets but found a mutual way to interact. They then acknowledged their different personalities through their puppets. In making a new attempt to interact, they discovered their similarity (possibly reflecting their acknowledgment that they all had autism) and it was through this that they were then able to create a more positive interaction. Shared play experiences are key to how children are able to make use of the various elements of communication in ways that are intentional, spontaneous and rewarding.

Being attentive

It has already been discussed how the creation of a play space provides a supportive framework in which the play partner can establish a sensitive presence for the child. Within this context the play partner seeks always to be attentive to the child and to how he or she is behaving in the play situation. Having established how long the play session will last it is essential that both the child and the play partner recognize this as a time to be fully available to one another. Attentiveness begins with the play partner making positive comments, using facial gestures and adopting a friendly, welcoming posture. In non-directive play such an approach is key to enabling the child to feel safe and begin to explore new and different ways to communicate. Any anxieties that the child may have about close proximity will also need to be considered in relation to the partner's physical response to the child. If the child is feeling uncomfortable then low intrusion can be established through burst–pause games or by gently mirroring the child's movements. Treating the child's withdrawal or avoidance of contact as intentional communication enables the play partner to make playful use of these actions while teaching the child that what they are communicating has meaning.

Aaron's parents and I had established how much he liked to use the puppets to tell stories and so I always made them available for him to play with. In one of our play sessions he took quite a dislike to one of the puppets, a brown, scruffy monkey with long arms and legs. He picked it up and placed it in his toy box out of sight and continued to play with other preferred puppets. On this occasion I did not ask him why he did not like the monkey and nor did he comment when I replaced the monkey at the end of our play session. On another occasion Aaron chose his favourite puppet, a bee. This time the monkey was not removed but he referred to it as 'not one of buzzy bee's friends'. The next time the puppets were played with was during a family group activity when his father chose the monkey for their story. Aaron took part in the story that he devised with his parents and sister by choosing a large colourful bird. It was a story with familiar activities that were obviously fun for the family where all the animals went to the park, played on a roundabout, ate some cake and then went back home. On this occasion Aaron was clearly more comfortable with the monkey and enjoyed their story. Since he felt safe with his father, who had the monkey, it made it possible for Aaron to alter his feelings towards it.

This example highlights how attentiveness does not just involve observing the child's actions but also their feelings and emotions. Creating an empathetic understanding also involves finding strategies to sensitively invite the child to recognize that what is being communicated is meaningful. Recognizing Aaron's anxieties, his father was still able to playfully introduce the puppet and reassuringly show how enjoyment and fun could be ascribed to the puppet. A further consideration in being attentive occurs as the father found a way to both wait for, and actively listen to, the child's actions and vocalizations. At the pre-intentional stage of children's communication development this mirrors the parent–child interactions of early infancy. Creative Listening is a technique applied to working therapeutically with children through the Children's Hours Trust, which uses a non-directive approach in its work with children. Pinney (1992) believed that being fully attentive to one person involves listening only to the other person who needs attention, the child. Creative Listening is non-judgemental and does not overdo praise. Instead, the maintenance of the support the child is receiving during the planned session provides the child with the confidence to explore more positive ways of communicating and behaving.

Another significant factor in establishing attentiveness is to follow the child's attentional lead. By focusing on what the child is playing with, the child's understanding of the language relating to that object is aided, while at the same time it enables the child to recognize how his or her behaviour is creating a communicative link with another person. Yoder et al. (1991) found in a study of preschool children with learning difficulties that when adults followed the child's attentional lead the children were able to learn more labels for objects than when their attention had to be recruited to a task or object. As the quality of attention is likely to be greater on an object of the child's choosing, it would appear that this enables the child to be more alert to the language structures that are linked to the object or activity. Bruner (1981) also recognized how the adult's focus of attention on the child's interest was the precursor for joint attention. The child becomes aware of being 'listened to' through the contingent responsivity that the play partner provides for the child. In children with developmental delays it may be harder to understand some of the non-verbal signals that they are presenting, and consequently this can lead to less contingent behaviour being used by the adult. The responsivity of the play partner to the social signals that the child is presenting therefore need to be carefully selected and enacted upon to give an appropriate response. Jones (cited in Cooper 1995) found that adult's perceptions and interpretations of children's behaviour was an important determinant in how they responded. It is the play partner's response to the child's communicative behaviour that will significantly help in shaping more conventional ways of communicating. In a similar way that a parent responds to the young infant, using different tones of voice, pace or facial expressions the play partner also needs to monitor his or her input in a way that is both relevant and contingent with that of the child's. Timing may also be considered essential for establishing a contingent response. If the child feels pressured into responding in a particular way he or she may be less likely to regard the interaction as a communicative experience. The timing of the input creates a framework that invites the child to share in a communicative exchange. Harris (1992) regards this pattern of interaction as fundamental to language development.

Jamie attended a residential school for children with autism. I had spent a day observing Jamie in his classroom with his peers and teachers and then in his house for after-school activities. Jamie, aged eight, was a quiet, very compliant young boy who was also non-verbal. He interacted with his peers only when he wanted to initiate contact but preferred to be a passive observer of their activities. In the playroom the following day, I observed him playing with one of his teaching assistants whom he knew very well. He was very physically active and enjoyed taking control of the play. When I played with him he was initially more apprehensive and uncertain of what to choose to play with. As he moved around the room I picked up an ocean drum and gently moved it about. He became interested in this and took it from me. For a few minutes he seemed to like moving it around and shaking it but then he put it on the floor and lay down on a small trampoline that was in the playroom. I approached him and, sitting next to him, picked up the ocean drum. When I shook it he sat up, and as he lay down again, I stopped. I matched the movement of the ocean drum to his movements so that when he sat up again and bounced on the trampoline I shook it very loudly and when he sat still, I stopped shaking it. Having established a pattern of interaction he then moved closer to me and gestured with his hand for me to shake the ocean drum so that he could bounce. We had engaged in taking turns and he was delighted with this. As his excitement continued and I responded, he looked at me and spontaneously vocalized by asking me to do it 'again'. He also said 'go' when I stopped shaking the drum. It was clear that by playfully engaging in this way with Jamie he had discovered his own capacity to extend his communication.

Spontaneous communication

In order to make sense of their own experiences and communicate them, children use a range of non-vocal, facial, physical and hand gestures to act as messages for others to interpret. Reaching out, grasping and pointing are all spontaneous hand gestures that young infants use initially to draw attention to their needs, whereas pulling away and turning the head are examples of their intentions. Piaget (1955) referred to these non-verbal channels of communication as *acted conversations*. This is an effective term as it emphasizes the link that children's non-verbal communication has with spontaneous bodily movement. In being contingently responsive to these movements, the play partner is not only helping to establish two-way communication but is acknowledging for the child that his or her communications are understood. Once these gestures are recognized as having meaning, the child is more likely to make use of them for social communication. The use of gestures for social interaction becomes an important component in the 'give and take' of conversation and the subsequent emergence of speech.

Potter and Whittaker (2001) carried out research that identified some of the ways in which children's spontaneous communication can be encouraged. A significant factor in their findings was that the adult's overuse of verbal prompting and questioning limited the extent to which children were able to communicate spontaneously. Similarly, when communication is engineered to meet the needs of the adult there is less potential for spontaneity and generalization of the acquired skill. It seemed that the most effective strategy was to encourage children to respond to environmental cues. Objects were presented in a way that a child had to initiate a request or choice, rather than wait for a cue by the adult.

Non-directive play allows for spontaneity through self-discovery and exploration and when this experience is shared with another person, it creates the potential in the child to make more use of spontaneous communication. With less adult-directed communication, the child has an opportunity to respond to toys and objects and even the play partner with more intention and independence than might previously have been observed. In being given time to think about the play and having an opportunity for actions to be reflected back either verbally or through imitation, spontaneity becomes embedded within the interactive framework.

It is within the established framework of the interactive play that the child comes to recognize that having choice and some control over the way in which objects are played with increases the desire for more intentional and spontaneous communication. As the child comes to acknowledge that the person is attending to him or her the involvement in communicating is heightened, and this is because the child is not dependent upon prompts to gain what he or she wants; instead, there is a mutual awareness and desire to communicate in more positive ways. After a parent workshop, I was contacted by a mother who expressed her joy that her daughter was now able to spontaneously give her eye contact after she had introduced interactive play sessions into their daily routine; once eye contact had become an act of communication that was not demanded, her daughter had discovered through their shared play that she could offer it unconditionally.

When he was three and a half years old Aaron was still very dependent upon verbal prompts and rarely initiated a conversation, despite having a good vocabulary. Over the months that we spent together Aaron's parents had noticed a particular change in his language development and during our play sessions Aaron would be talking constantly about his actions. His interaction with his parents was well supported as they learnt to reduce their questioning and instead comment on what he was doing.

In one of our sessions I gave Aaron a choice of red or brown sand to play with and he began to put the animals into the red sand; some of them he buried, whereas he wanted others to be upside-down in the sand. He was describing what they were doing but then announced that the bear did not like the red sand because it was too hot and he put it in the tray of brown sand.

This spontaneous reaction led him to extend his play so that the brown sand became snow and the animals went skiing instead. Aaron was developing his ability to think in more abstract and spontaneous ways when playing imaginatively, which provided us with a clear indication of the way in which his language was developing. Within the context of a one-to-one special playtime Aaron was establishing an understanding of the nature of interaction and began to make more use of conversation to share his ideas, which we hoped would transfer to other play situations with his peers.

The presence of a supportive play partner who becomes involved in sharing the communicative experience of the play aids the child's ability to generalize these skills and highlights the potential that play has for altering previously established patterns of thinking about the use of verbal and non-verbal language. Aaron became more confident in sharing conversation with his peers once he began school. His one-to-one play sessions at home had involved a specific communicative structure that he was able to transfer into school, which was equally supportive of his communication skills. Unlike language, which is a highly structured mode of communication, the pragmatics of communication are much more diverse and complex. For those children who have difficulties in comprehending the vast array of linguistic and communicative functions that are the basis upon which all relationships are developed, the need to sustain opportunities for more spontaneous ways to communicate will be essential for their understanding.

Imitation

Like many skills in communication, imitation will develop under conditions that enable the child to understand the pragmatics of social interaction. Despite well-documented studies (DeMyer *et al.* 1973; Stone *et al.* 1990; Rogers and Pennington 1991; Heimann *et al.* 1992; Smith and Bryson 1994; Sigman *et al.* 1995) that indicate the extent to which children with autism appear to have a central deficit in imitative behaviour, more recent research suggests that interactive approaches can be effective in aiding skills in imitation, joint attention and turn-taking (Dawson and Osterling 1997; Chandler *et al.* 2002; Wieder and Greenspan 2003). In their study, Beadle-Brown and Whiten (2004) found that despite the notion of a deficit of imitation in autism, children's ability to imitate occurred consistently as part of a typical developmental pattern. Skills in imitation improve with maturation and although the younger children in their study showed significant delay in what they were able to imitate, this did not appear in the older children. It is perhaps more significant to recognize the function of imitation, particularly in younger children. In early development it is through the imitation of facial gestures that children and their carers learn to match their behaviour. Hobson (2002) describes the ability that is now being identified in very young infants to copy the actions of another as communication before thought. Synchronicity and reciprocity, which are significant features of parent–infant interactions, are clearly early forms of imitative behaviour. Jones (1996) considers that children's ability to imitate a parent's oral gestures occurs not because of an innate response mechanism but as a result of the child's 'coincidental matching of interesting stimuli with the infant's behavioural expressions of interest and exploratory motivation' (p. 1968).

According to Nadel et al. (1999) the function of imitation changes around the age of three years from an act of communication to a tool for learning. Children will imitate the actions of others when they recognize the purpose for which an action or verbal expression is being used. Nadel and colleagues found that children with autism also used imitation as a major communicative tool and as such it is a good predictor of the social capabilities of children with autism. Beadle-Brown and Whiten (2004) point out that such findings have implications for early intervention programmes for children with autism and that promoting imitation by encouraging the child to imitate or by imitating the child will improve other skills in social interaction.

Dawson and Adams (1984) and Nadel and Pezé (1993) found that children with autism were more socially responsive, showed more eye contact and played with toys in a less perseverative manner when an adult imitated their behaviour. Most interactional approaches for children with autism emphasize the key role of the adult in imitating the vocalizations and actions of the child to increase awareness of the function of communication and promote the development of language. Imitation is an essential aspect of body and linguistic mapping, which are fundamental requirements for intersubjectivity and non-symbolic communication. Meltzoff and Gopnik (1993) also recognized that an understanding of others, including their mental states, is developed in the context of mutual imitation.

On my first visit I was able to observe Neema's behaviour in the home and discuss with her parents their concerns about her language delay, their difficulties in managing some of her behaviour and her social interaction. Neema was five years old and had just started school. Although she could occupy herself with play, she did not initiate or show a preference for playing with her parents or other members of the extended family.

In the first session with Neema I had a box of sensory materials from which she chose some coloured feathers. She explored them by spreading them out over the floor and then picked up a large handful and threw them at me. I responded with surprise and laughter at this gesture and so she repeated the action. When I had the chance I picked up a handful of feathers and threw them at her. She turned and laughed and picked up another handful to throw at me. I was able to build some anticipation into this game that she had devised and with my next handful I said 'ready, steady, go' to support my actions. She stood with her back to me and turned each time she wanted me to repeat the words and the actions. Reaching down to pick up another handful she turned towards me and said 'ready, steady. . .'. With a sense of building in her own anticipation she moved across the room, turned towards me and together we both threw the feathers at one another.

Within the close proximity of the playful interaction Neema was able to show her ability for vocal imitation following my imitation and extension of her actions. Her actions became meaningful for her once these were mirrored back in a repeated sequence. Her ability to engage with me was also an indication that she recognized how she could affect my behaviour. Where previously she had not played with toys as part of an interactive experience, creating the opportunity for two-way communication increased Neema's desire to communicate with more intentionality, which she then generalized in other situations.

In another session her mother had planned an activity for Neema to plant some seeds in a flowerpot. Her mother presented all the different things that were going to be used and talked about them. She let her feel the soil with her hands and then showed her how to put some soil in the pot using the spade. Neema then picked up the spade and copied what her mother had done. Her mother then counted out some seeds and Neema repeated this by pointing to the seeds and counting them. Neema was then shown where to put the seeds and followed her mother's actions. She needed no encouragement to pick up the watering can to put some water on the soil and was praised for her efforts and concentration.

As an important feature of social communication, Neema's capacity to imitate or engage in joint attention was dependent upon the motivational factors that were allied to the activity. When the activity is based on the child's interests, imitating and extending how a preferred toy or object is being played with can have greater impact on the child's responses than an adult-directed task or planned play sequence. Social understanding is also more likely to be generalized if the rewards are based on a shared experience that has intrinsic value for both partners. As Nind and Hewett (1994) state, of all human activities, communication is one for which extrinsic rewards are not needed, as first-hand experience is irreplaceably more effective than a learned experience; 'The reward for communicating is communicating' (p. 67).

Eye contact

Sharing eye contact with a communicative partner makes communicating more effective but it is not essential. Gaze avoidance is a common feature of how individuals avoid awkward or confronting situations and in a similar way staring or eye pointing can be used to send a specific non-verbal message to another person. For individuals with autism the difficulty in making eye contact with another person should not always be considered as an avoidant behaviour but it is the understanding of the use of eye contact as a tool for establishing a social connection. This implies that the use and avoidance of eye contact has a strong emotional component and, as in all aspects of social communication, it needs to be nurtured and encouraged rather than enforced. There are also cultural variations in the use of eye contact that need to be taken into consideration during communicative exchanges. Demanding eye contact or giving a reward when it is presented by the child short cuts its meaning; it is not an act of communication that the child has chosen to use merely for the sake of communicating, but is one imposed by someone else. If eye contact is given for tactical or strategic reasons it is devoid of its main purpose as a natural expression of interaction and connection with another person. Instead, the child needs more experience of contingent interactions that emphasize the expression of emotions through bodily movements and facial expressions such as in play, drama or movement.

Playful exchanges that create fun and enjoyment increase the likelihood of more sustained eye contact. This is because the giving of social smiles coincides with the giving of eye contact. What may initially be experienced as an uncertain gesture of communication is overridden by the desire to maintain the positive feelings that are provided by the communicative act. By responding to the child with enthusiasm it increases the potential for the child to respond with the same attentional eye gaze that the play partner is giving the child.

If the child's focus of attention is fixed on a specific toy or activity, it becomes very difficult to shift that attention to a person unless the play partner can provide the child with an equally stimulating and exciting reason for focusing on something else. Hence playing physical games that include an element of anticipation and excitement can be effective in developing eye contact because they allow for closer proximity and are less threatening and the communication is at a level that matches the child's understanding.

> Clara always showed more communicative behaviours when playing physical games with her father. To reduce the amount of time she spent playing alone, I suggested that this was a way in which he could create more opportunity for positive interaction. As her father laid on the floor she sat on his bent knees and, in anticipation, waited for his knees to drop after he had counted to three. Eye contact was established easily because she was looking down at him and he responded by looking at her as he counted. With her excitement she started to vocalize 'dadadada', creating shared enjoyment for both of them. The anticipation, eye contact and vocalizations increased their communication as she was learning to regard their play as a social experience and not just as an activity.

I also suggest to parents, if their child likes to be pushed on the swing, to stand in front of them. This way the child cannot avoid looking at them but they are doing so in a way that is being sensitively maintained through the physical activity they are enjoying. Many children also like to be swung in a blanket, enabling an adult to share eye contact with the child during a relaxing experience. The emotional connection that is established through making eye contact will have a profound effect not only at an intrapersonal level, but also on the subsequent development of the interpersonal relationship.

Intention

The child's ability to change their focus of attention from an object to a person shows a marked change in communicative competence. When Liam found the bubbles for me to play with, he was able to shift his attention from popping the bubbles to looking at me to request more. This implies a move towards more intentional communication and represents further understanding of causality and consequences. When the play partner responds to the child's efforts to communicate 'as if' that is what was intended it enables the child to recognize it as intentional. When a baby babbles, the parents invariably talk back by interpreting what he or she was intending to 'say'. This communication is based on the child's vocal and physical gestures, their emotional state and the context of the interaction. Repeatedly using this format within interactions and treating the child as an intentional agent provides an opportunity to begin to understand how another person might be thinking. Foster (1990) suggests that the development of communicative intent involves the child's ability to repeatedly combine the use of gaze, vocalizations and gestures with a person in an activity that reflects a 'meeting of minds'. These non-verbal signals of communicative intent are symbolic of the child's innate need to make sense of the social experience.

A teacher described how she was working with Tomas who had only one word of verbal expression – 'no'. It was effectively used to enable him to make a choice about what he wanted to do but it also meant that he would not always appear to want to follow her instructions or requests. He had been playing with a tray of shaving foam for some time, spreading it around with his fingers and making patterns with it when she told him that it was time to stop. He wrote 'no' in the foam so she wiped it out and wrote 'yes'. He responded by wiping out her 'yes' and writing 'no'. As they took turns in writing these words he began to show some understanding of the communication that was taking place between them. The teacher, describing this as their 'yes–no game', recognized that he clearly understood how to use the language and the social meaning that the words conveyed.

Tomas' desire to communicate with intent was mirrored by the motivation he had towards the play activity and the more positive response he received from his teacher. Tomasello and Farrar (1986) found evidence that such joint attention episodes contributed towards the development of verbal language. Embedded with the shared communicative experience were the affective meanings that gave both of them the opportunity to understanding each other's intentions. Situations that foster a pattern of interaction that includes vocalization, gesture and mutual attention will increase the potential for both play partners to coordinate their intentions. Such appropriate responsiveness alters the perception of the social experience that can bring about a change in their mental as well as their affective states. Intentionality also involves the ability to make decisions that will include how and when the child chooses to communicate. Although this is indicative of the bursts and pauses that are part of the natural pattern of communication, in children with autism this is often interpreted as a behaviour that indicates a desire to withdraw from social contact. The child on the other hand is still learning how to establish their intent to communicate and can only do so when motivational and mutually attentive experiences are available to them.

Spoken language

The impact of non-verbal communication on children's language development is widely acknowledged but it would appear that spoken language, as a means of conveying messages to one another, is still regarded as the most important measure of an individual's communicative competence. Children will only be able to gain recognition of their own communicative competence when they have social experiences in which the communicative partner responds to any attempt to communicate, regardless of its mode. Both play and language are symbolic representations of thought that are related to an action. Lewis's study (2003) suggests that there are a number of key factors that account for this relationship which are not so clearly defined in relation to play and language development in children with autism. However, she cites the research of Carpenter et al. (1998) who found that when parents synchronized their behaviour and verbalizations with those of their child during play, there were significant gains in linguistic development. Kobayashi (cited in Richer and Coates 2001) describes how the establishment of emotional communication and the nurturing of a social experience can become transformed into different perceptual modalities. This includes not just hearing language but gaining an understanding of its meaning and usage. Parents will express a deep desire for their child to begin talking but often do not recognize the profound ways in which non-verbal communication of bodily movements, gestures and facial expressions that are taking place in their daily routines are providing the foundations for receptive and expressive language. The imitation of vocalizations and actions in the context of play means that language is not presented in an intrusive way, but developed through the emotional connection created by the adult's attentional focus on the child.

I received a request to meet with a mother and her six-year-old son Zafar, who were visiting London from abroad. She described her relationship with him as very positive; he liked cuddles and rough-and-tumble and was very attached to her. She desperately wanted him to talk but felt she had not been given the right strategies to help him and was worried that it might never happen. I spent twenty minutes with Zafar and during this time I observed his play closely and briefly interacted with him. He chose to bounce a soft ball on a low table and when it rolled away I pushed it back to him. He pushed it back to me and then I was able to build in some anticipation before rolling it back to him. After a few turns of this he gave me eye contact and smiled. I then picked up a wooden puppet that has a moving mouth when shaken. He picked up a similar puppet and I began to move mine around making different vocal sounds and actions with it. Each time he copied me, making the same vocal sounds and approximating the actions. His mother sat watching amazed at the extent to which he was able to express his communicative abilities to the point where he began using some familiar words. It then emerged from our discussions that what she had described as his inability to talk was actually his inability to have a conversation with her. She also became aware that during those times when they were physically close and playful she rarely used language to describe his actions or respond to his vocalizations but now recognized how she could do this to help him develop his spoken language.

Jordan (2001) describes this mismatch between language and communication as a significant characteristic of autism in that some children never acquire an understanding of the use of language for communication, whereas others can use language to block communication. Regardless of whether or not a child has a language delay, an awareness of the pragmatics of language follows a biological and developmental path that is dependent upon the adult maintaining a flow of dialogue that is both verbal and non-verbal. What is essential for children is that through their encounters they simultaneously experience all the channels of communication available to them. Children's play provides an essential context for learning about communication and language.

Experiences that enable the child to initiate and maintain joint engagement facilitate the acquisition of the conventions of conversation and the ability to respond to the actions and language of another.

Providing a narrative also shows an interest in what the child is doing, creating an empathetic response that builds on learning language in the context in which it is used. The narrative is kept simple and maintains a natural flow. Children with delayed language need to hear the rhythm of spoken language that matches their pattern of movement and interactions with objects. Making the speech disjointed breaks down the language into isolated chunks and reduces opportunities for the child to learn about the flow of two-way conversation. Commenting on the child's activity rather than directing it enables the child to develop an awareness of language forms. This internalizes the experience for the child and teaches them how language relates to their actions, objects and emotions. Children, whether or not they have a language or communication impairment, often find questioning difficult. A question is often too demanding and fails to get a response because it involves a complex set of linguistic structures associated with knowledge of one's own personal perspective. Imposing questions on the child may significantly reduce the child's intention to respond and lead to lack of an understanding of language that is required for use in other contexts. As Rogers (1961) points out, often questioning is done to support what the partner is wanting or needing to know rather than focusing on how the child is able to express what they are doing.

Creating a non-threatening atmosphere that provides a space for reflection and intention is not too dissimilar to having a conversation marked by significant pauses and even silence. When interactions are informal and include an element of fun and humour this adds a richness to the understanding of communication so that the child feels more confident about offering a verbal response. Using 'I' and 'you' in the narrative or conversation is essential for developing the child's concept of self. Using the child's name is appropriate for giving instructions as in 'Julian, come here', but the same format does not need to be used during informal exchanges that are describing what the child is doing. Attributing actions to the child helps him or her to understand the functional use of language. For example, rather than 'Mary is running and Mummy is going to catch you' it is preferable to use 'You are running and I am going to catch you' as it follows the more normal patterns of syntactic structure in language.

As the child is exploring and developing new ways of interacting, all attempts to communicate verbally and non-verbally must be praised and encouraged. The child should not be made to feel that they are not communicating correctly if they cannot offer eye contact, nor should the flow of interaction be interrupted to gain a response based on the adult's expectations. This spontaneous and natural approach to language acquisition builds on levels of communicative competence even in children with autism whose receptive language skills may be significantly more developed than their expressive language.

Children with autism may develop spoken language initially by imitating what someone else has said. Although this is typically how language is acquired, some children appear to get stuck in their understanding of the use of language and continue to use language in this way. According to Williams (1992), however, this echolalic speech suggests a strong desire to want to communicate and interact. Echolalia can therefore be regarded as having a functional communicative role and one that can become part of a playful verbal routine. Even when children imitate the same intonation, echoing the child's vocalizations and bodily movements using songs and musical instruments can be turned into a spontaneous interactive song.

In the play context, the capacity to use single words to label familiar objects that have both intrapersonal and contextual relevance will result in more efficient internalization and generalization of new concepts. Moor (2002) describes how she had tried to help her child understand prepositions by showing him picture cards but it only made sense to him when she actually made a game of sitting 'under' the table. The kinaesthetic approach to learning language establishes the links between thought and action and enables spoken language to become more relevant.

When I visited Neema's home for another session her mother informed me that Neema had been hiding her toys in the garden and she did not know what to do about it. I suggested that we taught her 'hide-and-seek' and found three of her favourite toys to 'hide'. Of course we did not hide them so that she would have difficulty looking for them but placed a toy on the patio wall, one on a hedge and another next to the washing line. We ran around the garden using the phrase 'where's the doll?' and when we found the doll made reference to it by saying 'here's the doll'. We repeated this with a train and a car and Neema was getting the idea of placing objects and them finding them again. At the end of our time in the garden Neema was verbalizing 'doll', 'car' and 'train' when we found these objects. The following week when I returned, Neema's mother explained that they had spent all week playing 'hide-and-seek' and, in addition to naming the objects she found, Neema was now running around the garden saying 'where is it? where is it? where is it?'

Through play Neema discovered not only why language was important for communication, but also how it became a catalyst for expressing herself in different ways. For those children who have good language skills, there will be certain types of play, drama or even the written form of language that can help them to represent their thoughts and feelings; Jackson (2002), in describing books as his doorway into other worlds, manages to achieve this by providing a vividly clear picture to others of his life as someone with Asperger's syndrome. Spoken language, like written language, is a symbolic representation of thoughts and words. In the same way that spoken language is more meaningful when it involves activities and events that the child is enjoying or is interested in, so the ability to play needs to be used for the same purpose.

Fraser had moved home with his family during the time that I was working with him and while he had very positive views about the new house his parents felt that through his behaviour he was possibly expressing some anxieties about the move. I asked him to draw a picture of his house and the only rooms he drew were his bedroom, the playroom, the dining room and the kitchen. He specifically described the decorations and used different colours to represent the different rooms. Even although there were only four members of his family he drew six places around the dining table. He did not draw the lounge where the family normally spent most of their time. On completion of his picture he shared it with his parents who were surprised about the six-place setting at the dining table, which he said represented places for his gran and grandad who had not yet had a meal with them in the new home. When his mother asked him why he had not drawn the lounge he said it was because he was angry with his brother for trying to play the new piano when he wanted to. Also, he did not like the wallpaper in that room and had been reprimanded for tearing it before his parents had had a chance to decide what to replace it with.

Like Fraser, some children develop the capacity to use language with increasing spontaneity, complexity and humour. This is discussed further in Chapter 6 where the role of play and drama in developing children's creative and figurative use of language is described. Opportunities to play with their peers in socio-dramatic play not only enables children to develop social skills, but also to mutually explore ways to master the rules for communication and language. Like drama, interactive play enables children to experiment and discover narrative rules within the security of the relationship. Other children that a child might be playing with often have more capacity than adults to use language that reflects their mutual engagement in play. This is because the motivation to maintain a flow of dialogue with the play overrides the need to question or instruct what should be taking place. 'It is through play rather than verbal discussion that they are able to give us an account of the most significant aspects of their lives' (Schmidt Neven 1996: 21).

Companionship

The ability to participate in a communicative act has its origins in the mutually engaging behaviours between the child and his or her main carers and it is these interactions that provide the foundation for more complex communication with others. Children with autism can be supported in the transition towards an increasing understanding of communication through the establishment of cooperative and enjoyable patterns of interaction that provide both companionship and challenge. This sense of being with others is important for the development of communication, as the experience of this relational interdependence leads to an increased awareness of an intentional responsiveness towards them. Children who have not had sufficient experience of early forms of play and interaction may become limited in their capacity to engage in meaningful interactions with others. They are more likely to have language difficulties and may show a preference for being alone rather than sharing the company of others. It is in this context that Stern (1985) refers to the 'undrawn' child rather than the child who has become withdrawn. As the relationship between the child and carers develops through the reciprocal, affective patterning of playful interactions there is a sense of reacting to the social stimuli that will transform the child's interpersonal world. The experience of security that the relationship provides will add to the desire to share communication, whether this is with parents, siblings or people outside of the home. Children who have difficulties with this core connectedness are likely to have an altered perspective of social interaction and helping to overcome this usually requires a therapeutic intervention to provide experiences in sharing affective states, joint attention and intentional responsiveness.

The development of communication lies in the sharing of play experiences that include excitement, enthusiasm and the joy of being together. An interactive approach is incompatible with the notion of obtaining social interaction by coercion or compliance. Furthermore, positive communication that includes play creates greater potential for interpersonal discovery and social and emotional competence. This includes the use of non-verbal communication, spoken language and affect-laden experiences occurring within a social context. The child, having experienced the self, then comes to understand the self with 'other' and seeks to maintain the communicative connection to support the sense of self.

> Billy, at three and a half years old, preferred to play with others on his own terms. Consequently, he found it very difficult to interact with his sister who was twenty months older than him and he had difficulties playing with his peers at nursery school. His parents wanted to make his play a more enjoyable experience so that it did not become too disrupted by his need to control what was happening. I introduced a game for him to play with his father that involved blowing a cotton ball across the room with a straw, but they had to rely on looking at each other to start each turn. Billy became very excited at the prospect of competing with his father but he also had to learn how to make the cotton ball move. Having mastered this it was interesting to observe how he and his father both wanted to win. They made repeated attempts to be the winner and the game of 'blow football' was maintained by scoring who had won. The game was then introduced to the rest of the family and in the context of playing with his Mum and sister he showed more willingness to take turns and accept that he was not always going to be the winner. Billy's motivation to share in this play together increased his ability to cooperate and through the excitement created he was able to experience a more positive way of being with his sister that had previously been difficult for him to attain.

An increase in Billy's ability to use expressive and receptive language provided more opportunity for others to engage in a verbal and physical dialogue. When this matched his level of linguistic understanding there was greater potential for social adaptability and awareness of how to relate to others. The emotional content of his play increased his awareness of his father's attempts to win and this enabled him to respond more competitively when the family were playing together. Non-verbal gestures, facial expressions and behaviour remain key to how individuals express their social relatedness, while having language extends the ability to negotiate and explore others' emotions and actions. The tools of thought and the capacity to understand the vast panorama of social situations are constructed on the basis of interpersonal relationships and the nature of the communication that takes place between them. Relationships are certainly not static – they frequently change on account of the differences in social understanding and the perceptions and communications of those involved. All individuals will find themselves in some kind of relationship but it is the ability to sustain it through positive communication that will affect how it develops. An important aspect of communicative adaptability is the way in which the child learns to collaborate in social acts, as this in turn will influence their level of social understanding. It is through interpersonal relationships that the understanding about the self as a communicator emerges.

A communicating environment

According to Potter and Whittaker (2001) there is overriding evidence that children with autism benefit from environments that provide the most opportunities for them to develop spontaneous communication. Children's communicative understanding and language are more likely to develop in an atmosphere that facilitates self-initiated, intentional behaviour that is responded to positively. The importance and frequency of these communicative opportunities should enable children to:

- gain and maintain the attention of an adult;
- request and initiate an adult's help;
- express emotions;
- influence the feelings and actions of others;
- follow the ideas of others; and
- gain independence.

The development of these communicative competencies needs to take place in an environment where the parent or carer has a clear sense of what can be achieved rather than manipulate opportunities to meet specific goals. Adults will be keenly aware of those environments in which the child expresses more motivation to communicate. When a child expresses pleasure in spending time in a particular environment, it is usually because the play experience is supporting the child's sense of well-being.

As the communicative and linguistic competencies of individuals with autism can be defined in terms of the contextual nature of the interaction, both indoor and outdoor environments should be accessible to children as they provide low demand and more naturalistic, responsive conditions for maintaining the interaction. The extent to which the child makes use of both functional and social communication will be dependent upon how the play partner adapts his or her language and communication to the child's comprehension level, and adults will need to establish those conditions that support the child's communicative experience with the world.

> In one of our play sessions Aaron had a soft springy hammer that he was banging on the floor so that it made a loud squeak. It was one of his favourite toys and each week he would ask for the 'boingy thing'. He hit it on the floor a few times so that he could enjoy the noise it made but then it broke. Concerned that he might become upset I picked up the toy and held it to my ear. I pretended to talk to it and ask why it had decided to stop squeaking. Then I told Aaron that 'boingy thing' wanted to be a quieter toy and just make a 'tap-tap' noise, to which he replied, 'boingy thing hasn't got a boing, it's called "thing"'.

Having established the communicative partnership, there is greater potential for the child to respond to others and develop new ideas for both play and interaction. The important factor for the play partner is to have much higher expectations for the child's communicative capabilities, which will lead to an enhancement of the interaction. Communication is not just an exchange of ideas or an opportunity to solve problems and gain mastery over experiences; it is essential in defining a relationship with another person. The capacity for children to participate in a diverse range of communicative experiences is determined by their motivations, temperament and response to stimulation, as well as the system or environment that makes up their social world.

Chapter 5

Creating meaning

If children are not able to attribute meaning to their experiences, it is difficult for them to exist in a fundamental state of relatedness with others and their environment. A crucial component in the construction of meaning is an innate drive to make sense of the world and when this corresponds to individual motivations it increases the internalization of the experience and the likelihood of more permanent changes in behaviour. Interactive play not only contains the experience in a way that it is meaningful to the individual, but also provides an integrated mode of learning that supports cognitive development and social understanding. This occurs as the adult provides playful activities that focus on extending the child's conceptual awareness, encouraged through self-discovery and the exploration of objects and ideas. Socio-cultural theories recognize that the adult's involvement in the learning process is one of establishing a co-construction of meanings through which individuals communicate their shared thoughts and emotions (Bruner 1990; Trevarthen 1995). Vygotsky (1978) stressed that the internalization of the experience is predominantly understood within the context of an individual's relationship with their environment and, in particular, their social interactions. It is therefore essential that the value placed on play re-affirms the significance of a child-centred approach to the development of knowledge about the world and, in particular, social relationships. The personal relevance that individuals attach to explorations of the world around them is based on their own perceptual understanding and this influences how it comes to be interpreted and acted upon. This chapter argues that in order to mediate in children's play and learning, it is essential that their perceptions, behaviours and interactions are valued and seen as meaningful to each individual.

Siegel (1999) points out that it is both personal representations of the world and interpersonal experiences that will shape cognitive development. Therefore interactive play has an adaptive function in that it is based on the creation of a shared system of experience and any learning that takes place occurs when the activity is extended beyond that which the child would otherwise reach alone. It is in the construction of a dynamic spiral of support that children will then be able to develop more active skills in concept formation, language and symbolizing.

The transformation from sensory representations to symbolic representations is highly dependent upon experiences that assist in activating different modes of thinking. This is inextricably linked to emotional reactions both in terms of how information is processed and the levels of arousal that activate chemical changes in the neural pathways. At the prelinguistic stage cognitive processing originates predominantly from the experientially based interactions with the environment. As patterns of interaction become established so they reinforce how information is processed and stored in the brain. This involves a memory base deep within the limbic system that becomes the foundation for acting upon all subsequent experiences. According to Dawson and Fischer's (1994) research it is as a consequence of an increasing awareness of others and the establishment of significant relationships that these memory states have the capacity to transform into more complex representations, such as language. The acquisition of language significantly affects the way in which experiences are processed. Language has a role in integrating experiences, adding further conceptual understanding to how an object or event can be remembered. Although any experience can have relevance at a preverbal level, in terms of concept development language adds meaning, making it possible to increase symbolic representation and abstract thought.

Because interactive play provides a positive framework for helping children to understand the meaning of their thoughts and actions they have the potential to develop a more coherent sense of their own personal and social world. Franklin (1994: 530–2) describes the search for coherence as being embedded in activities that are representative of the human drive to create meaningful realities. Each of these realities, in addition to being interrelated, is regarded as a means through which understanding is formed.

- we seek to know the world around us;
- we seek to know the social world;
- we seek to organize our experiences;
- we seek to make sense of our inner world;
- we are actors in the world of our own lives;
- we are closely connected to other human beings;
- we are driven towards making things;
- we move towards gaining competency and mastery;
- we are always stretching boundaries;
- we need to express feelings and ideas.

For children, these behaviours are predominantly achieved through their play and become more complex and sophisticated as new experiences alter their thoughts and behaviour. Hence they are equally relevant to the ways in which adults engage in their work and leisure activities. It is also significant to recognize that these realities are not dependent upon a set of intellectual competencies but are highly individualized and will be influenced by a whole range of social and cultural experiences. The process of intellectual growth is dependent upon the need to establish feelings of competence, not just in terms of making sense of experiences via thought and action but through the emotional significance that the individual gives to them.

LeDoux (1996) believes that children who are deprived of play opportunities or who are not sufficiently supported in overcoming difficulties in social interaction will have a weakened ability to develop conceptual understanding and abstract thought. Rather than view children with autism as having a weakened ability to play, it is crucial that the shared play experience is seen as aiding conceptual development, representation and abstract thought. Bailey (2002) also recognizes that play functions as a cause as well as a consequence of the child's ability to develop self-awareness and to understand fantasy and reality, and even the intentions of others, and, as such, adults have a significant role in creating the conditions in which to develop these skills.

The origins of experience

The establishment of meaning and its analogies with construction is useful as it implies that specific foundations have to be put in place in order for any permanent structural changes to occur. In the developing mind, the activation of sensory information is assimilated through the emotional reactions to an experience. Sensory experiences that originate from a psychobiological basis are also essential for concept formation about the self and the self in relation to other people and objects. Any difficulty in integrating sensory information will affect concept formation but this should not imply that as an experience it has any less relevance for the individual. Sensoriperceptual processing is at the core of concept development and involves not just the physical sensation of the experience, but also what it represents or comes to symbolize.

Anna, a parent, described how her son could not tolerate the noise of traffic on the road (prior to a diagnosis of autism that explained why he had difficulty with sound sensitivity). At two years old, he would either scream if the noise became too loud for him or he would block out the sound by covering his head and closing his eyes so that he was then not looking around and absorbing other things in his environment. For him the concept of 'car' was not as an object that he enjoyed going in to take him to places he liked but something that he came to fear because of the pain it caused him. She therefore exposed him to outdoor sounds in different ways, by letting him watch cars on the television, buying him remote control vehicles for which he could control the sounds and taking him outside in the evenings when there was less traffic. When he began to describe the sounds of traffic as 'good' or 'bad' at around the age of three and a half, she realized his ability to make a crucial link between his knowledge and the emotional reaction to the experience.

The foundations of experience are not, as is often assumed, from the child's isolated state, but from the sense of being connected to others and the environment. Kernberg (1980) believes that the acquisition of knowledge is not based on separate units of information but on the unitary nature of experience. Because the self, objects and people are not experienced as separate this implies that there is a sense of interconnectedness towards them. Initially experiences are understood not in fragments but as 'wholes'. Experiences and images, and even other people, lack form and structure until sufficient information is assimilated. Perceptions are internalized as sensoriaffective experiences until the build-up of memory traces transforms how the object or experience is interpreted. Williams (1998) suggests that when some children have difficulty moving to the next stage of sensing and developing knowledge of self, others and objects, they remain at a sensoriperceptual level where they feel more secure. The separating of self from 'other' is an ongoing process of assimilation and interpretation that is dependent upon the nature of the caregiver's interactions and not something that the child can achieve alone.

In a Key Stage 1 class for six pupils with autism, I frequently observed Ben's play behaviour. Despite being offered a variety of toys and play activities he was only interested in scattering them or breaking them up into smaller pieces. When he played with water he did not use any plastic beakers or toys but just splashed his hands in the water. Outside he would continually wander around the play equipment rather than play on it. There was no apparent form or structure to his play other than the repetition of the same actions with the activities he preferred and there was no evidence of containment or construction in his use of objects. As a child new to the class I was also aware of the profound difficulties he had interacting with the other children and although he had some spoken language, he did not use it to initiate a conversation with the adults or children. He appeared 'isolated' in all his behaviours in the classroom until I began to play alongside him, imitating the same actions that he used to play with his preferred activities.

I was able to position myself opposite Ben at the water tray and he also let me put my hands in it at the same time as him. I imitated his actions and accompanied them with words. As I used the word 'splash' he was soon able to build in some anticipation of when I would splash him. As staff, we made sure that we always played in the same way with him so that he could develop an understanding of the words and actions and that we wanted to interact with him. We then introduced other wind-up toys into the water that would splash when they popped up or moved around. In this way we were extending his play; not making any demands on him or introducing an activity that was not meaningful to him or that he might not enjoy. By carefully placing a selection of these toys next to the water tray, we observed him picking one up and putting it in the water. It was important that we continued to support his play and help him to wind up the toys he wanted in the water, especially when another pupil came over to the water tray to see what he was playing with. From the apparent formlessness of his play, the interaction we established with him enabled him to develop the capacity to merge his actions into thoughts and relate to objects in a way that continued to interest him.

It is in the creation of the social and emotional dependency of the adult–child relationship that the child began to develop the capacity to respond and make sense of his experiences; children with autism who predominantly engage in exploratory and manipulative play rather than pretend or symbolic play may be doing so, not because of an inability to represent but owing to the delay in establishing a more competent sense of the self and 'other'. They may need more time to explore an object because the mode of processing they are using means they have difficulties abstracting the separate elements of it and therefore they are less able to recognize its function. Hence there is a danger of making assumptions about the play behaviours of children with autism as being related to a specific cognitive deficit.

The cognitive processes that underpin the internalization of experience cannot be separated into structures of thinking, perceiving or affect, as they all impact on how information is stored in the memory. Isaacs' (1966) early theories of intellectual development recognized that 'children's cognitive behaviour is not a set of separate relation-finding units but a complex and dynamic series of adaptive reactions and reflections' (p. 52). Furthermore, although these structures exist, they cannot be developed without the appropriate stimuli. Isaacs' theory of cognitive development does not focus on hierarchical intellectual structures as Piaget's did but suggests that a key factor in children's capacity to develop more abstract and causal concepts is their interest in the experience. Early relational play is at the beginning of this process and it is from their own explorations and discoveries that children naturally come to establish a mode of learning in which they feel secure but equally able to change. Developmentally, children may adopt a predominant learning disposition through which they gain knowledge and understanding but this does not imply that other modes of learning will be excluded. Individuals may be predisposed to use certain patterns of cognitive processing but it is how experiences are integrated that will affect how meaningful they become.

The construction of meaning is not based on intellectual competence but is a model of cognitive processing that has at its core the experience-dependent relationship. Experiences initially lack form and structure but as new information is acquired so more selective perceptual processing takes place and this will influence how it is understood. The continuity of the experience provides time and space for the child to develop the capacity to fuse together the significant features of the experience that may subsequently lead to a transformation in functional and conceptual understanding. Even if skills have to be relearnt or become more complex, the same pattern of cognitive processing applies. This is accompanied by a level of independent action that is manifest by the child's own motivations, enabling him or her to abstract the most relevant aspects from the experience. Embedded within an experience-dependent model is a growing awareness of the separateness of the self from others that is crucial to the child's ability to interpret and gain further knowledge and understanding.

Shared meanings are more likely to emerge when conscious acts of relatedness are established and linked to a set of internal representations about the 'self' with 'other'. Without a level of social stimulation children will be less able to develop new concepts about objects or use them in a representational way. Likewise, children who remain at the exploratory phase of object recognition will have a less developed sense of self than those who are using objects to represent their thoughts. During one of my parent workshops a concern was expressed about using the child's object of interest to engage with her as 'feeding the obsession'. There are several reasons why this is not likely to happen. First, while the adult may mirror the actions of the child who is manipulating the object they will not share the same intensity in the affective qualities of the object. Mirroring the behaviour acknowledges the child's sensory perceptual preference for the object and this enables the adult to explore other ways in which it can be manipulated. At the same time as maintaining the child's focus it also sensitively invites different ways to creatively explore the object. In this way the child is given the opportunity to extend his or her repertoire of behaviours, making connections between different modes of play and creating more flexible ways to think about it.

> The parent described how her daughter Susie was 'obsessed' with ribbons. It had become an issue of behaviour management for the parents because she would demand a new ribbon every time they went shopping together. She always had to have matching ribbons in her hair and became distressed if she could not wear the ones she wanted because they were being washed. As an activity in the workshop I then presented the parent with a large dance ribbon and suggested that she explored what she could do with it. She moved around the room making large and small shapes with it, shaking it and letting it ripple on the floor. She began to laugh as she realized how ribbons could be more fun. She thought about using a dance ribbon with some of her daughter's favourite music and how synchronizing the shapes they could make together would help Susie to respond more positively towards her and give them both a chance to get more exercise!

By extending the use of the preferred object or activity, meanings will not be destroyed in the process of reorganization but can be re-experienced. In this way they would both be seeking ways to make interaction more enjoyable and meaningful. There is a sense of equilibrium that is maintained while new and different concepts are introduced. Brosnan *et al.* (2004) suggests that the inability to process relationships between elements is undermined in autism but they imply that when the stimuli is presented visually or kinaesthetically children show greater achievements in Gestalt processing. Increasing access to play using toys and other materials that can be used in a variety of ways implies a greater potential for concept development, emerging as a consequence of a reaction to stimuli and the ability to discriminate and recognize relationships. Typically children develop the capacity to utilize these skills quite rapidly in early development not only because they are essential for physical survival, but because they help to establish meaningful interactions with the world.

Building concepts

As children continue to be encouraged to spontaneously explore objects through the sensory modalities, perceptions become transformed and rooted in the individual's drive to abstract the significant features of the experience. Because of the emphasis on sensoriaffective experiences in early concept formation, learning can therefore be described as impulse driven. Such impulses expand the neural pathways and lead to more effective integration and awareness of the social and emotional aspects of their lives (Hughes 1991). The construction of concepts is based on shared experiences that provide high levels of stimulation and where the child's understanding is fostered by acknowledging his or her interests in the world. This is a further reason to observe how the child's play fits into an existing conceptual framework or schema.

Neema would explore objects by scattering them on the floor. She would do this with the family photos but did like looking at them and identifying people she recognized. If her mother was distracted, Neema would find something from the kitchen such as a packet of frozen peas and scatter these. Interestingly, the first activity that she engaged in with me was with a bag of coloured feathers that she scattered on the floor. When I became part of her scattering activity she was able to increase her interaction with me and discover different ways to explore feathers. She made throwing them into a game and used them to gain a response from me. Her communication was extended to using language, giving eye contact and developing an understanding of the cause and the effect that her actions had on me.

This example shows how interactive play increases the likelihood of change in the child's actions and representations that were accommodated within her existing patterns of thinking and behaving. Commenting on or attending to what the child is doing increases the child's awareness not only of the activity but also his or her mental state. This provides a linguistic and conceptual scaffold from which the child can begin to understand how mental states influence behaviour. The ability to make this connection indicates a new pattern of cognitive processing that is essential to the development of concept formation and symbolic understanding.

How children relate their conceptual knowledge of physical, social and emotional experiences to objects and people is highly dependent upon the contextual nature of play and how others interact with them. Where there is a delay or interruption to this developmental pattern, regardless of whether it is pathological or environmental, it will affect how children respond to new experiences. If the adult's response to children's play behaviour implies a weak ability to comprehend the nature of their actions it undermines their potential to acquire further skills in abstracting thoughts and developing their own ideas. On the other hand, the presence of a play partner helps to promote the child's awareness of the significance of their actions and achievements. Although the ability to attach emotional significance to an experience is fundamental to a child's concept development, he or she is also reliant upon others to value it for its originality.

Toby was two and half years of age and had recently received a diagnosis of autism. He attended a preschool setting where it was felt he would benefit from an early intervention programme. He was seated at a table and had been given a set of stacking cups. This was an activity he recognized as staff had modelled it for him on previous occasions and he had some knowledge of what he was being asked to do. He put one cup on top of the other in the correct sequence but then became distracted by wanting to explore one of the cups by putting it in his mouth. The cup he was sucking was green which happened to be his favourite colour and, as a consequence of this, he was unable to return his focus to the activity he had begun. When I sat opposite him, he looked at me briefly but continued to suck the green cup. I picked up a cup to continue stacking but he reached out to stop me. Acknowledging my presence in this way indicated his ability to shift his attention from the green cup to me. I picked up the cup again and imitated him. He smiled and watched me place the cup on top of the two he had stacked. It was not correctly placed in the sequence so he removed it and placed the green cup there instead.

Williams *et al.* (2001) consider that parents and caregivers have a crucial role in demonstrating and highlighting the use of objects and using verbal narratives and physical activity to help the child engage in play. Providing that the activity is presented in such a way that it is meaningful to the child and that he or she is not purely responding to the adult's expectations, only then are play behaviours likely to develop beyond basic exploration and involve more functional and representational interpretations. If play is only seen as meaningful for the child when an adult determines that it has some functional relevance, it becomes goal directed rather than experience based. The fragmentation of a play activity into smaller tasks can result in the child assigning less relevance, leading to weaker generalization and poor transferability. Although a functional analysis of play and play objects may serve to highlight the benefits to children's learning and development, there is a danger that the measurement of certain play skills is too simplistic and either undermines the aesthetic nature of the experience or obscures a function that is more relevant to the child. Describing certain types of play as functional implies that other modes of play are not as relevant to the child and his or her developmental needs. Although it is not appropriate to define all play activities as goal directed, they are not functionless.

Robert, at six and a half years old, had a significant delay in his spoken language but good receptive language skills. He had been diagnosed with autism as a result of a metabolic disorder that had affected his physical and sensoriperceptual development from birth. Robert lived with his parents in the country where they were surrounded by fields and farm animals, and his love of tractors and farm machinery was frequently evident in his play with representational toys. To support this I offered him a chance to play with his tractors in the sand tray, but, because of his uncertainty about touching the sand, he moved away from it and instead requested a drink of water from his mother. He came back to the room where we were playing and poured some of the water into the sand tray. 'Tractors in mud,' he exclaimed and then proceeded to happily move them around, getting a tractor 'stuck' and using another vehicle to push it out. His father was surprised by the way in which Robert had linked the idea of mud to the lane in which they lived, which was often very muddy. It was interesting to observe how he only played with the sand when it resembled something he was familiar with.

By having insight into the child's inner world, the support offered creates the potential for extending how particular objects can be presented. In the development of awareness of the separateness of self from objects, children will shift between moments of integration and disintegration with their environment. The facilitation of the play experience provides a secure base from which children can increase their understanding of separateness and develop an ability to discriminate, make associations and solve problems. An increase in the associations a child is making through play will result in being able to discover more uses of the object and enable him or her to develop more flexible ways of thinking.

Robert would frequently play out the same scenario with his representational farm vehicles and farm animals. This involved putting all the animals together in a box and then taking them out one at a time and placing them on different vehicles and moving them across the room from one side to the other. His mother was unsure how she could share in this activity as he was very clear about what he wanted to do and he did not like her interfering with his pattern of play. She wanted to change the way he played with the toys and to teach him to do something else with them. When she distracted him with another game or toy he would stop playing and leave the room. She frequently admitted not knowing what to do with his play so it was important to focus on what they did like doing together. Because Robert had been quite inactive as an infant she had spend a lot of time singing to him to keep him occupied so we discussed how she could use this during their play together. When Robert next played with the animals and tractors during one of our sessions, I encouraged her to observe his play and to support it by singing 'Old MacDonald'. When Robert picked up a certain animal she would incorporate it into the song. This gave meaning to his actions but also enabled him to respond to her so that she was then anticipating which animal he would pick up next. His mother needed to feel that she was participating in his play while he became more aware of his influence on her response. She gradually discovered that it was more enjoyable to join in with him rather than become upset when he did not play with his toys in ways that she wanted him to.

Through the inherent need to establish a sense of relatedness to objects, children can be guided by adults to develop concepts not only about the physical nature of objects, but also about their existence within a social world. It is because interactive play is experienced in the present that children develop the capacity to assimilate relevant information that leads to further concept formation and subsequent knowledge about social relationships. Having a fixed repertoire in play or using the same toys does not mean that the child is not able to increase the range of associations or combine them in novel ways. When the child's focus in play is to line up objects this indicates a core ability in sensoriperceptual processing that involves the establishment of organized structures, patterns and shapes. Froebel (1974) suggests a more powerful use for the establishment of lines that is evident in children's early play and states that 'the representation of objects by lines soon leads the child to the perception and representation of the direction in which a force acts' (p. 76). The significance for the child does not have to be in the establishment of the line but what it represents. In other words, there is an energy to the child's thoughts that acknowledges the relevance of the action: it involves a number of different thought processes, which include a level of self-absorption, concentration and creativity.

Ahmed always liked to take the same collection of animals with him when he went out to visit relatives or new places. He liked to create his own story scenario with the animals and would also line them up and sit looking at them until he decided to alter the sequence in which he had placed them. He had been playing with them outside in the garden but when he brought them inside one of the animals was missing. He found it difficult to continue to make a story without one of the animals and picking up the elephant he took it to his father and told him, 'Elephant is very strong. It needs to find blue horse.' His father then responded by going to find it for him.

Even when a favourite toy is lost, the child came up with a unique replacement that suggests a creative ability to solve a problem. Such actions give rise to more spontaneous interactions and this aided his ability to develop more abstract ways of thinking. The need to organize experiences is an essential feature of concept development that is dependent upon repetition and practice. Play that enables children to categorize, recognize patterns and sequence objects or events raises the potential for increasing levels of abstraction. Hence the organization of play into specific repertoires can also be seen as an attempt to create meaning. Establishing preferences for certain types of play or particular play activities ensures that the salient features are securely explored and mastered.

Toys and activities that provide representations of familiar experiences not only further how children make sense of the world around them but also how they make sense of their personal world. Through the use of representational toys and objects children will be able to project their knowledge as well as their feelings about experiences that are significant in their lives. Children will first make use of toys and objects and even people for the novelty they provide. However, they soon learn to reject or prefer particular items for the saliency that they attach to them. Children should be offered toys and objects that give them the opportunity to learn through their own explorations; they do not have to have a specific function but should present the children with an appropriate level of curiosity and stimulation for them to solve problems and make their own discoveries. I would express some concern about the overuse of 'cause-and-effect' toys with repetitious sounds and visual stimuli, of which there is a vast array available (usually made of plastic), which seem to be extensively used as 'occupiers' in classrooms for pupils with severe or profound learning difficulties. The physical similarity of the stimuli means that they provide only a basic causal mechanism for learning, which encourages the ritualization of the experience with no opportunity for spontaneous error correction, rehearsal or transferable knowledge. However, I have observed children using both 'cause-and-effect' computer programmes and electronic sensory equipment that provide different levels of skill and therefore have an inbuilt motivational factor to stimulate learning; through the stimulation they provide levels of physical and sensory activity are combined, aiding the development of more concrete and abstract thought processing.

The use of different resources and toys for interactive play activities should provide opportunities for experimentation, construction and representation, which enable images and ideas to be given an objective form. It is within the shared experience that the potential for shared realities and shared meanings emerges. The use of objects also enables children to formulate rules, categorize and plan, and, as a consequence, they are able to develop more abstract ways of thinking and responding. With opportunities to practise what they already know, children can revisit the same concepts and build new ones. In this way they can gain mastery and the confidence and capacity to extend their knowledge and understanding.

Creating coherence

Individuals are drawn to organize their experiences as a result of the sensations, actions and tensions that have occurred from the moment of conception. The interpretation of events is fundamental to how they are stored in the memory and will remain inactive at an unconscious level until associations between stored information and current experiences can be made. The individual's inherent need to create coherence and establish patterns of behaviour will aid the development of independent modes of action and thought. Logical thought is an essential component in understanding the meaning of events and through play children will have increased opportunities to establish links between literal and symbolic thinking. The ability to structure knowledge aids skills in planning, categorizing and problem-solving and creates the potential for more interpretation and the development of ideas. According to Bruner (1986) interpretation is the earliest form of representation that can either remain as thoughts or be expressed through action and language. Language is a symbolic representation of thought and therefore fundamental to concept development. The emotional significance of the interactive play creates the potential for more symbolic acts to develop as internal representations that are formulated via the interpersonal experience. Stewart (2001) recognizes that symbol formation follows a developmental sequence that originates in the parent's responsiveness to the child through language and interaction. Through interaction, language and thought become more active when successive experiences promote concrete levels of understanding and imagination.

Lizzy was twelve years old and had attended a school for children with autism since the age of five. Her parents encouraged her with many of her interests at home and in the community. She enjoyed singing and music, the computer, drawing cartoons and attended a dance club. She had activities planned for her, or she was left to occupy herself, which she could do quite happily. From my observations she was encouraged to take part in activities where she was frequently questioned about what she was doing and prompted to take part in activities that would keep her occupied. Although this admirably showed her parents commitment to her involvement in social experiences, there seemed little opportunity for her to use her leisure time in more spontaneous ways that would enable her to express her own level of independence and her parents had requested some ideas about how they could develop this. I began by singing to Lizzy to introduce myself and help her to feel relaxed with my presence. She soon started to copy the tune I sang but made up her own phrases to sing back to me. Because I joined in with her song, she became more interested in maintaining something that she was enjoying. She continued to think of humorous phrases to sing, which she repeated. This revealed an ability to use language spontaneously and in abstract as well as concrete ways.

Shake my hand, shake my hand
hello Lofty
shake my hand.

We moved on to another activity that involved story-making using different fridge magnets on a magnetic board. I placed one of the magnetic shapes on the board and used a narrative to describe it. She then imitated what I had done and gradually she added more to the board, but as she seemed unsure of creating a narrative I made one for her that involved rhythm and repetition. As she added and removed the shapes it became her story, in which she was able to use some of them to represent characters from a television cartoon that she liked. Her excitement and pleasure in her new skill became evident in her use of language, which became more spontaneous and conversational as a result.

As her use of language altered she was able to integrate the experience and became aware of how meaningful it was for her both personally and socially. Her behaviour became more intentional and there was an increase in her use of language, so that she was able to make crucial connections between her ideas and share them with me. Helping children to integrate their experiences through positive interaction is essential if they are going to develop a more coherent sense of self and understand the impact of their actions on others. It is the nature of the shared experience that exemplifies how play influences the development of symbolic communication.

Rather than view play simply as a means of occupying children that has no set purpose other than being intrinsically satisfying to the individual, there is now a fundamental recognition that it assists in the organization of thought processes by influencing functioning across both brain hemispheres. Perceptual processing deficits in autism have been associated with a weak 'central coherence' in cognitive functioning and this suggests that because processing is local (left hemisphere) rather than global (right hemisphere), information is not processed in context, leading to a fragmented perception of the world. Further studies by Happé (1999) and Rinehart et al. (2000) also indicate weak global processing affecting the ability to identify how elements of a visually presented task relate to one another. However, none of these studies focuses on the role of affect on the individual's ability to establish coherence. The affective qualities of an experience, whether or not it involves play, increase the likelihood of children being able to integrate their experiences and act upon them in more meaningful ways. Emotional reactions bring about biochemical changes in the neural systems between both brain hemispheres that can either act as a block to extending knowledge and understanding or assist in creating more coherent ways of thinking and behaving (Siegel 1995).

Affective experiences that are play based are part of the cohesion and detachment that influence central thought processes, and they are likely to increase the level of global conceptual understanding by giving meaning to the wider realities of the experience. For example, the heightened anticipation of a trip to the park to play on the swings incorporates a variety of other perceptual experiences that must be retained and acted upon to make the preferred activity the focus. Gestalt therapists, such as Oaklander (1989), prefer to consider the holistic nature of the context in which the child is functioning, as no single element makes an experience meaningful. The Instrumental Enrichment Programme (Feuerstein et al. 1980) also recognizes the pervasiveness with which altering one aspect of cognition, for example the affective response, will impact on the potential to understand the 'whole'.

Children with autism do not differ in their ability to use organizational strategies to help them make sense of their experiences, and the complex processing mechanisms that they use to organize their actions should not be underestimated. Rather, it is the way in which information is processed that affects how they relate it to others; this includes how emotional reactions are used to aid their interpretation of what is meaningful. Instead of focusing on differences in cognitive ability it is more essential to recognize how different levels of functioning co-exist. Individuals with autism may be more dependent upon routines to provide them with some predictability in the face of constantly changing realities but these are also essential for the maintenance of cognitive and affective stability, which are inherently human characteristics. Children often appear to look for more complex structures and interpretations, whereas at other times they can be content with the simpler and more obvious ways of handling experience.

Piaget's notion of 'equilibration' within cognitive structures, which aids children's ability to make links between their internal schema and external realities, indicates the drive to make sense of experiences, and in so doing helps them to establish functional relevance. Consequently, when children use play to organize their thoughts and actions it shows an in-built capacity to solve problems and establish some coherence with increased complexity. Once these organizational structures are in place then the child can gain new insights into different ways of thinking and behaving. All play, regardless of its mode, consists of internal and external organizational principles that will support and encourage concept development. Coherent patterns of thinking and behaving are more likely to emerge when children are given opportunities to engage in activities that provide them with the time and space in which to develop symbolic understanding.

Feeling competent

An activity in which the child is eager to engage will contribute psychologically to the promotion and anticipation of new actions. With the adult's presence, it raises awareness of the significance of the child's acts so that he or she gains more understanding of what took place as well as the processes through which this was achieved. As children become more aware of their own intentions to act, this impacts on the responsiveness of the adult, creating a context for increased exposure to one another's mental states. Social interaction therefore becomes key to how children develop the intellectual ability to understand the difference between what is real and imaginary. This occurs when the adult provides activities that encourage autonomy and competence, creating the potential for children to modify and extend their conceptual and symbolic awareness. Play symbolizes the child's need to understand the realities of the world around them and when this is simultaneously supported within a positive relationship it allows for new boundaries to be explored.

Meins *et al.* (2003) studied the critical period in which maternal responsiveness facilitated the acquisition of a theory of mind. Their results indicated this critical period to be during the attachment phase when joint attention and the linguistic labelling of the child's mental states and behaviour helped to draw the child's attention to the functional relevance of their actions. Children who have significant difficulties in socially and emotionally relating to others will continue to benefit from the same interactional patterns that parents provide for the young infant to establish a secure attachment. Using language and creating a context where children are treated as intentional agents increases the potential for developing more mind-mindedness and awareness of others' feelings and intentions. As Bruner (1986) states,

'It is not that the child does not have the capacity to take another's perspective, but rather that he cannot do so without understanding the situation in which he is operating' (p. 68).

The domains of understanding are multidimensional, making it difficult to imply that deficits will occur in particular areas of cognitive functioning. For example, the child's ability to engage in more intentional behaviour towards another is indicative of not only cognitive processes that involve planning and decision-making, but also those that are influenced by affect and the ability to be reflective about one's actions. Intention is evident at the prelinguistic stage of development but may be more reliant on behaviour and gestures to elicit shared meaning.

David was five years old and non-verbal. He had a visual system of communication but was not using it to request objects he wanted and usually had to be prompted to use it to request food at snack time. The use of the symbols for communication had not been fully established and as a result it was felt that he would benefit from an Intensive Interaction approach to increase his understanding of communicative intent and relating to others. David was given one-to-one sessions in the soft play room on a regular basis. The staff were encouraged to join in his play and mirror his actions. The focus of the thirty-minute sessions provided an effective space in which to develop his awareness of us and enabled the staff to establish more understanding of his play and interaction. He clearly enjoyed the physical nature of the interaction and repeatedly wanted to be bounced on the large physio ball that we had placed in the room. In the classroom he would not initiate any play with the toys or other pupils and referred to the staff only when prompted. On one occasion we observed him taking a chair to the cupboard where the large physio ball was kept and trying to open it. Not achieving this he got down from the chair and went and stood next to a member of staff until she realized what he wanted. The Intensive Interaction was maintained for several weeks and we frequently used the same activity during these sessions. During one of these sessions, while I was bouncing David on the ball, I stopped and asked him if he wanted to 'go again'. He would either give me eye contact or gesture by bouncing on the ball. This continued until I stopped and waited for him to bounce or gesture that he wanted to continue but instead he looked at me and said, 'Go again'.

The onset of language adds a further dimension to understanding the intentions of others and the need to formulate more understanding is heightened (hence the reason for so many 'why?' questions from typically developing three- and four-year-olds). For David, the framework for establishing meaning was defined by the interpersonal process that had been created to support the development of his communication. Although the extent to which the shared experience increased his emotional understanding is not clear, it does indicate the importance of the social and contextual influence on his communicative competence. Children are more likely to respond intentionally to an experience when it corresponds to their desires or motivations, and it is important that they are exposed to a range of experiences in which this can happen. This leads to the formation of further mental representations that are consciously or unconsciously linked to an awareness of emotional states.

Bornstein *et al.* (1996) noted in their research that an increase in representational and symbolic competence was significantly influenced by parents facilitating the play experience. They also found greater improvements in cognitive functioning when the interactions were reciprocal, positive and supportive as opposed to those that were directive and intrusive. Using interventions that are dependent upon a learned response too early in the child's development could potentially undermine the need to internalize experiences in ways that more effectively aid the development of abstract ways of thinking. The externalization of knowledge only occurs when various concepts have been internally represented, mentalized and generalized and built into a child's existing repertoire of behaviours.

Kwan's parents had recognized his interest in creating regular patterns and sequences with the wooden blocks. They had become so used to seeing him line them up, focusing his attention on making sure that they were correctly positioned that they assumed he played in this way 'because he is autistic'. He could sometimes spend up to an hour arranging them on the floor and, even if his parents joined him, he would give them blocks and expect them to do what he was doing. They at least felt that this was an attempt to share in his play and accepted that this was what he did with blocks. When I observed his play, he had carefully balanced a series of blocks to form several bridges of different heights. His box of vehicles was in the playroom and I picked up a car and pushed it under one of the bridges he had made. His father did the same with another car and then Kwan copied him and picked up a bus.

As the bus was bigger than the cars, the bridge was too small for the bus to go under. We watched as Kwan spent several minutes re-adjusting the size of the bridge using more bricks and checking to making sure it would not fall down when he pushed the bus through. Had his father or I intervened to help him achieve this he would not have had the opportunity to formulate his own ideas about what he needed to do to solve the problem of the bridge being too small. He had already established skills in how to manipulate the bricks, to which he applied the same determination to the new sequence of events that we had presented to him.

The ability to project ideas through objects indicated how Kwan was making use of representations and patterns of thinking that had been established from earlier experiences. Unless children are given the opportunity to explore these projections with another there is little motivation or need to learn anything new from the play with objects. They have become stuck in a preferred schema that not only impacts on their knowledge of self, others and the environment, but also reflects their emotional states.

Block play provides children with an instant opportunity to use a plain object to represent something else. Just by placing a few blocks on top of one another it becomes a tower that can be knocked over and rebuilt. There is also the added incentive and problem-solving task to build it in such a way to prevent it from falling down, a feature I have often observed when fathers are playing with their children! Block play enables children to make representations of familiar objects and in this way it becomes a self-initiated meaningful experience. An interesting study by Le Goff (2004) found that the motivational aspects of Lego™ amongst a group of children with autism led to an increase in their social interaction skills when shared play sessions were set up. Although the planned play sessions were devised to facilitate social interaction, the outcome of the research would also suggest that it was their sense of relatedness to the Lego™ activity and their ability to be creative with the blocks that was a key factor in helping them to relate to one another. This adds to the discussion about the holistic nature of play and its role in helping to integrate both the local and global aspects of cognitive processing.

Play helps children to move between what is real and imaginary but they cannot achieve this independently of their interactions with others. Peter (2003) recognizes that participation in shared play and drama aids the internalization of mental representations by enabling children to take different perspectives which are then given meaning. Pretence becomes a route to social competence as the child is given a focused opportunity to play out familiar situations and stories that have personal relevance for them.

The strategies that many children with autism adopt in their play that may be interpreted as isolating, repetitive or lacking in symbolic representation might imply a lack of competence. This tends to be inferred because of the difficulties in the social referencing of the activity. Instead, by making reference to the meaningful aspects of their play it emphasizes the skills they have in equating the internal and external representation of the experience. Play is rooted in the child's capacity to represent thoughts and to make links between what they know. It is equally important that adults are able to infer meanings to children's play and interactions as this helps to build further representations and symbolic understanding. Interestingly, it may not be an adult but other children who have a far greater capacity for interpreting a child's play and they more readily adapt their own actions to fit in with how the child with autism is playing.

It is not just about using play to acquire meaning but, more crucially, that play exists to give meaning to the child's actions and thoughts. Interactive play provides a greater opportunity for integrating knowledge and increasing awareness of the social impact on learning that the child would not be able to achieve if they were left to play alone. Children need to feel supported in establishing their own rules, solving problems and making decisions through their play and other significant interactions. For children with more severe and profound learning difficulties it is so often the case that they are given fewer opportunities to extend their thinking in this way. Erikson's (1980) theory of psychosocial development suggests that, unless children experience a sense of mastery or competence in their interactions with others and the environment, they will have a weakened ability to make sense of the self, emotionally or cognitively. The integration of the psychosocial model of development and cognitive growth suggests that rather than a measure of cognitive ability, play is a significant factor in the development of cognition.

Variations in the play behaviours of children with autism do not just relate to intellectual ability, as it is the stimulation and level of involvement in the activities that will invite them to respond in different ways and create meaning from the experience. In this way there is no variance between their approach to play and learning and that of their typically developing peers. The child is continually involved in perceiving and interpreting stimuli through which they construct meaning. Likewise, the possibilities for perceiving and acting are also unique because of the ways in which each individual has established an understanding of the world in which he or she lives. According to Dunham et al. (1989), having positive affective experiences increases the child's motivation to participate in more socially contingent relationships. The adult's role is one of having higher expectations of the child's abilities to use their play to respond in ways that reflect their knowledge and understanding. Pretti-Frontczac and Bricker (2004) also suggest that when interventions are provided within the naturally occurring activities in the child's environment their functional and generalizable skills are more likely to develop. The creation of meaningful experiences will not only aid the child's conceptual understanding of social behaviour, it also gives them time to show us what they know and understand about their personal and social world.

Chapter 6

Developing imagination

Within the affective resonance and reciprocal communication of early interaction, children learn that their responses to activities are meaningful and, as a result, this enables them to develop more complex interpretations and expressions of play. Spontaneous exploration via sensory experiences results in highly personalized interpretations or perceptual images that are the earliest form of representation and fundamental to the development of imagination. As the infant's play becomes more intentional and there is an increase in curiosity and exploration, crucial connections are made between ideas and actual events that result in more symbolic acts being created. In early development, the ability to play imaginatively emerges from the individual's drive to abstract the significant qualities from a range of intra- and interpersonal experiences and transform them into thought and action.

According to Hobson (1993) it is the nature of the shared experience in early parent–child interactions that exemplifies how both play and language influence the development of symbolic communication. For example, when a young baby learns to reach for a soft colourful toy that is being presented to her, she does not shake it in imitation but puts it in her mouth. It is not only the exploration of the toy that is significant at this stage, but also the taking of it, which symbolizes an interpersonal connection to another. It is as a consequence of the cognitive and affective influences involved in altering patterns of behaviour that children become more competent in using different thought processes to communicate, interpret and solve problems in their play and interactions. The integration of the social experience and the ability to respond to experiences in unique and innovative ways is an essential feature of the creative process, and playful interactions that include elements of spontaneity and enjoyment will have a profound influence on a child's ability to develop flexibility, symbolic awareness and representational thought. This capacity for creative thought is vividly shown in this poem by a young boy who has autism and significant difficulties with verbal communication:

When you are trying to think blue
And end up thinking black
You can be sure to be frustrated
Time and again it happens to me
And I get quite helpless
Otherwise why should I get up and spin myself
Spinning my body
Brings some sort of harmony to my thoughts
So that I can centrifuge away all the black thoughts
I realise that the faster I spin
The faster I drive away the black
When I am sure that the last speck of black
Has gone away from me
Then I spin back in the opposite direction
And pull the blue thoughts into myself
It depends how much blue I want
If I want more blue I have to spin faster
Otherwise not so fast
It's just like being a fan
The trouble is when I stop spinning
My body scatters
And it's so difficult to collect it together again

(Mukhopadhyay 2000: 101)

Contrary to much of the literature that describes individuals with autism as having an impairment in imagination, thought and flexible behaviour, this is not universally disordered in their play or ability to express themselves creatively. Since the 1970s, much of the research into the cognitive functioning of people with autism has resulted in educational or treatment programmes focusing on remediating left-brained deficits and emphasizing the rigidity of thought processing and weak central coherence. Unfortunately, there has been less recognition given to how right-brained activities that involve non-verbal processing, intuition and creative expression can assist in bypassing the difficulties in perceptual and emotional responsiveness. Where play and the creative arts have emphasized self-expression and spontaneity, they have tended to be regarded as additional or alternative to the curriculum and this has undermined their essential role in children's cognitive development. The key to enhancing learning potential for children with autism is to adopt more creative approaches to teaching that incorporate play and the creative arts to support the integration of both brain hemispheres, strengthening the weaker neural connections and aiding the development of imagination and creativity. A further reason for promoting play and the creative arts is the social dimension that enables children's inclusion and identity with a wider range of sociocultural experiences.

There are many people with autism who are able to express their intellectual skills and creative talents through music, art, literature and mathematics, indicating the capacity for more abstract, symbolic and imaginative ways of thinking. The ability to express oneself creatively and imaginatively does not belong to the domain of those individuals with autism who are especially gifted or who are of higher intellectual ability. When opportunities for children's imagination and creative expression are facilitated and nurtured through play, the creative arts and associated therapies, this impacts on altering states of mind and well-being, both psychologically and biologically. This chapter attempts to demystify why some children with autism have difficulties in developing symbolic or imaginative play by emphasizing the socio-affective processes that are essential for developments in cognition. Frith (1989) makes the point that rather than look at deficits in brain function in individuals with autism it is more relevant to refer to the perceptual sensitivities to incoming stimuli. These perceptions are clearly linked to how children playfully interact with their environment. The ability to internalize and develop an emotional response to an experience becomes an expression of creativity and a powerful means of communication. A fundamental premise of the creative arts is that the utilization of the senses and the communicative dialogue between the child and adult lead to a more positive realization of the self as an independent, inventive and reflective thinker. Children who are deprived of creative or playful experiences or who are directed too much in their play will continue to relate to the world in either chaotic or rigid and inflexible ways. Regardless of their level of intellectual functioning all children will need opportunities to develop imaginative and creative ways of thinking, to develop confidence and experience a sense of wonder and enjoyment.

> Creativity is best construed not as a single power, which you either have or do not, but is multidimensional: Creative processes involve many different functions, combinations of skills and personal attributes. They involve special purposes for familiar mental operations and the more efficient use of our ordinary abilities, not as something profoundly different.
>
> (Boden 1990: 259)

As the National Advisory Committee on Creative and Cultural Education (NACCCE) Report (1999) points out, creative possibilities are pervasive throughout everyday life; more importantly, creative activities not only involve the use of imagination, but they are also fundamental to developing it. Imagination can therefore be defined not just as a mental activity involving analysis and reason, but also as a synthesis of ideas that influence expressions of creativity. Russ (2003) questions whether it is play that reflects the processes important in the development of imagination or it is the play processes that facilitate imaginative and creative abilities. This discussion is linked to play activities that encourage problem-solving and the mastery of skills and the more pleasure-giving aspect of play that children engage in with spontaneity and for enjoyment. According to Thomas (1997), the concept of imagination can be described both as a distinct product of mental imagery and as aesthetic originality that is the source of creative thinking. This suggests that what is required is a more holistic approach to understanding the development of imagination, which views the process of play in all its manifestations – occurring from birth through to adulthood – as key changes in patterns of thinking. This includes the symbolic interpretation of events and the creative use of objects, as well as the ability to engage in imaginative and sociodramatic play. Creative experiences that allow children to consciously and unconsciously represent themselves through their use of sensory materials, narrative and the arts will influence how they relate to others and, in response, how others relate to them. The key components in the development of imagination that are explicitly represented in play and the creative arts are clearly linked to the affective processes that are nurtured in playfulness, spontaneity, creativity and humour. The motivation to explore, experiment and represent, which is embodied within the creative process, will impact on children's cognitive development and is implicit within an interactive play approach. 'With the right approach a plain white hat and a plate full of yarn spaghetti can contribute to a young child's cognitive development' (Bodrova and Leong 2003: 50).

Playfulness

In recognizing the difference between learning how to play and being playful, Lieberman (1977) argues that there is a distinct relationship between playfulness and the development of creativity and imagination that is not always evident in more functional types of play. Playfulness emerges as an element of play that is linked to the development of physical, social, emotional and cognitive spontaneity and therefore manifests itself differently from other play behaviours. In creating dance-like movements in response to a favourite piece of music, enjoying chase games or hiding an object in a box to create a surprise for the recipient, it involves an emotional relatedness to the experience that allows for originality and more divergent ways of thinking that emerge from a knowingness and desire to alter aspects of the interaction. Not being bound to specific expectations, children are able to make their own unique contributions to the play experience and discover their creative potential.

Sami, aged seven years, was non-verbal and had autism with severe learning difficulties. His sensory preferences were shiny objects and pieces of material that he liked to hold on to or flap, so a variety of these were made available to him in the playroom. In our first session he explored some shiny material that crackled, putting it over his head, standing on it and moving around the room so that he made a noise with it. Sometimes he stood quietly with the material around his feet and at other times he moved around excitedly, enjoying the noise he was making. Sami repeated these actions in the following session but this time I found a shiny rattle, which I shook as he moved around the room. I stopped shaking it as he stood still and began again when he moved. His realization that I was moving with him resulted in him taking the rattle from me and jumping up and down on the shiny material shaking the rattle. When he gave me eye contact and smiled it illustrated his ability to playfully relate his actions to another person. The creation of the shared ideas and responses equated to an informed awareness that motivated him to attend more to the pleasurable aspects of playing together so that he was driven to investigate further the qualities of the experience.

Playfulness describes the essence of play in which spontaneity, pleasure and humour reside. Although this can occur when children are playing on their own, relational play with a partner has the potential to heighten the qualitative nature of the play. Having a playful disposition impacts on their emotional well-being and personality development and undoubtedly how they relate to experiences throughout their lives. My observations of interactive play with children who have autism have identified that the characteristics of playfulness are in evidence before the acquisition of more functional play skills. There is a marked capacity for physical alertness, spontaneity, curiosity, enjoyment, active participation, self–other orientation and humour, which Lieberman (op. cit.) identifies as the 'global behavioural dimensions of playfulness'. The key to the development of playfulness and children's creative and imaginative potential emerges from sharing in their focus of interest and providing opportunities for more authentic communication. Hadley

(2002) describes this as 'getting inside the flow of children's play' so that through their actions and awareness they are able to become more reflective and consciously alter ways of thinking about things that are familiar to them.

In many educational and childcare settings, and even in homes, playfulness is often equated with being out of control, lacking in purpose and discouraged as an activity that could make a mess or be regarded as inappropriate. Adults tend to prefer children to remain seated or quiet when playing or to take part in activities that have set rules and functions, such as computer games or sports. These may be helpful activities for teaching specific skills, but too much of this type of play can result in the development of rigid patterns of behaviour and a lack of creative thinking. I am not suggesting that children cannot be creative when using computers but that they also need opportunities to engage playfully at an interpersonal level. Often it is when the adults themselves are uncertain about the benefits of play that they are unaware of how to engage playfully with a child. During my workshops adults are always given opportunities to playfully explore objects and toys, to be creative and interactive and to give themselves time to internalize the feeling of playfulness. Usually there is a sense of relief that they can be with children in this way and recognize that the same learning goals can be achieved through a less directive and more play-oriented approach. One parent told me at the end of a workshop that she always thought that when her son came home from school she had to continuing working with him to help him to learn and now she realized that he could learn when they were playing together. Another parent arrived at one of my workshops exhausted from coping with the demands of her family. She spent some time playing and by the afternoon appeared more relaxed and was joining in conversations with other parents. When asking the parents at the end of the workshop what they wanted to do when they got home this particular parent told me that she was looking forward to making a treasure box for her child with autism so that she could have more fun with him. The presence of playfulness leads to a marked change not only in the quality of the play but also in the relationship. One of these qualities includes a mutual consciousness that communicates a safe context in which to explore different ways of thinking and playing. It is the containment of the playfulness within the relationship that therapists in the arts recognize as fundamental in bringing about a change in an individual's view of the self and interactions with the world (Oaklander 1989; Wilson *et al.* 1992; Jennings and Minde 1993; Landreth 2002), otherwise such play can be seen as impulsive, lacking in focus and with little potential for development. Being present with another, the child is able to experience the *play in its fullness*, observing in more detail the differences as well as the familiarities and acting upon them in ways that will impact on affective and cognitive processing.

Humour can also be an element in playfulness that adds a different qualitative dimension to the experience. Being humorous is reliant upon the ability to abstract ideas and alter meanings; it is also an expression of affect that can contribute not only to the maintenance of the social interaction, but also to the development of imagination and creativity. Many individuals with autism are able to understand and share in the subtleties of teasing and joking and enjoy the 'slapstick' type of humour that is not dependent upon linguistic skills or complex knowledge of social interaction. Humour is often related to novelty and surprise, which are both significant elements of playfulness and can sensitively be used to counterbalance more rigid and inflexible ways of thinking.

In one of our sessions Aaron did not want to play as cooperatively as he had done on previous occasions and decided to hide in his large wicker toy box. I put a puppet on my hand and tapped on the box to ask if the duck could play with him instead. He opened the lid and told me that the puppet was not a duck because it was not white.

I picked up a white chicken puppet: 'This is white, is it a duck?' I asked him.

Aaron: 'No, it's a chicken, it's got a red thing on its head.'

I picked up a white sheep: ' This is white, is it a duck?'

Aaron: 'Nooooooo. That's a sheep!'

I made some sheep noises.

Aaron: 'Sheep wants to eat flowers.'

I picked up a flower puppet: 'Will he eat this one?'

Aaron: 'No, that's got a smiley face on it.'

I picked up a wooden painted flower: 'He'll eat this one. This hasn't got a smiley face.'

Aaron: 'Well it'll have to go to the smiley face shop and get one.'

Aaron hadn't realized that through the spontaneity and fun with the puppets we had actually been playing together. He had accepted my teasing him by correcting me but had also found an imaginative way to express himself.

As a component of playfulness, humour functions as an expression of affect and cognition and as a result it contributes to the imaginative and creative process. When a parent wears a box on his head and calls it a hat or tries to put on the child's coat instead of his own, it results in an attentiveness that enables the child to respond differently and extend how the experience is received. Within the familiarity of the play situation the impact of the emotional experience will assist children in making leaps into more imaginative ways of thinking.

Creativity

Creativity is seen as a product of imagination because it involves the conceptualization and integration of original ideas with the mental ability to reflect on experiences past, present and future. Duffy (1998) defines creativity as a way of thinking that helps previously unconnected ideas and experiences to become connected in ways that are meaningful to the child. The manifestation of creativity within the arts adds an additional dimension to any definition beyond that which describes it as an aspect of cognitive functioning. In play, drama, dance, art, music and literature, creativity is defined not solely in terms of the mastery of a skill, but also in the non-verbal, intuitive sensing and individualization of the experience.

Rather than attempt to define creativity, researchers and educators tend to refer to expressions of creativity and the creative processes that are reflected in an individual's behaviour, activities and experiences in order to understand its relationship to cognition. According to Robinson (2001) creativity is not just an internal mental process but involves action – playing with ideas as well as objects and representing them with originality. Consequently, a child's first scribbles on paper or their collecting and lining up of toys are acts of creativity that denote an approach to life and an increasing awareness of the creative self. A further component in the development of creativity is an intrinsic motivation and ability to attend to an experience that is meaningful. 'Creativity is rooted in flexibility, fluidity, inventiveness and above all playfulness, experimentation and discovery, which lie at the heart of artistic expression' (Berggren 2004).

Play, regardless of its mode, can be described as a creative act because children are constantly acting upon different experiences, and consciously or unconsciously exploring the relationship among themselves, the object and the activity. Evans and Dubowski (2001) describe this as a creative dialogue that results from the child developing the ability to symbolically represent or create something new from what is familiar. Inherent in every individual is the need to create, and when this is achieved through interaction, encouragement and spontaneous exploration, they are increasingly able to represent and attach different meanings to their experiences.

As an intentional behaviour and non-verbal method of communication, play makes use of symbols that help children to redefine their personal view of the world and understand the actions of others. Symbols emerge through this creative expression and provide shared meanings in which concepts are formed and relationships can develop.

In my last session with Fraser and his family I wanted an opportunity to talk with his parents alone and set up an activity for Fraser and his younger brother that would encourage them to play cooperatively, share ideas and create something together. I presented them with some sheets of newspaper, string, sticky tape and some pegs and suggested that they should try to make something to sit in. I gave them a time limit of thirty minutes and encouraged them to work together using a set of friendly 'rules'. This took place, to their parents' amazement and obvious pleasure, without any disruptions. Towards the end of the time given to them to complete the activity, they had stuck pieces of paper together in a large rectangular shape and put pegs all around the edge. They requested help from their father to thread the string through the pegs and when completed they pulled the string tight and both sat down inside the boat that they had made together. Working collaboratively had enabled them to experience communication through shared meanings and, through the creative use of materials, to engage in a shared symbolic act.

Play as a symbolic form of communication signifies further how children come to develop more divergent ways of thinking beyond the literal and specific. The use of symbols in play can help children to bridge the gap between reality and fantasy by eliciting a sense of meaning in an otherwise confusing situation. Symbols also support the child's ability to differentiate between the real and the imaginary. Increased access to supported play reduces the difficulties some children with autism may have in differentiating between fantasy and reality because the adult, aware of the individual's emotional and intellectual strength, helps to develop a greater awareness of the cognitive and affective processes that are taking place when they are playing together. By giving time for the child to reflect on the exploration and manipulation of the play objects that are being mirrored by the play partner, it heightens the child's symbolic understanding and aids the development of the imaginative use of the object. In therapeutic terms this is at the core of the creative process.

This was illustrated in a play session I had with Liam when I had spent some time establishing our relationship by responding to his non-verbal request to tickle him and roll him to and fro in a blanket. As his confidence in making contact increased, he stood on my feet and I walked around the room, holding on to him, pretending that together we were a monster. I made 'monster' noises and talked about being a monster, which he clearly enjoyed and did not want to stop playing. The following day, after he had gestured for me to remove my shoes, he stood looking at me. 'Do you want to be a monster?' I asked, and he stood on my feet and held on to my arms.

Providing the stimulation for more creative acts is dependent upon the individual's curiosity and the intrinsic and extrinsic rewards that are likely to influence how objects and ideas are explored. Creativity also involves elements of risk-taking and challenge that are key to cognitive development and underpinned by the individual's affect and attitude towards the experience. Although for many people being creative occurs in isolation from others, there are also those whose creativity can be encouraged by the nature of the positive interactional process that is made available to them. Craft (2005) identifies the following factors as significant in stimulating children's creativity and sees the need to:

- develop children's motivation to be creative;
- provide an environment where children can be rewarded for going beyond what is expected;
- use language to both stimulate and assess imaginativeness;
- help children to find personal relevance in learning activities;
- encourage additional and alternative ways of being and doing, celebrating their courage to be different;
- give children time to incubate their ideas.

(p. 13)

This chapter continues with examples of how an interactive approach has enabled children with autism to spontaneously explore a range of sensory materials and creatively express their ability to differentiate between the real and the imaginary in the play experience.

Sand Play

Sand Play has been used within the therapeutic context since it was recognized that the manipulation of the sand and the use of small world objects provided a powerful means of non-verbal expression and an opportunity for individuals to reveal to themselves the nature of their thoughts and feelings. The malleability of the sand, which for many is an enjoyable experience, is the first important factor, followed by the way in which objects are chosen to create a scene in the sand. Lowenfeld's (1979) 'Small World Technique' has promoted the use of sand play as a therapeutic tool, but sand can also be effective in enabling children to explore its creative qualities and gain some control over how they manipulate objects within the safety of the sensory experience. It is important to make the distinction between playing in a sand box with buckets, spades and pouring cups provided and offering children an individual sand tray and a choice of small world objects to put in it. In most Early Years settings, sand is available as a sensory play activity but, personally, I regard this as an under use of a valuable resource that should not only be functional (or only available in Early Years settings), but should also provide opportunities for enhancing self-expression and symbolic play in a supportive and non-judgemental environment. In the Sand Play process it is significant that the small world objects are not chosen at random. Because the choice of the objects is significant to the individual, it enables them to be used symbolically. At a preverbal level there is also an emotional significance to the manipulation of objects in the sand and an opportunity to enter into a personal dialogue that helps the individual to move forward in his or her thinking and interactions. When a child is using the sand tray, the presence of the play partner provides a supportive role that gives time and space for the child to creatively explore aspects of the self.

I always began our sessions with Fraser in the family group, to give each member an opportunity to talk about significant events of the past week. A common occurrence that affected all members of the family was the arguments between Fraser and his mother, particularly over his taking food from the kitchen when he wasn't allowed to and shouting at his mother about getting ready for school in the morning. Following one of these discussions, Fraser expressed an interest in using the sand tray and a range of small world and natural objects. I explained that in the time available he could use the sand and objects in any way that he wanted and that I would not be telling him what to do but, if he wanted, I would talk with him about what he was doing. He began quite enthusiastically looking at the range of different objects and manipulating them. He did not touch the sand and kept it completely flat in the tray. He then made a pattern of shells around the edge of the sand tray and explained that he wanted to use them because they reminded him of going to the beach where he liked to walk the dog and go bodyboarding. He found a number of plastic snakes and laid them on the sand, moving some of them towards each other before placing them in lines on one side of the sand tray. Next he chose to put a motorbike near the snakes and then placed a bus on the sand, which he told me represented the school journey he would be going on the next day. With any available space on the surface of the sand he placed more shells. When I informed him that he had just five minutes left he asked if I wanted to know what his picture was all about. I did not impress on him to tell me but this was something that he wanted to do. He explained again about the shells and about the bus and we talked about where he was going with his class. He then told me that the snakes represented him and his mother arguing and the turbo motorbike represented his dad. He went on to explain that although his dad liked motorbikes he didn't have one. Fraser wanted to show his parents what he had done in the sand tray and first explained it to his mother in the same way that he had told me. When his father came to look at the sand tray and Fraser described it again, his father pointed out to him that using the snakes to represent arguing with his mother was very interesting, especially as Fraser knew that she did not like them. In Fraser's sand tray there were expressions of both the literal and the symbolic: the bus for the school trip and the snakes representing him and his mother arguing. Unconsciously Fraser had used the sand tray in a thoughtful and sincere way to represent significant and meaningful aspects of his life that encompassed a range of different emotions: the comforting, pleasurable reminder of the beach, the excitement of going on a school trip, the discomfort of arguing with his mother and the ability to empathize with his father. When we joined together again as a family group, Fraser appeared a lot less anxious and was more receptive to writing a Social Story with his mother entitled 'Let's Stop Shouting'. Somehow the focus on the sand play and the explanations that followed seemed to give Fraser some space to think where, owing to the busy activities of his home and school life, he had not had time to reflect on his actions and feelings about himself and towards others.

Kalff (1980) recognized that sand play is a contemplative process for the individual and, at the same time, a creative act. She sees these processes as intimately related and therefore effective in the stimulation of the imagination. It is the transformation of ideas and feelings into the concrete reality of the objects in the sand that enables the child to redirect his or her energies into creative channels of self-expression.

As a group activity the sand and small world objects can also be used for story-making, when the adult supports the development of a story or uses one that is familiar and the children introduce chosen characters and objects in the sand as the story continues. The three-dimensional use of the characters, objects and changing landscape provides a kinaesthetic experience that aids the development of imaginative thinking. Such activities also encourage cooperation, promote language and give children an opportunity to initiate their own ideas and negotiate how the story can be developed. Because the experience is motivational and contained within the structure of the narrative, it enables children to make use of their creative energies, helping them to build a shared symbolic language.

Clay and play dough

In the same way that sand and water are familiar tactile materials, playing with clay and play dough represents a desire to spontaneously explore the qualities of natural elements. It can be pressed, rolled, pinched and squeezed and instantly change its form if that is what the child wants to happen. It is through the sensory experience that children can then find the freedom to create patterns and shapes and make representations of familiar characters and objects. In the Reggio Emilia approach the three-dimensional use of clay for sculpture-making is regarded as an opportunity for young children to learn more deeply about how to represent aspects of themselves and their world. They come to recognize through the qualities of the media that they are working with that there is an emotional understanding about the nature of their work through which they can make transformations and rethink ideas. The materials also provide them with a creative language to describe the qualities of their work that also persists in other art forms.

Neema had played with the play dough on several occasions but this had invariably resulted in her pressing the play dough out flat and then emptying all the shapes and beads onto it. She showed little interest in exploring other ways to manipulate the play dough so I modelled for her, forming different shapes with it and decorating them with beads. When she was offered the play dough again I gave her a choice of beads and a variety of small world objects. She chose the beads and spent twenty minutes carefully placing them in the play dough that she had pressed down on to the table. I sat with her as she did this without modelling the activity with her, as on this occasion she seemed to want to attend only on what she was doing and I enabled her to do this. Having covered the play dough with beads she reached out for the other objects I had initially offered her and took two candles. She placed these in the play dough and looked at me, vocalizing 'addy burday do you'. I found some matches and lit the candles. Together we sang the 'Happy Birthday' song and then she pointed to me to help her blow out the candles on her pretend cake, which we followed with cheers, claps and laughter. Being unable to have a conversation with me about what she was making she had found her own way of expressing something that represented a familiar, enjoyable experience. This may not have been her initial idea when she began pressing the beads in the play dough but with the discovery of the candles she had created something that she recognized as being meaningful to her.

The use of these different objects that interest the child, rather than prepared shapes, not only enhances spontaneity and motivation, but also gives meaning to the exploration of the different forms and textures that are an important aspect of the creative process. During a visit to a school I observed the children making clay pictures relating to a class topic on buildings. Having been shown how to cut a rectangular piece of clay they then pressed more clay into the shape and made patterns with different tools to create different door designs. Engaged in their own work, the children found a way of creatively expressing what they had been learning about that extended their knowledge and led to more representational ways of thinking and using language to describe what they had done. Newson and Newson (1979) recognize that if it is a relaxing experience, clay is one of those materials that 'seem to occupy just enough of the attention to free the rest of the child's awareness for creative and imaginative thought' (p. 17). The working of clay or play dough can be a soothing experience to many children (and adults) because they are able to create and re-create shapes that are meaningful to them. The focus of working with clay or play dough is not just about the final product but the engagement with the material during the process.

Story and narrative

The affective processes involved in play enable children to extend how they creatively represent their knowledge and understanding of the world. Therefore, play becomes a social act in which shared meanings can be expressed through language and action. Stories and narrative that are stimulated from children's own experience become an essential component of the developmental process through which they come to learn more about themselves, their culture and their physical world.

As part of a school project I ran a literacy session with a class of ten- to thirteen-year-old boys with autism and Asperger's syndrome. The aim was to develop more creative ways for the children to express their use of language and also to develop more cooperative interaction. Staff were included in the group to model and support the activities with the pupils. I explained that we were going to make a story and each say a sentence of the story when the ball was rolled towards us. The following script emerged from this activity, which we then discussed, particularly in relation to the emotions that might have been expressed in the story.

The Boy in the Woods

Staff: Once upon a time a boy went for a walk in the woods.
Staff: He found an enormous hole.
Pupil: He went down the hole and heard some spooky noises.
Staff: So he went to investigate and he saw a big purple monster.
Pupil: He looked scary.
Pupil: He stamped on the monster.
Pupil: And then the boy ran away from the monster.
Pupil: And went to watch ITV.
Pupil: In a haunted castle.
Pupil: The haunted castle was full of zombies.
Staff: That were all made of straw.
Staff: So he decided to build a fire.
Pupil: But the fire burnt down the castle.
Pupil: The boy ran away from the castle.
Pupil: He went to the big Buddhist temple and sat with Buddha and prayed and said I want to be with you. The end.

We discussed how the boy might have felt when he was walking through the woods and when he discovered the monster, whether he would feel bad about burning down the castle and what it might have been like to sit next to Buddha. The shared story provided the boys with an opportunity to project their knowledge, thoughts and feelings within the boundaries of the narrative form.

According to Bhattacharyya (1997) the context of the narrative allows for the integration of imagination and reality that is key to an individual's psychological well-being and cognitive growth. Stories impact on children's behaviour and affective processing, regardless of whether they are creating their own stories, retelling or listening to familiar stories from books, videos or films. Stories invariably provide examples of empathy, problem-solving, social behaviour and symbolism that enable children to interpret and redefine those aspects that are significant to them. Understandably, children will seek comfort in repeatedly referring to the same texts or narratives, as the pupil had done in talking about 'watching ITV' in the story above.

The use of objects and characters in story-making enables children who are less competent in verbal communication to create narratives via a visual and tactile experience. Blakemore-Brown and Parr (1996) describe how the multi-modal delivery of stories helps to embody both inter- and intrapersonal skills.

For a less able class of children, some of whom were non-verbal, I used a magnetic board and a collection of fridge magnets of different designs and characters to create a story together. Each of the children chose a magnetic shape or character that they wanted and our story developed as each child made their contribution to the magnetic storyboard. For those children who were unable to describe their character or object and link it to the story, they simply placed it onto the storyboard and I gave them a simple narrative. The teacher was pleased with each child's contribution to the visual story, which motivated them to want to create another one. This time they recalled a favourite story, *We're Going on a Bear Hunt*, and used the magnetic shapes and characters to create their own version of it. Again the non-verbal children in the class placed their objects on the magnetic storyboard but this time the other children provided the narrative.

Although children's interest in books and stories may extend beyond their competence in reading and spoken language, it highlights the importance of using a kinaesthetic approach to narrative and visual imagery. Favourite stories can be extended to incorporate real situations or the child as a character in the story, so that he or she can explore different ways to think about what is familiar. Children's own involvement in their story-making allows them to transform, alter or even repeat situations that can result in an increase in their ability to attend to the shared experience. It is within the safety of the relationship that has been created that they are able to draw on their own interests and experiences to create and invent something new.

Art

In the literacy session with the class of boys the following week, we used the same story-making sequence and although it began in the same way it became more elaborate as each one of them contributed more detail to the story. At the end of this story it was decided that we could make a picture of a fairground, which was one of the places that the boy in this story had visited. A large sheet of coloured cloth was laid out on the floor and a wide range of three-dimensional objects, small world figures and natural materials were made available to create a picture. One of the boys decided that he wanted to make a roller-coaster and found some straws, which he placed across the material. He asked another boy to help him and then he used the straws to make a Ferris wheel. Unprompted, another boy wanted candy floss and found some pink fluffy balls to put on the picture. Small representational toys were found to make a ghost train, along with a mobile phone in case someone got lost! The boys took turns to describe what they were putting on the picture and why it was significant. One of them wanted to put some chocolate on the picture but had difficulty selecting what he could use to represent this. I gave him a choice of some counters, beads and shiny pebbles and he decided he liked all of them and placed these all over the picture to represent his love of chocolate. In making the creative connection between story and art the boys were able to select relevant language not only for social purposes, but also for extending their thinking about what they were creating. Staff also observed how the boys were able to select objects to represent their ideas and how aware they had become of one another's contribution to the whole picture. Like the story, the creation of the picture had vividly captured their attention, extending their skills of representation while maintaining an interpretation of a familiar event.

The three-dimensional use of objects not only supports the developmental process, but also for some children it avoids a preoccupation with glue and paint that may interfere with their creative use of different media. Children need access to a wide range of natural and manufactured materials so that they can explore their potential use within any artistic format, but I would not suggest that these are presented simultaneously as this may again negate any creative exploration. Instead, selected materials or those that relate to the child's sensory preferences can be made available. A child's interest in wheels and circles could be expressed through using them to make patterns using paint, sand or clay. Carefully displayed, this provides an opportunity for the child to be reflective about something that he or she has created and to consider it more from an aesthetic rather than a purely functional perspective. When children show a preference for using a particular colour it can be explored through a range of different media so that used creatively it can become an object of self-expression. The use of colour can be seen as a liberating as well as an emotional experience, that once revealed can have a profound effect on how the individual feels about seeing the self represented in this way.

With a group of fourteen- and fifteen-year-olds in a specialist school for children with autism we were using art in one of their lessons. The focus of the lesson was personal and social awareness and creating a gathering circle at the beginning of the session helped to draw the group together with some discussion about circles. Immediately one of the students said it reminded him of a football, another pupil said that it was like a ring. Each student was then given a circle shape and encouraged to decorate it with art materials of their own choice. Some chose to colour it in, others made it look like a football and one pupil used glue and shapes. Each circle was personalized and then shared with the rest of the group. Some of the students said they did not like the circle because it was too uniform and they wanted to make a different shape. It was important for this group of students to maintain a sense of containment with the activity and I suggested that this time they drew a leaf to paint or decorate with their own choice of materials. Each leaf shape was different but they observed one another and the way in which they used the paint so that a few of the leaves were multicoloured, with paint dribbled on them. We brought the finished pieces to the circle to share them and one of the pupils became very articulate about his circle and his leaf. He had coloured the circle in completely using orange crayon but had previously said he did not like it. When he looked at his leaf he noticed that he had used yellow and red paint that had merged together. 'Oh,' he said, 'that's orange too but I like it like that.'

Within the context of the mutual experience the creation of something new enables children with autism to increase their confidence in using a range of different art media to make representations and develop insight into more complex ways of communicating that are not dependent on language. Jontes (2005) recognizes that what children communicate through their art is clearly linked to the developmental process and their core emotional needs. It involves a visuospatial intelligence and an expressive and aesthetic awareness that all children have the capacity to develop when given the appropriate experiences.

Music and movement

Like art, music and movement are highly effective in communicating both physical and emotional states of being. The rhythmic 'to and fro' of non-verbal body language, the synchronicity of movement and the emotional 'tuning in' to the qualities and attributes of the other person are unconscious elements of music and movement that individuals come to recognize as being essential to learning about interaction. The child's vocalizations and spontaneous movements are at the core of musicality that need to be encouraged and supported with songs and expressive actions during playful routines (Alvin 1978).

It is often interesting to observe how children make use of the space and silence to try and understand their personal view of the world in which they live. The view of the self is likewise reflected in body movements and hence creates a language that is communicated to others. In one of my workshop activities I asked the participants to move in a similar way to a child that they knew and for it to be observed by a partner. In gaining an awareness of these movements they came to understand at an unconscious level, rather than a conscious level, what was being communicated and therefore sought to create or mirror a movement that would support this. The response from the person who had initiated the movements was one of feeling supported and understood, so that as the movements were extended by the partner he or she felt more confident to explore other creative ways of moving and interacting. Using movement in this way has therapeutic benefits for children who have difficulties with their own body awareness and relating to others. By focusing on how a child is moving or using objects and mirroring them, it can enrich the way in which he or she develops a deeper understanding of his or her own creative potential.

When Abdul had chosen the toy he wanted to focus on I observed his movements as he explored its properties. He picked it up and let it drop; he twisted it so that it would spin and holding it he stretched it out and watched it go back to its smaller shape. To this he added his own actions so that when it landed on the floor he jumped up and down, when it spun round he would do that too and when he stretched it out he moved his arms up and down. Through his non-verbal response to this toy I was able to join in with his movements and as he continued to play with it he anticipated my actions. His capacity to go beyond the spontaneous exploration of the toy showed insight and an awareness of the impact of his ideas and actions on another.

Likewise improvizational music with chosen sounds and instruments symbolizes the interplay between the qualities of the individual's internal state and external expressions of creativity. When this takes place in the presence of another it offers a dynamic experience that helps the child to create new sounds and movements so that, in the safety of the relationship, alternative patterns of behaviour can be explored. Using musical instruments or songs that mirror these feelings shows an empathy and desire to develop a relationship with the child.

When Jo became very excited during a play session and started to run around the room, I introduced a song that matched his actions.

'Jo is running round the room, running, running very fast.
Jo is running round the room, running, running fast.'

I used an instrument to support his actions and played it in accordance with his movements so that I could adapt the tempo and slow down or speed up the song. As Jo became attuned to the sound of the instrument that was mirroring his actions, he responded by making sounds to match his running. I then introduced a new verse to the song.

> 'Jo is moving slowly now, slowly, slowly round the room.
> Jo is moving slowly now, slowly . . . , slowly . . . , stop.'

As this developed into a game it maintained the interaction so that he was not only listening to the sound of the instrument but was becoming aware of his own movement. By establishing synchronicity within the relationship and mirroring his actions and vocalizations it strengthened his confidence in responding to me and enabled him to enter into more improvizational behaviour that included spontaneous speech and initiating contact.

Through music and action, the reciprocity, attention and focus of the shared interaction represent the child's and the play partner's capacity to organize and present ideas differently. In group music sessions a variety of interactive songs can be used to invite children to add their own suggestions of words, characters and actions. The familiarity of the song provides them with a framework for their spontaneous responses and therefore the capacity to invent new ways of responding. Because each child's actions are valued it offers an emotionally supportive experience that is taking place within a creative and social context.

Puppets

Puppets can also be used to support non-verbal and verbal communication as they are naturally engaging and they allow for both creative expression and facilitate cooperation within significant relationships. The different characters and animals can be useful symbols for thought and action and provide children with a means to differentiate between reality and fantasy. The familiarity and enjoyment with which most children explore the qualities of the puppets provides a valuable resource for the development of language and imaginative thinking. In addition to being used with a child on an individual basis, they also assist in creating more positive interactions both in the home and with peers. Stories can be developed using puppets that are represented by each individual in a way that is meaningful. It gives children an opportunity to learn more about themselves and their play partners through the characters presented.

In another session with Fraser and his brother they created a story using two puppets. Little assistance was given to them in their preparation, as they already understood the framework for creating a story. I remained with them, however, to provide support in maintaining the positive interaction as they devised the story together. Fraser chose a hedgehog and his brother chose a monkey. Fraser decided his puppet was the teacher and his brother made his puppet the pupil who was not well behaved in class. Their story involved arguing and bullying and was only resolved when the brother used another puppet, a bear, to invite the monkey home to tea. When their mother observed this story she was overwhelmed by the accuracy of the portrayal of their actual relationship with the use of the puppets. After using the puppets in this way Fraser was able to verbalize how he found his brother's behaviour frequently annoying to him and that he often took control as a way of trying to change what was happening between them. His brother expressed how he wished that there could be happier endings and wanted to try and recreate this with their mother playing with them to make another story.

A familiar story can enable the children to develop their own interpretation of it or, because of the internalization of the qualities of the puppet they have chosen to play with, they can also create a story without words. As Walters (2004) identifies, stories using puppets enable children to:

- model responsiveness;
- develop autonomy;
- regulate emotions;
- reduce tension;
- provide structure and consistency;
- promote competency;
- encourage playfulness.

Peter was a five-year-old boy who had been adopted and had recently had a diagnosis of autism when I began working with him. In one of our sessions he gave me a hedgehog puppet and then found a small zebra finger puppet. He told me that the zebra had lost its Mummy and that the hedgehog would have to look after it. He gave it to the hedgehog that I was holding and then, as he looked for other puppets he wanted, he found a large zebra puppet, which he put on his hand and said, 'Here's its Mummy, baby zebra's going to be happy now.' His ability to empathically represent the need for nurture and support within a loving relationship through the use of the puppets powerfully illustrates the capacity for emotional understanding that is often assumed to be lacking in children with autism.

Both of these examples highlight the children's capacity to merge themselves into the characters of their puppets. As Gergen (1994) suggests, the self is a continually changing history of relationships that alters and affects an individual's identity. As a result, the interpersonal connectedness that is established through playing with puppets supports the capacity to represent the self symbolically and has greater potential for the development of imaginative and creative thinking.

Drama

Role taking and sociodramatic play can also been seen as opportunities for children to represent themselves in relation to others and explore concepts of reality and fantasy. The capacity to both transform and develop awareness of oneself has its origins in the spontaneity and playfulness of early adult–child interactions. According to Pinciotti (1993), early interactions nurture a sense of improvizational dramatic sequences through which the child learns to integrate real and imagined experiences. Engagement in familiar play routines can also result in the extension of the play into a dramatic event that is invariably based on a real experience. For example, when an adult hides a toy for an infant to find he 'acts out' looking for it using gestures, vocalizations and facial expressions that invite the infant to take part in the scenario. The playfulness of the situation enables the infant to gain knowledge of real and imaginary situations and to become more skilled in responding with humour, surprise and delight.

Peter (2000) emphasizes the value of dramatic play sequences in aiding the development of thought and language and as such it has a key role in children's social development. As children are encouraged to make physical and mental connections between an imagined experience and their actions it transforms their understanding of their own and others' behaviour. Unlike imaginative play that can take place in isolation, drama is essentially a social act that provides opportunities for children not only to express their own thoughts and ideas in novel and interesting ways, but also to have those ideas challenged and extended by others. A further key factor in the creative use of drama is the role of a facilitator who provides a framework for the actions of the children and sensitively guides them in the shared experience.

As part of a school project I worked with a small group of three girls. Two of the girls were competent verbal communicators, whereas the third pupil showed less confidence in social interaction or communicating verbally and it was felt that she would benefit from some playful interaction in a small group setting. At the beginning of our second session one of the girls announced that it was her birthday so it was decided that we should have a birthday party to celebrate. We discussed what we would need for the party and it was decided that we should have something different to wear and some food to eat. The girls chose hats and scarves to dress up in and staff in the group also became involved in creating colourful outfits. We asked each of the girls what they would like to eat at the party and using play dough we moulded different shapes and decorated them using a variety of beads, shiny shapes and shells to make cakes. When one of the girls used some coloured sticks as candles in her cake to represent the candles we all made sure that we did the same. Once we had placed our cakes on the cloth that we were using as a table, the girls continued to add other food using coloured counters for chocolate buttons and cotton wool for marshmallows. It was then decided that we needed some music to dance to and I used a song in which everyone was able to suggest something they wanted to bring to the party. This continued until it was time to finish the session. The birthday theme was clearly one that each of the children was able to relate to, making it easier for them to represent it. The girls were able to make their own creative contribution to the play activity and through the fun and excitement it helped to establish both group cohesion and a sense of friendship. The group activity also enabled them to develop a sense of shared affect that maintained their positive interaction, negotiation and collaboration.

When children are able to hold on to images from something that is familiar and transform objects and props and even themselves in drama or imaginative play it increases their ability to develop more complex mental connections and to process information 'as if' and act upon it.

These metacognitive skills enable children to communicate more effectively and by increasing the potential for language and abstract thought it highlights the essential role of drama and the arts in children's learning and cognitive development. Rather than see imagination and creativity purely from a developmental perspective, it is perhaps more pertinent to recognize that the ability to imagine is rooted in the realities and perceptions that are highly personalized and meaningful and that occur within a context which gives the individual a feeling of 'psychological safety'. As human beings we create our own realities based on how we make sense of what we know and the emotional impact becomes an integral element of the experience; individuals may look at the same object but see it differently, listen to the same piece of music but hear it differently, touch the same object but feel it differently. How these are perceived is how they are interpreted and, consequently, how they come to be imagined. Individuals will behave in ways that express their imaginings.

A key component in the development of imagination and creativity in children who have autism is that it remains embedded within a child-focused philosophy. Otherwise there is a danger that too many expectations and demands are placed on children to perform in ways that do not reflect their abilities, interests or personalities. Creative experiences are multidimensional in nature and this enables children to explore simultaneously the relationships of colour, form, movement and pattern, and of order and chaos, language and silence.

Another vital element of the creative process is the individual's potential for greater self-realization and interaction. If adults want children to develop their creative and imaginative thinking then it is essential that this includes elements of playfulness, spontaneity, enjoyment and humour. For children with autism, opportunities for creative expression should be evident in homes and educational settings where quality interactive experiences incorporate child-led, self-motivated and individual modes of exploration and learning that not only help to develop relationships but also allow for their creative potential. 'The creation of something new is not accomplished by the intellect but by the play instinct acting from inner necessity. The creative mind plays with the objects it loves' (Jung 1952: para. 197).

Chapter 7

The smile programme for families

Children's development is inextricably linked to the family context that exists as the primary social group for developing understanding about interpersonal relationships. The family system also offers a unique context for caring and nurturing individual members and promoting emotional well-being. Patterns of interaction are frequently changing and the ways in which they are maintained, broken and repaired are key to how individual members learn about socialization. Regardless of its cultural background, the family exists to provide a dynamic system of support for all of its members and each individual contributes uniquely to this process.

Following an interactive play workshop, a parent shared with me how she had shared one of the workshop activities with her daughter aged six, and her nine-year-old son who has autism and ADHD. They played with a balloon and each time one of them hit it they called out their own name. Then they chose to call out their favourite colour. The activity continued with them taking turns to suggest a favourite TV programme and this meant that the game lasted for half an hour.

The use of the children's names encouraged each child to acknowledge him or herself as being present with the other, making the shared activity meaningful to each individual. Making their own choices helped the children to recognize that they can appreciate that others can have different or the same ideas as their own. As the activity continued it encouraged more flexible, reflective thinking. Although this focused activity was based on shared enjoyment, a range of skills was also being encouraged that could then impact on other interactions.

When the activity finished her son went to his room and began to play his recorder. He was practising to play it at school but then called to his mother to sing with him while he played. She had been delighted by this response, as it was not something he had previously asked her to do. She felt that by making the time to play together he had wanted to find a way to continue to engage her in his activity.

Interventions that focus on the repair or establishment of reciprocity in relationships can clearly benefit those families in which a child's development has been affected by neurological or physiological damage. The use of relationship-focused interventions has highlighted a fundamental shift away from the focus on individual difficulties in social responsiveness, to recognizing how individual family members will have a major influence on the child's social development. Relationship-focused interventions provide a distinct set of principles that emphasize:

- the importance of the parent–child relationship;
- positive ways to engage with the child;
- the use of developmentally appropriate play activities;
- the supportive role of the facilitator;
- the maintenance of the interactive strategies.

These principles will be discussed in this chapter in relation to the establishment of the attachment between a parent and child, sibling relationships and the use of interactive play to develop emotional and social responsiveness. Any reference to working with families also acknowledges that many children with autism will be living in settings other than the family home. Where the professional responsibility becomes equated with that of a parenting role, it is important to recognize that the same principles of relationship-building can and should be applied.

Parents or main carers take much of the responsibility for the maintenance of the family and they are constantly vigilant to the ways in which different circumstances in the life cycle alter how the family system functions. For many families, having one or more child diagnosed with a disability significantly impacts on relationships both within the family as well as externally with other family members and the wider community. Rivers and Stoneham's (2003) study supports the findings of Powell and Gallagher (1993), who found that the effects of having a child with autism in the family resulted in both positive and negative influences on family relationships. Therefore, by working developmentally with the family it provides a more effective means of looking collectively at the whole system, rather than just the child who is having difficulties with social integration. Webster *et al.* (2004) point out that many parents of children with autism seek external support to help with their child's behaviour and developing communication skills but are rarely guided to look at patterns of interaction and play to aid the development of communication or alter problem behaviours.

When I first met Clara's parents, one of their immediate concerns was that she woke very early and this significantly impacted on the way in which they were able to run their own business for the rest of the day. After discussing the pattern of Clara's day it was clear that she was getting a good night's sleep but went to bed very early as she had little to occupy her after her evening meal and before bedtime. We considered how a half-hour session of playtime could be included in her daily routine before her bath and bedtime, and her parents thought they would try to maintain this for a week. On my next visit to the family they were pleased to tell me that they now got up an hour later than they had done previously because they had used a special playtime to encourage Clara to have more interests that were engaging for her so that she did not go to bed too early. Their shared enjoyment and playful interactions with Clara meant that they felt more relaxed and able to work more effectively during the day.

Behavioural interventions may be considered effective in the short term by removing or reducing the impact of the behaviour on the child and the family but it will always be more pertinent in the long term to focus on changes that are taking place at intra- and interpersonal levels. Interventions that are relationship based assist in reducing the sense of isolation experienced by those with autism who may see the social world as a challenge. By acknowledging and working with all aspects of the child's development there is a growing sensitivity towards the individual's social understanding as it is on this basis that all mutual interactions are made. Dunn (1993) argues that the quality of relationships is not dependent on differences in social or cognitive competence but the extent to which social understanding is used within a relationship. It has been a key theme in this book that socialization is not something that is done *to* a child but *with* the child in a complex system of emotional regulation and communication.

The capacity for social understanding is also highly dependent upon the maintenance and continuation of the emotional sensitivities and responsiveness that were established during the attachment phase. Bowlby (1969) was keen to stress that attachment patterns are not exclusive to early childhood and, although they change, they remain a significant feature of interactions across the lifespan. This view has been firmly supported by others who have been involved in more recent studies on attachment (Marrone 1998; Steele and Steele 1998; Holmes 2001; Belsky 2002). Early forms of play provide positive opportunities for parent–child interaction and contribute to the emergence of a secure attachment relationship. If this pattern of interaction is not well established or becomes altered too quickly it can interfere with the hardwiring of the brain and the ability to assimilate the social and emotional cues necessary for maintaining positive relationships. It is for this reason that relationship-based interventions that emphasize playful interaction and positive communication will need to be continued well beyond infancy for many children with autism.

Lazarus (1991) recognizes that changes in the pattern of socialization, from early affective states to more complex interactions, increase the need for adaptability in both affect and behaviour. Individual differences in the responsiveness of the child and of the parents and carers are seen as key to the establishment of social behaviours and the level of social understanding that the child develops. It is also the case that children will develop different relationships because of the sensitivity and responsiveness of the significant people with whom they come into close contact. Studies have shown that the ways in which fathers interact with their child is very different from that of the mothers (Lamb 1977, 1981). Fathers tend to engage in more physical games, whereas mothers tend to engage the child with toys and use more language. Differences in adults' nurturing styles of interaction are not only vital to the development of the children's social understanding but also in the development of their personality. The reason why the family is seen as an important context for establishing patterns of social behaviour is because it consists of a small intimate group committed to the psychological and physical well-being of each individual. It is important to acknowledge therefore that the child's earliest experiences are predominantly social, and regardless of any subsequent change in the child's neurophysiology this remains key to how experiences are remembered and interpreted.

A family focus

Interventions that assist in supporting the family system as a whole while acknowledging the integrity of each individual's contribution within it are likely to bring about more positive changes in family interaction. Working systemically with families focuses on the strengths and needs of individuals within the family and any priorities for change are recognized as those that the parents or carers currently regard as essential to the family's well-being. Involving and empowering the parents or carers in this way increases empathetic understanding between the family and the professionals working with them. Studies in family systems have shown the impact that this has had on helping to bring about more long-term improvements in socio-emotional functioning across the family lifespan (Bott 2001; Woody 2004; Eisenberg et al. 2005). According to Mahoney and Perales (2003) and Webster et al. (2004) many interventions for children with autism involve a great deal of professional input that might result in undermining parenting skills. For many adults living and working with a child who has autism, there is a tendency to see the autism as overshadowing what would otherwise be regarded as child-like behaviour that is part of a developmental continuum. When professionals only focus on devising coping strategies for managing the child's behaviour or overcoming communication difficulties, many parents can be left feeling inadequate if they are unable to maintain the strategies or fail to see the improvements they want for their child.

Any difficulties a child has in expressing social and emotional reciprocity, regardless of the aetiology, will undoubtedly affect the responsiveness that parents have towards the child and this can influence their own expectations and beliefs about their parenting. The same applies to how siblings develop relationships and how these alter across the lifespan. It is not that parents or siblings of children with autism fail to stimulate the child to play, but that the child's capacity for emotional arousal may be incompatible with that of their desire to interact. A parent once expressed how uncomfortable she felt with some of the strategies she had been shown that would make demands on her son to participate in activities to develop his social communication skills. She commented that 'using interactive play has enabled me to be more spontaneous with my child, knowing that he is learning all about how to communicate'.

Relationship-based interventions offer a more holistic approach in which the objective, regardless of the activity, is to focus on improvements in socio-emotional functioning. The goals set do not have to be task-specific but are integral to the spontaneous ways in which parents and family members are encouraged to interact with the child who has autism. By assisting parents or carers in setting the goals they can begin to feel empowered and regard themselves as more competent in playing and interacting with their child and in achieving the developmental outcomes they want for him or her.

Danny would spend hours occupying himself playing with puzzles and because his parents knew that he liked them he had quite a large collection, which his parents and other friends and family had bought for him. His parents were pleased that he could request a puzzle and recognized this as a positive communication. He was also very precise about making sure all the pieces were in the right box and this too was felt to be very useful, unlike his brother who was less tidy about his toys. The puzzles had become a barrier, however, to Danny's parents' desire to interact and play with him and they wanted some ideas for extending his interest in other toys and activities. His mother expressed some concern that Danny had not wanted to play outside in the garden and as it was summer she certainly wanted him to have the opportunity. In responding to a request for a puzzle his father took it outside and placed it on a table. Danny was uncertain about this but, after putting the puzzle on the table, his father had walked over to the trampoline and started bouncing on it. He made quite a lot of noise and was 'clowning' about on it and because Danny was completely distracted he came over to watch his dad. It was not long before Danny was on the trampoline, bouncing and laughing with his dad.

As Gil (1994) points out, parents and carers participating in play enhances their understanding of the play experience for the child and creates the possibility for deeper emotional contact. Individual family circumstances, parenting styles and cultural influences need to be carefully considered when implementing strategies and the need for professionals to work with an unconditional positive regard for the family becomes essential to the success of any intervention programme. In particular, in many cultures fathers may see themselves as having a different role in their child's development. Likewise many fathers may have less of a nurturing role in the care of their child with special needs or can feel excluded from much of the professional input the child is receiving.

A professional approach that is not judgemental or critical enables parents and carers to recognize their own skills. They then come to regard themselves as having a greater understanding of the ways in which their child is learning how to make sense of interacting with others. The smile programme suggests the use of strategies and activities that acknowledge that family members will all respond to them in different ways. With the focus on relationship-building and emotional well-being rather than on acquiring skills, it aims to enrich the lives of individual family members. In recognizing how important this is for the family it becomes central to plan a programme together, which focuses on situations that enable the child to express his or her communicative competence. Being responsive to the child's communicative behaviour is fundamental in helping the child to establish more confidence in communicating with others. The reciprocal nature of interactive play provides a safe context in which to create the socio-emotional bonds necessary for the child to express a willingness to engage in more complex acts of communication. For those children in whom specific brain damage may result in an inability to acquire spoken language it is important to highlight the value of non-verbal methods of interaction that are key to the development of the relationship and encourage families to look for mutually enjoyable ways to make contact, which are not dependent on verbal communication.

A parent attending one of my workshops had received confirmation of her son's diagnosis of autism just three weeks previously. He was three years old and she had been told to expect nothing but problems for a few years until her son was at school and had hopefully by then developed some language. Her emotional connection with her son enabled her to look more pro-actively at his development and she was keen to establish some positive ways to encourage his communication and language. She commented that he loved books but used them mostly to flick through rather than focus on the content. He did have certain favourite books that he would let her read to him but he would often want her to repeat the same story over and over again in one sitting. I suggested that she could try to use objects or toys that represented the characters in the book and either let him hold them or use them to tell the story. I also encouraged her to focus not just on the activity and how this was helping him with his language development, but also to be aware of the experience of being together. He would cuddle into her as she read the story and these feelings of comfort and warmth help in creating a heightened emotional sensitivity towards the activity; how this is remembered will help the child to learn and become more competent in understanding relationships.

At the core of socio-affective development is the nature of the initial attachment relationship that both the child and the parent create together. One of the key elements of the smile programme is to assist parents and carers in recognizing the nature of the attachments within the family, including the extended family, where this is appropriate. The emotional and behavioural adjustments that families make when there is a child with a disability in the family will significantly affect relationships between family members (Hornby 1995; Carpenter 1997; Sanders and Morgan 1997) and any changes that consciously or unconsciously take place as a result of intervention will alter the quality of those relationships. Relationships based on physical and emotional nurturance are fundamental for developing positive life experiences and imparting social/moral values, and the family provides the most valuable context in which to establish these.

Attachment relationships

Attachment is a consequence of the early physical and emotional bonds that have existed both pre- and postnatally. A crucial factor in developing attachment is the quality of the interpersonal relationship that is not solely determined by the main carer but is something that the child and adult create together in an ongoing reciprocal relationship. Bowlby (1969) saw attachment as the psychobiological need for survival that is achieved through the emotional bonds created between the child and the caregiver.

The development of empathy and mutual attunement involves the child's ability to internalize the sensory stimuli offered by the parent and the sensitive modulations of the parent's behaviour towards the child. Although this process of positive arousal and interactive repair is not dependent upon early reciprocal play, such interactions contribute in a major way to the development of the loving relationship. Playful interactions help to determine the development of trust in the relationship and act as a key indicator of attachment security. Both trust and unconditional acceptance are significant features of a caring relationship. As James (1994) suggests, 'A secure attachment is a love relationship that is caring, reciprocal and develops over time. Attachment provides the nurturance and guidance that fosters gradual and appropriate self reliance, leading to mastery and autonomy' (p. 24).

Dallos (2006) refers to an attachment system that is based on the adult's responsiveness to the child's attempts to communicate and it is this pattern of mutual dependency that supports the emotional needs of both the parent and the child (Figure 7.1).

Due to the difficulties that children with autism have in establishing reciprocal interactions and developing an internal model of the 'self'

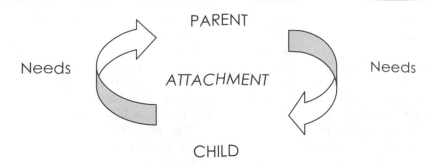

Figure 7.1 Attachment needs as mutual (Dallos 2006).

and 'other', there is a difference in the quality of the attachment pattern that can result in a disrupted or disorganized relationship with the main carers. Studies by Shapiro *et al.* (1987), Rogers *et al.* (1993), Capps *et al.* (1994), Dissanayake and Crossley (1996) and Yirmiya and Sigman (2001) have identified that children with autism were able to develop secure attachments but the motivation to interact was more dependent on core needs such as for food or comfort, or self needs such as requesting preferred objects, people or situations, rather than an intentional desire to share an experience with another. Schore (2003) believes that the disregulation of 'mutually affective cueing' occurring with increased frequency can lead to the child reducing attempts to seek out the security of the parents. These socially and emotionally impaired behaviours come to impact on the main carers by creating a sense of 'redundancy' that subsequently affects how they interact with their child. However, one vital feature of the brain during the early years of development is its plasticity. This suggests that the capacity for the brain to create other neural connections should not be undermined, but is only likely to occur when opportunities to promote positive interaction are extended (Bowlby, 2003).

Cognitive–behavioural models have dominated much of the literature and research on autism and influenced educational programmes for the past thirty years, but increasingly psychologists are becoming interested in the neurobiological influences of attachment which are believed to hold the key to understanding the developmental psychopathology of autism (Sroufe 1996; Rutter 1997; Maratos 1998; Brisch 2004). Neurological damage or developmental delay has been found to indicate similar behaviours in children who have specific attachment disorders (Richter and Volmar 1994; Hughes 2003; Brown-Macdonald 2004; Mukaddes *et al.* 2004). These include:

- superficial engagement;
- indiscriminate affection to strangers;

- not affectionate on the parents' terms, only their own;
- destructive of self, others and materials;
- no impulse controls or frequently hyperactive;
- delays in language development and deficits in communication;
- lack of cause-and-effect thinking;
- poor peer relationships;
- bizarre behaviour patterns.

Studies by Dawson and Fischer (1994) and Schore (1994) have identified links between disorganized and disrupted attachment and brain development, and recognize that post birth there are specific areas of the brain that mature as a result of developments in the affectional bonds involved in attachment. Kanner (1943) noted that it was not a lack of awareness of other persons but a profound difficulty with emotional engagement that affected how a child with autism established reciprocal social relationships. Relationship-based interventions and arts therapies that focus on the repair of the 'inborn disturbance of affective contact' (Kanner 1943) are characterized by loving acceptance, emotional regulation and nurturance of individual personalities. By focusing on the development of global behaviours and natural patterns of engagement based on relevant developmental theories, it has become pertinent to take account of the impact of autism on patterns of attachment.

I worked with a family in which the mother described how she had experienced postnatal depression following the difficult birth of her daughter and she had concerns about the significant impact on Alice's subsequent development and relationship with her. Alice was now four years old and had recently been diagnosed with Asperger's syndrome. Her mother's reaction to the diagnosis had resulted in further concerns about how to engage with Alice in playful ways and she was keen to help her to develop more confidence in interacting socially. The activity I devised for Alice and her mother aimed to provide a positive way of relating that would help to re-establish a cycle of positive interaction. It was also important for the development of their relationship to consider how together they could rediscover a physical connection that is an essential element of nurturing and emotional well-being. The activity was based on the Theraplay® technique (Jernberg 1976) that focuses on enhancing attachment and strengthening parent–child relationships. Theraplay® is based on natural patterns of interaction that focus on the four essential qualities of nurture, engagement, structure and challenge (Jernberg and Booth, 2001). By creating an active and empathetic connection with the child it has an empowering influence on the development of the relationship and subsequent interactions. The primary goal of the Theraplay® treatment is to establish playful, attuned responsiveness that enables the child to gain more confidence in interacting and experiencing feelings of self-worth.

Alice and her mother sat opposite one another on the floor and, as her mother stroked Alice's hair, she sang her favourite song. Alice smiled and her mother commented on how beautiful she looked. She repeated this several times and Alice visibly showed pleasure in this. Her mother then began to gently massage her face by rubbing her forehead and making circles on her cheeks. She talked to her about what she liked to eat and Alice was joining in by suggesting more of her favourite foods. Her mother then put her hands on Alice's shoulders and sang 'Row, row, row your boat' which gave Alice a sense of them moving together. Following this her mother rubbed her arms with firm strokes. To finish, Alice's mother made big circles with her hands on Alice's tummy and then surprised her with a tickle. Alice clearly enjoyed this and repeatedly asked for more. This ten-minute structured activity ended with a cuddle and experiencing such physical and emotional closeness towards Alice visibly affected her mother. The session continued with us swinging Alice in a blanket and letting her roll on it. Alice then wanted her mother to play 'Ten in the Bed' with her and they rolled on the blanket together. The activity finished with blowing bubbles for Alice to catch and she reciprocated by blowing bubbles for her mother.

At the end of our time together Alice's mother was clearly very moved about what had taken place. She shared how this had made her feel differently towards Alice and that she felt more positive about wanting to spend time with her in playful activities. The challenge for Alice had been to experience being played with in a way that had enabled her to experience the fun and enjoyment of contact with her mother.

Stern (1985) describes the matching of the parent and child's affective patterns as an interactive regulation. During interactive play, the careful monitoring of different emotions by both partners heightens the communicative partnership. The extent to which the child reciprocates these emotions is dependent upon the responsiveness of the parents to attribute meaning to the child's emotional states. Marrone (1998) recognizes that there are similarities between this sensitive responsiveness and empathy but, whereas empathy implies the identification with the other's mental states, he suggests that, 'Sensitive responsiveness involves some internal negotiation between the momentary state of feeling like the other and the ability to react as a separate being' (p. 43).

Although for the parent this may be occurring unconsciously, it is the variations in the different modes and timings of the playful engagement that increase the child's capacity to process socially and emotionally relevant information. When this is maintained, the child has an opportunity to develop a sense of security and containment that can then be replicated when communicating with others.

Waddell (1998) recognizes that attachment relationships are a key factor in the link between children being able to separate and their ability to symbolize. For example, the sharing of an experience makes it possible to sense that others can have a mental state different or the same as one's own. Because playful interactions involve both verbal and non-verbal communication they become crucial in enabling children to regulate emotions and gain confidence in themselves as being separate. However, as the relationship matures, children need to regard themselves not as independent but as separate beings who are interdependent. The core features of interdependence and reciprocity are most likely to occur within the context of mutually enjoyable interactions. This is because the desire for action always involves an emotional connection. Schore (1994) states that the attachment bond leads to 'the growth of an internal system that is capable of appraising motivationally significant and emotionally meaningful environmental events' (p. 100).

The study by Yirmiya and Sigman (2001) made it clear that the secure attachments that were observed in children with autism were indicative of responsive and sensitive parenting, and suggest that this may also contribute towards the children's optimal development. This highlights the need to consider the extent to which the family system is essential to the maintenance and repair of interpersonal relationships, characterized by empathetic responsiveness, emotional regulation, proximity, trust and security, unconditional acceptance and interdependence. As the child's attachment relationship with the primary caregivers develops it undergoes a transition from dependency to increasing socialization with others. This will include siblings or extended family members and any subsequent peer relationships. Determining variations in social behaviour between different individuals provides a more effective framework for dealing with the emotional changes in these relationships and it is by acknowledging the uniqueness of each individual within the family that this allows them to express their personalities.

Sibling relationships

Several studies (McHale and Gamble 1987; Bägenholm and Gillberg 1991; Damiani 1999; Kaminsky and Dewey 2001) have acknowledged that the impact of having a child with autism in the family has no more or less influence on the psychological adjustment or development of the siblings than families that do not have a child with a disorder or disability. Other studies (Dyson 1989; Brody *et al.* 1991; McHale and Harris 1992) have looked at the age, gender and birth order of the sibling in relation to the child with autism and these too have not shown any significant variations in the nature of sibling relationships. To date, however, there have been few studies (Dunn and McGuire 1992; Stoneham 2001) that have focused on how siblings interact with one another and the impact that this has on the social modelling of behaviour and the development of individual personalities. Individual circumstances, temperament and parenting attitudes and styles are therefore seen as having a much greater impact on the development of sibling relationships (Verté *et al.* 2003). Rivers and Stoneham's (2003) study also reinforced the importance of the family context as being the main contributor in the quality of sibling relationships and as such this supports other developmental theories on the nature of sibling relationships. Sibling relationships are characterized by individuals involved in sharing similarities and differences in friendship and support, and as each individual matures so the dynamics and dependencies of the relationship also alter. It is suggested that children with autism who are less socially responsive and who have difficulties engaging in socio-affective behaviour with other family members will not be as receptive to the social modelling behaviour of the sibling. There may be less opportunity for reciprocal play and as a result the impact on the relationship is likely to follow a similar pattern to that of the parent–child attachment relationship. Given the complexity of the social, environmental and biological influences on social development it would appear inappropriate to make any assumptions about the quality of sibling relationships without further research into this sensitive area. I have certainly witnessed situations in a sibling relationship when there was considerable rivalry between two brothers, one of whom had Asperger's syndrome, but also others when compassion and warmth were essential features of the relationship. Play can provide a bridge for siblings to experience spontaneous and meaningful interactions and the frequency with which this occurs will support the establishment and development of skills in language, sharing and emotional well-being. Within the context of family support, the repair and maintenance of the sibling relationship becomes equally dependent upon the provision of opportunities in which to share similar interests and develop an empathetic awareness of each other's behaviour regardless of age or ability.

Carly's older brother was fourteen years old. He obviously had very different interests from his six-year-old sister and enjoyed spending time in his room playing his guitar and computer games. Carly's mother had difficulty recognizing her daughter's play behaviours as purposeful, particularly when she climbed the furniture or jumped up and down the stairs. I suggested that Carly's need for physical activity could also be channelled to play outside in the garden. When Carly's brother joined us he sat next to her on the swing and tried to match her speed and height. When she stood up so did he. When she got off the swing to go on the climbing frame he stopped and waited to see what she would do and when he did not join her, she went back to the swing. He had been able to establish a way of interacting with her that complemented her skills and interests but he also felt comfortable sharing this time with her, and there was evidence of their ability to modify their behaviour to maintain the interaction by playing together.

Balancing one's own needs and the needs of others in the family becomes an essential aspect of learning about social relationships. It is a significant feature of how family members experience a sense of connectedness despite the differences and similarities in their personality, age or ability. It is essential that any interventions take account of the siblings so that they recognize themselves as valued members of their family, able to contribute to sharing an understanding of the uniqueness of their brother or sister who has autism.

The family sessions

The smile programme uses three main principles of involvement with the family:

1 structuring time to be with the family;
2 facilitating and modelling how to interact playfully;
3 giving suggestions for parents and siblings to engage with the child in play.

An illustration of the smile programme follows using examples from sessions with a family, which highlight the process of increasing engagement and positive interaction between the parent and the child with autism and, in this case, the child and her sibling: Sophie is four and a half years old and attends a local special school for children with autism and severe learning difficulties. Sophie loves music, will sing familiar songs and likes to play with musical toys. She actively explores a range of toys and objects but was not using them functionally or symbolically. She occasionally uses speech to gain what she wants or make comments but is not yet using language to spontaneously engage in conversation. George is her brother who is six years old and he attends the local primary school. He has very good language skills and loves talking about characters in history and making up stories.

The sessions predominantly took place after school when the father was still at work, although the father was present for one of the sessions and for the final meeting.

The initial meeting

This was an opportunity to observe the interactional patterns between family members and in particular how the child with autism was interacting within the home environment. A large basket containing a few natural and manufactured toys and objects provides a focus of attention for the children while introducing the programme to the family. The intention at this stage is not to carry out any formal assessments that relate to the child's academic or play skills but to offer a supportive presence that focuses on creating an empathetic understanding of the parents' or carers' reasons for wanting to develop more positive and playful ways to interact with their child who has autism. These initial observations and discussions are then used to plan activities and individualized strategies for developing a special playtime within the family.

Sophie and George began by exploring the contents of the treasure basket at the same time. Sophie found one object that she wanted to hold on to while George continued to explore and talk about several of the objects he found. I observed that Sophie and George did not interact physically or relate to one another through the objects and toys they were playing with. However, they both remained in the room while I talked to their mother and this gave her an opportunity to express what she felt were the main areas in which she wanted help to develop Sophie's communication and play. We discussed the goals that she wanted for the following sessions: developing Sophie's spoken language, developing more interactive play between Sophie and George and extending Sophie's play skills. These goals may appear broad but there is a danger that by setting smaller targets the activities lose the spontaneity and focus on achieving a skill, rather than engaging in the experiences of interacting and playing from which the skills will emerge.

Each session follows the same format as this and provides a structure with which the children can become familiar, even if different activities are presented. Following the initial visit the facilitator is able to plan activities that reflect the way in which the child with autism is currently playing and interacting. Activities also have to realistically fit within the family context and may or may not make use of the toys that the children already have. Sessions always start with ten minutes to discuss anything significant that relates to the work we have done or will be doing together and any special achievements that have occurred between the sessions.

If permission is given, each session is filmed using a video camera to provide a way of recording the activities that take place and the impact these have on changing patterns of interaction and communication. Video Interactive Guidance (VIG) is widely used for observational and assessment purposes in a range of educational and therapeutic settings. A key benefit is the way in which this allows for positive feedback, a reflection of the interaction by the parents or carers and as a tool for planning future programmes. Use of the video helps the adult to interpret his or her own communicative behaviours in relation to the child's responses and, as a result, this has been found to be effective in raising attuned responses and communication (Burton 2002). Parents are encouraged to communicate in ways that support the child's actions and emotions and to reduce language that is demanding or questioning. This increases the likelihood of more positive interactions that assist the child in initiating responses that help to maintain the shared playtime.

An opening activity starts the session and includes the child and any other family members who want to join in. This is an opportunity to acknowledge each person's presence and to establish the focus for our time together. This is followed by a series of activities that will, if siblings are involved, include an activity with them, with the parent(s) and with the facilitator. Natural breaks occur, fitting with the child's need to withdraw, get refreshment or a have a comfort break. Because the activities are planned to correspond to the child's interests, the motivation towards the activity negates any need to coerce the child to take part. The session ends with a closing activity that can be a song, a story or physical activity, depending on what is appropriate in helping the individual move out of the focused activity onto something else. The session ends with a discussion to consider what was achieved, looking back at the video to look at patterns of interaction and highlight significant achievements. Recommendations and ideas for parents or carers to consider in between the sessions are also noted; this acts as a reminder of the positive ways in which they can interact with their child.

Session I

I began by singing a song about playing together and we all had a chance to hit the balloon as I sang. Sophie loves singing and although she did not know the words she tried to copy the tune. George was more interested in hitting the balloon than singing and was keen to move on to the next activity. When we finished the song, Sophie left the room and went to the kitchen to request food. During this time George chose to play with some play dough and started to make a picture in a tray by squashing the play dough to make waves and a boat. He started to tell a story about who was in the boat that was similar to one of his storybooks. When Mum and Sophie came back into the room they sat with us. Sophie picked up some play dough and put it in her mouth and her mother stopped her. When she did it again I tickled her cheeks. She looked at me and despite trying to eat more she anticipated my response and this distracted her from eating the play dough. George continued to try and tell his story but seemed distracted by Sophie's presence and broke up his picture.

Another activity was a simple game of 'hide-and-seek' with some familiar objects under a blanket. I wanted Sophie to seek out her favourite objects and for George to try and guess what they were by feeling them first. Sophie showed little interest in the activity and walked away once she had found one of her toys. George continued to hide objects around the room for his Mum and me to find. When Sophie came back into the room we had a 'snowball fight' using cotton balls. Sophie observed the game and when the balls were thrown at her she picked one up, pulled it apart and dropped it. She then ran around the room while we threw cotton balls at each other.

In our discussion Mum recognized Sophie's difficulties in staying with the activity but that she had briefly managed to be part of them. She had clearly acknowledged my presence when I was tickling her and had given me eye contact and smiles. In each of the activities there was very little interaction between Sophie and George. They played with the same activity but alongside one another and in very different ways. I suggested that, to encourage George and Sophie to play together, activities needed to focus more on sensory play that would appeal to both of them. It would appear that, because Sophie is not yet able to offer ideas for play with her brother, he is not able to reciprocate and play at her level of exploratory play.

Session 2

In this session I wanted to focus on what the family could do together and provided a large sheet of paper to make a family collage. Sophie chose the colours she wanted and walked all the way round the edge of the paper making long strokes with a paintbrush. George chose a corner of the paper and wanted to make a treasure box so painted a shape and then stuck sequins on to it. Mum also used one side of the paper, painting letters and shapes. Sophie spent some time reapplying paint to her brush and making long strokes on the paper. When she no longer wanted to paint after about ten minutes, she left the room.

For another activity George and Sophie were each given a treasure box containing five objects. The individual treasure boxes represent a gift to each child to help them recognize that they are both special and at the same time have an individual way of exploring the objects inside. They sat together looking at their objects and Sophie chose to spend most of her time exploring some coloured feathers. George made up a story with his objects and, using the whistle, he pretended to be a station guard. He was enjoying making up a story and then decided to use the whistle to lead us in a game of 'musical bumps'. Sophie was very happy and laughed as we danced around together and then sat on the floor when the music stopped. This time when we had a 'snowball fight' she came close to her mother and started to throw the cotton balls. Her mother commented that Sophie had been more involved with activities this week even though she had not been as vocal. Sophie's ability to join in with the 'snowball fight' implied that she felt more secure when she was being held by her mother, giving her the confidence to interact. Sophie's close attachment to her mother is clearly evidenced by her need to be near her mother or seek her out for comfort and pleasure. I was able to stress how valuable this was in terms of their attachment relationship and that this had enabled Sophie to gain more awareness of herself and confidence in her relationships with significant people in her life.

Session 3

In this session there was an opportunity to encourage more interactive play between Sophie and George. We used a blanket and they took turns to be swung in it. We also rolled them together and sang 'Ten in the Bed'. For about twenty minutes we covered them, rolled them and swung them together in the blanket, and there was a lot of laughter as we pretended they were too heavy to lift or had disappeared and we could not find them. Sophie left the room when we finished this activity but came back to investigate the objects in her treasure box. George used the five objects in his treasure box to tell a story and then Mum told hers. Sophie had not given much attention to their stories but when it was Sophie's turn she held a small baby bottle to the plastic doll. With her focus on this I provided a simple narrative while she continued to hold them together. Ending our session with the 'snow-ball fight' this week, Sophie independently threw some cotton balls and moved around the room as we threw them to one another.

Sophie had been much more engaged in the activities this week. Her mother was aware that Sophie had been more vocal and expressed more pleasure in today's session. She had spent longer with George and was more focused on the objects she had found. Her ability to use the toys in a representational way indicated the emergence of this skill and it was recommended that similar activities with small world objects should be encouraged.

Session 4

During the week it had been George's birthday and they had been to a party with a lot of a children at a local play centre. There had been soft play and entertainment during which Sophie had joined in with all the other children playing 'musical bumps' and had sat with them when they were singing songs that were familiar to her. For the parents it seemed that this had made it a very enjoyable experience. With Mum's suggestion, we continued the birthday theme and sat at the kitchen table decorating biscuits for a tea party with toys. I encouraged George to pass things to Sophie that she needed, but he was engrossed in making patterns and pictures with the icing tubes. Sophie meanwhile made some attempts to squeeze the icing onto her biscuits but was enjoying eating it at the same time. She frequently gave me eye contact and was saying 'anana' repeatedly, attempting to say my name. When we had finished decorating biscuits Sophie remained with us. I began to tickle her in praise of what we had done together and she started to use the word 'tickle' and move my hand to her tummy to repeat what I had done. Sophie and George were encouraged to go and find a toy to bring to the tea party but George did this independently and Sophie was helped to choose her favourite teddy. When we started to use some party poppers, she happily watched what we were doing and enjoyed gathering the coloured shreds.

I had become aware that during our sessions George did not play specifically with Mum usually because Sophie took most of her attention. In this session I wanted to find a way to enable them both to have one-to-one time with Mum after their shared activity. George chose to play with the puppets with his Mum and made up a story with the puppets they had chosen. With his monkey, George led the story and Mum had little opportunity to express how her puppet, a hedgehog, could take part. Sophie's time with Mum by herself involved exploring shaving foam and talcum powder. They sat close to one another and Sophie and Mum explored the shaving foam together. Mum rubbed it onto Sophie's hands and face and Sophie reciprocated. She smiled a lot when her Mum put talcum on her hands. She waved them about and enjoyed watching the powder fall.

In this session I also recognized George's reluctance to do things either with or for his sister. There was a genuine interest and concern for her, but it seemed their ability to form a stronger sibling relationship was affected by Sophie's difficulties in being aware of him as a play partner. It was recommended that their shared play activities could involve physical games where they could either pass objects such as a ball to one another or where George could give Sophie instructions when they were playing on the trampoline. This would appeal to George's interest in taking the lead and give Sophie an opportunity to become more responsive towards George.

Session 5

Dad was present for this session and this introduced a different dynamic to the activities. There was delight from George about the activities we would be doing and recognition from Sophie that I was there to play with her again. Just before my arrival Dad had asked Sophie to get dressed, to which Sophie had replied 'I don't want to.' This had thrilled both parents. Mum also shared how she had made some simple puppets with both children and that Sophie had spent some time holding it on her hand, looking at it and singing to it, whereas George had used his to make up a story.

We used a small trampoline and took turns to bounce on it. George was encouraged to listen to instructions to jump, clap or sit and also had an opportunity to give instructions to others. He showed a reluctance to give Sophie instructions probably because he knew that she would not respond how he wanted her to. We encouraged him to respond to Sophie's bouncing and clapping gestures as she was not able to give verbal instructions and in this way he would be imitating her actions.

In their treasure boxes this week George had five green objects and Sophie had five pink objects. George immediately began to make up a story, while Sophie found a lizard and explored it for some time. Dad appropriately sat opposite her and verbally reflected on what she was doing with it. As a consequence she continued to explore other objects in her box. She found a large pig and then picked out a smaller pig, as if making a connection between the two toys. Then she explored a sparkly pink ball. George used his objects to make a story by involving his parents. Sophie had continued to explore her objects while George told his story. She then picked up a flower and I responded by labelling it for her and making a sniffing sound. She imitated my sniff and then held the pig to the flower and sniffed again.

George wanted his dad to use the octagon shapes to make something and although they began making something separately they soon joined it together to make a spaceship. I sat with Sophie on the floor and her Mum sat opposite us. Mum reached over to tickle Sophie so I encouraged Sophie to do the same to her Mum. We developed this into a turn-taking game and also one in which if Mum tickled Sophie's hand then Sophie was encouraged to tickle her Mum's hand. As the game continued Sophie began saying 'tickle, tickle, squeeze' and it ended when she leaned forward and gave her Mum a big hug. The family 'snowball fight' was full of laughter and fun and George was able to tell me how much he had enjoyed the session. As he remained with us while I discussed the session with the parents I asked him if he could think of other activities where he could show Sophie what to do and he thought he would like to use the trampoline again. Playing in the indoor tent and having tea parties were more of his ideas. This showed a marked shift in his thinking about playing with his sister that may have come about from the whole family being together on this occasion. Evidence of Sophie's ability to use toys representationally suggests that this could be encouraged by involving her in play with small world people and animals that she was beginning to show an interest in. If George joins in or plays alongside her then he would be able to model for her how to play with the objects.

Final meeting

Having a closing session is vitally important as it provides a definitive point at which the family can consider the impact of any changes in the way in which the family functions and how they have incorporated the interactive play strategies into their family life. The video is used to reinforce the positive outcomes from the activities, highlighting developments in the growth of the relationship, communication skills, sibling interaction and play skills. Discussion is focused on the achievements and changes that have come about as a result of the sessions. Essentially this helps parents and carers to feel more empowered about using play and to recognize the effectiveness of their parenting skills in finding positive ways to engage with their child who has autism. Consideration is always given to the impact on the family as a whole and even to members of the wider family, as it is the family system that remains key to the impact of any fundamental changes in socialization and relationship-building. One key development for this family, during the time I was seeing them, had been Sophie's realization that she could use the toilet independently. Although not directly related to the play activities we had been doing together, it is possible that her increasing confidence in interacting and using language both at home and at school had increased her self-awareness. They also reflected on how George was responding differently to his sister and that he would now make a choice about the activities that he did want to play with her. Sophie was more able to interact with George when their activities were physical or fun for both of them.

The final session is drawn to a close with an activity such as a family picture or sculpture that enables the family members to express how they are currently feeling. The images and colours used will hold particular relevance to the individual family member and therefore to the family as a whole. George and his parents drew a large island on their picture and put on it their names and drew pictures of them. Mum was reading, Dad was relaxing on a chair and George was playing football. Sophie had been observing them and then stood on the paper. Mum drew around her feet several times. She then drew faces on the feet that showed different emotions. In seeing themselves represented in this way it can help parents to reflect upon what has taken place during the time that we have been working together. There had been significant emotional changes in each of the family members with regards to Sophie's achievements as she had learnt to take part in a range of activities with George and was developing more independent behaviour. The emergence of her representational play with figures and animals was an exciting development in Sophie's play. She was also beginning to respond with more imitative behaviour both in terms of her language and play. When playing with a ball she would comment on what she was doing using words such as 'bounce', 'up' and 'down'. Her mother was feeling more relaxed about her ability to engage Sophie in different activities and was able to reflect on the value and enjoyment of playing specifically with George, usually making up stories and acting them out. Encouraging George and Sophie to play together had helped George to be more accepting of his sister's difficulties in interacting with him. On one occasion he told a visitor to the home that because Sophie had autism everyone needed to make compromises for her! Although he still liked to play his own games he had also thought about and suggested activities they could enjoy together.

Two weeks after our sessions together had finished I received an email from the mother, which read as follows:

> Sophie initiated a game with George at a level he could enjoy! They were both in her bedroom. She was snuggled up in bed and reached out to grab him and pulled him gently into bed. She began to sing 'There were ten in the bed . . .' and they had about six rounds each of this. They took it in turns to be the one to fall out, then jumped back up on the bed to get in on the other side. Sophie was singing the song and shouting 'roll over' or 'night, night' depending on

whether it was her turn in or out of the bed. He loved it and so did she. This wasn't a game we've rehearsed with her at home although we've sung the song to her many times and read the book to her. The whole idea came from her interest and imagination.

This comment highlights how important it is to acknowledge that the responsibility for change is dependent not only upon the partnership created by the parents and the professional, but also on what the family believes is essential for the well-being of all its members. Any changes that occur have to fit with the realities that are meaningful to individual members, otherwise there is less likelihood of the family's achievements being maintained and developed. By focusing the family on what they consider are the priorities for development, the activities become more meaningful to them.

The smile programme encourages family members to engage regularly in play activities with the child who has autism and to see it as a purposeful way of gaining more positive interaction and developing communication skills. Although the activities chosen will be dependent upon individual circumstances, they are fundamental to how all families need to function for the emotional and physical well-being of their members, regardless of whether or not they have a child with a disability.

Further considerations

A key aspect of working with families is maintaining a supportive understanding of their interpersonal relationships and organizational style, while inviting opportunities for change that are realistic and effectively integrated into family life. Although the amount of time and nature of the activities is dependent upon individual family circumstances, it is important to make recommendations that the family feel confident they can adopt. Establishing interactive play is not about finding a mechanistic time to be together, as this may influence the outcome of the shared experience. Instead it is about valuing opportunities for focusing on sharing time to play and attend to one another. It is more likely to be effective for shorter periods of time on a daily basis rather than an extensive programme of activities that does not realistically correspond with the way that the family functions.

Reed *et al.*'s (2004) study of early intervention programmes found that the optimum benefit of any intervention was at fifteen to twenty hours per week. They also found that less intensity reduced parental stress. Too much focus on obtaining specific goals may undermine the value that parents would rather place on their interpersonal family

relationships and the impact these will have on the adaptive and social behaviours of their child with autism. It is also important that any
intervention is flexible enough to take account of the differing needs
of individual families such as demands on time and implementing the
techniques. No one programme or intervention should be seen as exclusive to the child's developmental achievements, as there will always
be a range of environmental, educational and biological influences that
will have more or less impact at any time during the child's life. With the
family as the primary social group, what takes place within the context
of the family will have the foremost influence on the child. Panskepp
(2001) describes how the consistent use of nurturance, tolerance and
playfulness during interactions optimizes positive growth in relationships and leads to a greater awareness of others' social and emotional
behaviour. One of the key aims of the smile programme is to provide
time for parents to see the value of play in helping to create the relationship they want with their child who has autism, while enabling
opportunities for the child to discover the warmth and enjoyment of
the loving relationship that the family has to offer.

Chapter 8

Interactive play in schools

Promoting learning through play has been problematic particularly in the education of children with autism. Many practitioners have been led to question the relevance of teaching through a play-based curriculum and how interactive styles of teaching can be incorporated into the more structured approach to the curriculum that is widely used in schools. This perspective has historically been allied to the view that deficits in the play skills development of children with autism are considered to undermine the benefits that learning through play affords. Even in the light of recent curriculum developments to promote play and creativity in children's learning, there still exists a discrepancy between learning and the value and relevance of play in schools. Theories and ideologies have tended to focus on early development and ignored developmentally appropriate and even cultural perspectives of play. Throughout, this book has emphasized the commonalities rather than the differences in response to the play experience, and affirms that individual potential will be determined by the adult's mode of intervention.

As a consequence of the legislation that has heightened the status of play in Early Years education, provision for children with special educational needs has increased in both special and mainstream school settings. Access to quality play experiences is therefore deemed an essential right for children regardless of whether or not they have a learning difficulty. As Nind and Cochrane (2003) point out, the development of a more formal curriculum framework in special education has resulted in interactive approaches being regarded as an 'add on', resulting in a two-tier curriculum. Consequently, approaches such as Intensive Interaction, Interactive Play and other interactive creative arts programmes have tended to be viewed more as 'therapeutic' rather than educational, a perspective that could potentially undermine children's entitlement to a broad and balanced curriculum. Peter (2000) argues that play and the creative arts have a powerful contribution to make in developing children's sense of self-advocacy, problem-solving and gaining knowledge of shared meanings.

Instead of focusing on resources, a significant factor in transforming curriculum practices for children who have special educational needs is that of overcoming previously held assumptions about children's development and learning needs (Barton 1997). In describing autism as a profound difficulty in social and emotional interaction rather than a set of behavioural characteristics it becomes a challenge for schools to develop strategies that will ensure children have access to a more socially inclusive curriculum. Rather than focus on deficits in pupils, play and the creative arts support an inclusive curriculum model by engaging both the teacher and the learner in an interactive process. Although educationalists may perceive that formal approaches to teaching provide more effective methods of assessment and have more clearly defined goals than interactive approaches, this does not have to be the case. As Sayeed and Guerin (2000) suggest, the outcome of the play experience and the learning that takes place is invariably contingent upon the adult's involvement and expectations of the child's ability and potential to play.

For all children it is essential that play is used as a medium for curriculum delivery. All children should be encouraged to be autonomous, active and playful in their approach to learning, regardless of their age and any learning difficulty. Children need to learn in an environment that provides opportunities for free play, structured play and scaffolded or guided play. In this way, each child is actively engaged in his or her own learning while being exposed to new experiences that are mediated through adult intervention. Although curriculum practices at primary level may imply more flexibility in the inclusion of play-based activities, it is not always evident. For teachers it is invariably the justification for the provision of play that gets in the way of their own beliefs about the educational value of activities that involve fun, spontaneity and ownership. In secondary schools, there is a natural progression from play towards the effective use of the creative arts, outdoor activities and personal hobbies and interests that should maintain an interest and enthusiasm for learning.

For children with autism, the role of interactive play in schools offers an integrated approach that acknowledges how children's learning can be enhanced through play, while providing a safe, therapeutic space in which to explore aspects of the self and significant relationships. Play impacts on the development of cognition and learning by placing value on the dynamic process of self-discovery, the manipulation and symbolic use of objects and the interpersonal connection with a supportive partner. Key to the effectiveness of interactive play is to ensure that the adults have sufficient confidence to engage in positive and playful ways with children. This can only be achieved when all members of the school community understand the principles of an interactive approach and acknowledge its educational value.

A model of training and consultation was established in one school that wanted to implement an interactive play approach into the school curriculum. Having access to the consultant beyond the initial training enabled staff to engage in collaborative problem-solving and develop strategies for supporting pupils' communication and social interaction. Nind and Cochrane (2003) also identify the value of project-based training as an opportunity for staff to see the expertise not only owned by another, but also accessible to them through their own repertoire of behaviours and professional knowledge. Importantly, by adopting a more holistic approach, staff in this project felt more confident about using a range of strategies that would extend children's communication, cognition and social functioning.

Accessing the curriculum

A major dilemma for practitioners working with a goal-driven curriculum has been to legitimize the time made available for well-planned play experiences and the availability of the adults to maximize the benefits for individuals and groups of children. In redefining the curriculum, teachers have also become acutely aware that the content is only one dimension of the educational experience and that what most effectively aids the development of children's knowledge and understanding is the interactive process between the nature of the activity and the individual's response to the learning experience.

From a cognitive perspective, Jordan and Libby (2000) acknowledge how play incorporates intention, interrelatedness, emotional directedness and narrative ability. Children with autism are therefore likely to benefit from increased opportunities to take part in activities that will assist in helping to overcome any difficulties they may have in developing these skills.

The effectiveness of any curriculum, regardless of whether it is in a special or mainstream school, is the extent to which adult-directed activities and collaborative learning are seen to engage the child in the process of discovery and generalization of skills. Curricular approaches that do not provide opportunities for pupils to negotiate aspects of their own learning or review what has been learnt will reduce the motivation to explore different ways of acquiring information. Although there are some children who will not be able to function independently in their daily lives, it should not be assumed that they cannot make decisions or elicit some control over the experiences offered to them. The provision

of play-based experiences within the curriculum is considered essential
for enabling participation in a wide range of social and cultural events
that provide the context for the majority of children educated today.
Regardless of age, ability or cultural background, play and the creative
arts aid children's inclusion into society. Although the focus here is on
establishing interactive play as an inclusive practice, it is considered
relevant to this discussion to acknowledge that special and mainstream
schools will implement the National Curriculum in different ways and
that strategies for accessing the curriculum through play will vary according to the age and ability of the pupils.

Ouvry (1991) devised a curriculum model for pupils with profound
and multiple learning difficulties that can also be applied to teaching
individuals with autism across the whole spectrum of ability. By providing a curriculum that places emphasis on the National Curriculum, a
developmental curriculum and an additional curriculum involving specific therapies, Ouvry's holistic curriculum model demonstrates an interconnectedness that aims to provide the breadth necessary for teaching individuals in accordance with their developmental needs rather
than age-related programmes of study. This offers a more pragmatic
approach to the curriculum because at any time the learning needs of
individuals may change and there may be priorities in some areas and
not in others.

Special schools

For many children with autism who are functioning at the earliest stages
of development, their learning experiences will be encompassed within
a developmental curriculum that provides a suitable forum for the implementation of interactive play. The focus on early communication
and playful interaction through sensory exploration is seen as creating
the foundations for the development of conceptual understanding and
may have a significant role to play in reducing some of the secondary
behaviours that can arise as a result of the profound difficulties in relating to others. The positive feedback that is received through interactive
play teaches the child about the nature of interrelatedness so that together there is mutual recognition of how it can impact on future learning experiences. The child's level of involvement will be contingent on
how the adult interacts with the child as well as the context and the
activities that are provided. Longhorn (1993) refers to these mutually
engaging experiences as the prerequisites for learning and emphasizes
that a curriculum should ensure opportunities are planned not only to
establish these but also to enable them to develop.

Jordan and Powell (1995) also recognize that, regardless of age or
developmental level, individuals with autism throughout their lifespan

will always require opportunities to reinforce these skills. If, for example, a teenager with autism and severe learning difficulties continues to gain a lot of enjoyment from sitting on a swing or see-saw in the park, should this be discouraged because he is of an age where he should be taking part in more socially appropriate group activities? Teachers in special schools or specialist provision recognize that a person-centred approach to the curriculum is likely to be more relevant because it acknowledges the appropriateness of activities in relation to the individual's emotional and developmental needs rather than their age.

Early years

In pre-school and Early Years settings there is little doubt that play is central to the curriculum and regarded as the most effective medium through which children learn (Curriculum Guidance for the Foundation Stage: DfEE 2000). Practitioners plan play-based activities that focus on areas of development with no attempt to compartmentalize children's learning experiences. Structuring play is an essential feature of well-planned play provision for children with and without learning difficulties. However, it is vital that practitioners clearly understand the distinction between structuring different types of play to provide a range of meaningful learning experiences, and structured play that refers to the mechanistic teaching of skills to obtain specific outcomes. Practitioners have a responsibility to maintain quality by ensuring that, in addition to scaffolding play skills, there is access to free play that enables children to develop their own preferences and responses to their environment. In the Te Whāriki Early Childhood Curriculum, quality learning experiences are defined as those that invite rather than compel children to participate, by which children can develop their own interests and views of the world and in which adults have an important role in aiding the development of children's understanding and knowledge (Ministry of Education, New Zealand, 1996).

Early diagnosis is essential in identifying causation of the difficulties in social communication but there is a danger that it creates a label that then governs the implementation of interventions that might isolate children from learning alongside their peer group. Lantz *et al.* (2004) suggest that Early Years educators should continue to plan programmes that target developmental and socially beneficial play when developing goals for children with autism. If a child remains isolated in their play then practitioners have to question what needs to be altered to increase the child's interest in playing with others. This will require adults to work more frequently on a one-to one basis to enable the child to develop skills in play and social interaction. Individual sessions have the advantage of providing more positive opportunities to model play with their peers and offer a more natural setting for the generalization of social skills.

Mainstream schools

The transition to primary school invariably implies a reduction in the opportunities that children are given to learn through play, but for many children play-based activities may continue to be the most effective way in which they can access the curriculum. Hadley (2002) argues for the need to reassert play within the classroom beyond Key Stage 1, not specifically for the teaching of play skills but to enable children to rediscover a playful disposition and emotional responsiveness towards their learning. He expresses concern about the 'ghettoization' of play into the Early Years curriculum and quotes Claxton (2000), who describes the challenge now facing teachers' professional view of the role of play.

> We need a more powerful rhetoric to defend what we know which is that play and learning aren't different things. Rhetoric however is not enough and one might argue that what we need is a general theory of play which argues not just for its importance as a stage of development but which reasserts its presence in the continuum of our lives as learners.
>
> (cited in Hadley 2002: 11)

It is likely that discrepancies over the role and status of play will continue to be a significant feature of both formal and informal educational debates. A common feature of structured programmes for children with autism, such as TEACCH, is the promotion of a 'work then play' approach to the curriculum that could potentially undermine opportunities for integrated learning and the generalization of skills. Of greater concern is a view that access to play, independently or with a play partner, is contingent on an individual's compliant behaviour or earned as a reward. Likewise if play is regarded as an activity to *entertain* the child, to compensate for the perceived difficulties in accessing a subject-based curriculum, this only serves to devalue the role of play in children's learning and could limit their entitlement to a broader and more relevant curriculum.

With the curriculum developments in mainstream schools there is now a much greater emphasis on identifying children's learning dispositions rather than their differences and this has given teachers a much clearer understanding of how to develop teaching strategies that are more child and play focused. This shift in thinking has emerged simultaneously with the inclusion of pupils with special educational needs in mainstream schools and as a result there have been significant adaptations to the ways in which all children access the curriculum. The potential benefits of using visual, auditory and kinaesthetic methods of teaching have received much attention but, in terms of assessing pupils' learning outcomes, are yet to undergo any rigorous research. However, in the publication 'Excellence and Enjoyment: a Strategy for Primary Schools' (DfES 2003) a review of the principles of learning and teaching recognizes the need to ensure that every child succeeds through a culture of high expectation, to build on what the learners already know at a structure and pace that enables them to learn and to make learning vivid and real – an enjoyable and challenging experience. This is to be achieved by matching teaching techniques and strategies to a range of learning styles that will build skills across the curriculum and enrich the learning experience by enabling children to become partners in their own learning (p. 29). It is within this framework that the opportunity to learn through play and develop creativity should be endorsed.

In deciding on the most effective strategies for teaching pupils with autism, teachers will want to ensure access to small groups as well as individual sessions in which their interests can become the focus of an activity. Studies in peer-mediated learning (Wolfberg and Schuler 1993; Lantz *et al.* 2004; Whitaker 2004) found a significant improvement in the ability of children with autism to play socially and imaginatively through the imitation of their peers. In each study the peers initiated the play using the same interactive principles of joining in with an activity that the child with autism had chosen. The sessions were structured by the adult to support the play activity but, over time, the children developed their own patterns of interaction and engaged in mutually favourite activities that resulted in increased enjoyment and enthusiasm. As Wolfberg (1999) found in her study, the children generated more spontaneous and diverse forms of play and appeared to be able to follow a sequence within the symbolic and social dimensions of the activity. These studies support the view of Gopnik *et al.* (1999) that there is a drive in all children to understand how another person might be thinking and that they come to learn more about themselves through the self-reflection that emerges from their observation of others during playful exchanges.

There remains some debate as to whether the same principles can be applied to pupils in secondary schools where subject-based teaching may not enable more interactive styles of teaching. As suggested, it is most likely through the creative arts and, in particular, drama that pupils will have opportunities to explore different social relationships, roles and symbolic meanings through the structure and sequence of narrative and action.

The role of the adult therefore is to plan and provide quality interactive experiences that will stimulate and reinforce the child's desire for exploration, conceptual understanding and acquisition of skills. An entitlement to the curriculum will be of little value if it does not have relevance for the individual. Defining the content of the curriculum and children's access to it ultimately rests with what educators recognize as their priorities for individuals, the prescribed national requirements and what is unique to the school community.

Planning interactive play sessions

A vital component in fostering children's development will be to define how the learning experience is offered rather than what is expected to take place. Child-directed teaching strategies place no more pressure on teachers in terms of planning and implementation; rather they enhance competency because they are based on the teachers' intuitive knowledge of how children learn. Key considerations for structuring the interactive play sessions will take account of the setting, including staffing and resources, and a highly individualized set of activities that ensure that the experience remains firmly within a positive learning framework. Planning sessions of interactive play should be seen as integral to the organizational structure of the topic or subject-based teaching with specific relevance to the needs of the individual or group. Teachers in discussion with colleagues will be able to make judgements about those children for whom individual sessions would be considered most relevant and those who would benefit from small group or peer-mediated play. This should be determined in terms of the developmental needs of the individual, as intellectual functioning and age may not be compatible indicators. Many children are likely to benefit initially from one-to-one sessions with an adult, whereas for others it may be relevant to be part of a group that focuses on developing social skills or sociodramatic play. In an educational context, child-focused interventions should complement any learning intentions by ensuring that they are:

- *Embedded in everyday activities.* For learning to be effective it has to involve transferable skills. As there is no single formula to teaching that can achieve this, educationists need to plan for children to be offered a range of different teaching styles that are developmentally appropriate and provide the right level of stimulation, sensitivity and autonomy. The non-intrusive nature of play with a supportive partner increases opportunities for children to learn about differences in social interaction and allows more authentic communication to take place. Using toys and activities that children are familiar with in other contexts during the interactive play sessions provides an emotional security that contributes towards an increase in their repertoire of socially responsive behaviours. Integrating experiences across a continuum of need rather than in isolation will be more beneficial to children's development and their social inclusion.

- *Individualized.* Naturalistic teaching strategies emphasize a more individualized approach than instruction-based teaching strategies. Regardless of whether a child is in a special or mainstream school, individualized programmes of learning will be an entitlement based on his or her specific educational and personal needs. Child-focused interventions require more specialized knowledge of the individual and increased opportunities for support in those areas of identified need. Consequently, sessions of interactive play will vary in content and pace depending on the child's response. When the child selects how an object or toy is to be manipulated and explored, the adult ensures that his or her response does not extend the experience in ways that are too complex but introduces challenge only in so far as it aids the child's thinking and emotional well-being. This approach emphasizes how the process-led play and interaction provides a positive and supportive environment for increasing expressions of autonomy, self-esteem and confidence.

- *Focused on the child's motivations and interests.* Interactive play sessions should always have an activity focus to enable the child to engage in a shared experience. Even if the child is intently focused on his or her own movements and initially shows little interest in the presence of another, it is possible to make a game of hiding or peek-a-boo that will invite the child to respond to a different set of actions. If toys or other sensory materials are available then the play partner will observe how the child is interacting with these and sensitively join in with the activity. The same applies with being part of a social group. The child with autism will want to have a level of competency in an activity before sharing the experience or being invited to respond to others' ideas.

- *Based on spontaneous communication and positive interaction.* Classroom settings that offer too rigid an approach to the curriculum provide fewer opportunities for children to respond spontaneously and, as a consequence, this reduces possibilities for developing more flexible ways of thinking and self-regulated behaviour. The more naturalistic setting of the interactive play also means that the use of picture symbols is not advocated during the sessions, as this will affect the flow of the interaction and the emotional connection that is being created. Interactive play alters the dynamics of the relationship because it is based on a more intuitive response to how the child is playing and what is being communicated through his or her behaviour. When communicative behaviours are modelled this raises enjoyment of the shared experience and extends opportunities for the development of play skills. Rogers' (1961) person-centred approach provides a number of conditions for creating a therapeutic relationship that are relevant to helping the person facilitate growth and improve his or her functioning:

- being perceived as trustworthy, dependable and consistent;
- being able to communicate unambiguously;
- experiencing positive attitudes towards the other person;
- being secure enough within oneself to allow the other person their separateness;
- allowing the person to express their own personality rather than modelling who they are on someone else;
- entering into the world of his or her feelings and meanings and seeing these as he or she does;
- accepting each facet of the other person;
- ensuring our own behaviour is not perceived as threatening to the other person;
- not being judgemental;
- meeting the other person who is in the process of *becoming*.

Not only is it important to acknowledge the feelings and attitudes of another person but also by understanding them there is greater potential for empathy and mutual engagement. Having a positive regard for another means that each person in that relationship discovers more effective ways of communicating. When children's actions (communications) are responded to positively they learn that their presence with another person is valued and they are more likely to make attempts to reciprocate the interaction.

- *Structured within the boundaries set by the adult.* Teachers will have the responsibility to plan the time for interactive play sessions that are conducive to other timetabled curriculum sessions. With the focus on language and communication, interactive play can be incorporated in the Literacy Hour and other activity-based or creative arts subjects. Making a regular time available for an individual or group establishes an understanding of the sequence of the interactive play session. In individual sessions, even although the play will be non-directive, the session is structured in so far as the adult has made available those materials and toys that match the child's sensory preferences or interests so that they can become the focus of the interaction. The session begins with a welcoming activity that aims to provide reassurance to the child or group that it will be a nurturing and enjoyable experience. In individual sessions the child is then given the opportunity to explore and engage in his or her chosen activity, which is supported and extended by the presence of the adult. An activity, which could include a song, ends the session and lets the child know that the special time together has finished. Group sessions will follow a similar format but activities will be planned to enable children to express their own ideas, for example in a story or drama sequence. Interactive play must be set within those boundaries that maintain the interaction in a safe space both physically and emotionally for those involved. The adult will need to make clear to the child what those expectations are so that the play together remains a positive experience.

Assessment

An effective curriculum model is one in which observations and assessments inform both child- and teacher-initiated activities. This is likely to occur only when an environment for play is provided, when children are encouraged to be autonomous, active and playful in their approach to learning and the adult intends to use play to assess and plan in relation to the curriculum. Unlike structured play that is task based, interactive play is an experienced-based approach that focuses on developing skills for learning through the adult's awareness of the processes involved in actively engaging the child in a shared experience. Newton (1988) suggests that, along the continuum of assessment, the most valuable information gathered is through observation and participation in children's play. In this way practitioners can make use of more intuitive assessments that form the basis of understanding what the child knows and can do. As interactive play is based on what is happening *between* people to make the learning experience more meaningful, this influences the nature of the assessment. It is irrelevant to measure what the child cannot do but to identify the potential that exists as a result of the support being offered.

Formal check-lists have a tendency to enforce what and how a skill should be taught, resulting in more inflexible strategies being adopted and little opportunity for spontaneity in learning or teaching. A rise in the use of play-based assessments has emerged as a result of changes in Early Years education but problems may again occur in trying to *make them fit* many children with autism who will have isolated areas of skill that do not correspond with developmental stages of play. These assessments tend to make more reference to functional play skills and emphasize the social dimension rather than the nature of the play itself. By not taking account of variations in the developmental process this could result in children missing out on experiencing certain types of play or having their play interpreted as inappropriate when it is relevant to their emotional needs and therefore a purposeful activity. For example a child may spend a long time picking up leaves in the garden, throwing them up in the air, twirling herself around or sitting looking up at the leaves moving in the trees. It would seem inappropriate to interpret this as 'not playing' when in fact it represents for the child an emotionally charged activity that includes exploration of natural objects and a fascination with movement. Were someone to join in with this activity it would heighten the experience for the child and offer new possibilities for action.

A rigid approach to teaching play skills does not provide the same experience-based, playful interaction that enhances communication and play skills in the same way that a shared experience has built-in opportunities to do so. As a consequence, a more dynamic and interactive approach to assessment is required, particularly when a child has an irregular developmental profile and the adult plays a strong mediating role in supporting the learning experience. Unlike developmental check-lists, the key to achievement in a dynamic interactive assessment is not dependent upon the context, materials and activities but the extent to which the adult is involved in the learning process with the child. These factors are highlighted in Laevers' Experiential Education Model (1994), in which he places assessment within a conceptual framework that is reliant upon the child's well-being and level of involvement to ascertain the likely outcome of the learning experience. He implies that this is dependent upon a particular teaching style that offers sensitivity towards the child's learning needs so that appropriate levels of stimulation are provided to engender high or low involvement. 'Involvement means that there is intense mental activity, that a person is functioning at the very limits of his or her capabilities with an energy flow that comes from intrinsic sources' (Laevers 1997: 2).

The Process-oriented Monitoring System focuses on observations that will indicate the quality of the process and the extent to which teachers make sufficient effort to secure the emotional health and progress in specific areas of development for each child; through this process teachers receive immediate feedback on the quality of their work and are able to establish intrinsically motivating targets for the child (Laevers 1997). Interactive analysis suggests that teachers look for interpretations beyond those that are immediately obvious and consciously take account of the within-child factors and their own responses to the child that will have a bearing on learning and behaviour.

The interactive nature of the Dynamic Assessment (Feuerstein 2000) recognizes the mediator's role as key to any intervention that might lead to change in the child's level of functioning. Feuerstein's theories have effectively been applied to play so that as the child and adult engage in an activity together it is possible to gain valuable information about 'the motivational and emotional aspects of the child's behaviour as part of the child's learning potential' (Sayeed and Guerin 2000: 89). This is achievable because the adult mediates not by directly teaching the task but by helping the child to acquire the learning principles through a repertoire of activities that repeatedly focus on the child's competencies and the sensitivity with which the adult challenges him or her to think and behave differently.

The Interactive Play Profile (Figure 8.1) is based on the process-led theories of Feuerstein and Laevers and focuses on the potential for modifying and extending cognitive and social functioning when the adult provides opportunities to encourage the child's curiosity, autonomy and communicative competence. The nature of the adult intervention is therefore seen as an essential part of the dynamic process of assessment. The Interactive Play Profile records achievements in the acquisition of skills for learning across social, communication and cognitive domains. As play provides a forum through which skills can emerge simultaneously, any assessment of these can be undertaken with the same rigidity as other more formal assessments. Significantly, in each of these domains there is an emotional component, as any change in a performance will be dependent upon the affective qualities of the child's intrapersonal state and their unique response to the experience.

The Interactive Play Profile can also be used during observations of group sessions or peer-mediated play and, as a consequence, provides a unique picture of children's learning across different contexts. In contrast to product-led assessments, this is a key difference in recording achievements that are process led. By recording the experience that led to the acquisition of the skill it reduces the demands on the child to perform in a specific way and enables the adult to introduce challenge in a way that aids the child's cognitive development. Across a number of sessions there may well be evidence of progress in a particular area of skill, through which the teacher will be able to identify the depth of learning and understanding that the child has acquired.

There is little value in teachers recording what the child does not know or has not yet achieved, as required with many check-lists; rather the skills that the child is acquiring to make the learning possible should be identified. Furthermore, there is increased flexibility in how the activity is offered and in the different strategies that an adult might adopt to extend the learning. Rather than feel the constraints of certain methods of assessment, teachers may then have an opportunity to explore ways to use assessments more intuitively and creatively. Sessions may be videoed or photographed for use within an individual portfolio as a record of achievement or used alongside other assessments to plan relevant targets.

In maximizing children's learning potential teachers will be aware of the need to use a range of assessment tools to inform individual

The Interactive Play Profile

Name:	Date:

Play context:

Experience:

Social communication skills

Awareness of partner(s); initiating contact; shared participation; engagement with partner(s); spontaneous eye contact; joint attention; taking turns; imitating; vocalizing; requesting

Emotional skills

Reacts to interaction; emotional response, e.g. relaxed, excited, happy, uncertain, confident, humour; engagement with partner(s); emotional reciprocity; emotional expression; regulating emotion

Cognitive skills

Initiating actions; spontaneous exploration; curiosity; generating new ideas; solving problems; building concepts; developing understanding; memory; representation of objects; pretend play

Key achievements:

Planning notes:

copyrightDSeach2006   photocopiable resource

Figure 8.1 The Interactive Play Profile.

programmes. Individual Education Plans (IEPs) are designed to identify targets for learning and the strategies for achieving these. Targets are usually based on curriculum subjects, social skills and behaviour with no requirement for play-based targets. Paradoxically, it is planned play experiences that will enhance children's access to the curriculum and have a significant impact on their personal and social development. However, Wood and Attfield (1996) point out that educators need to be aware of what children can learn spontaneously and what requires specific teaching. In particular, there is a danger when teaching children with autism that targets are more task based and do not allow for achievement in a skill to be recognized unless they meet the specific criteria identified on the IEP. As an example, the target 'Ashuk will give eye contact when asking for a drink' is written for a child who does not give spontaneous eye contact. An essential component in the child's learning is the extent of the adult's intervention and it may well be that in another context that involves sharing a motivating activity that Ashuk frequently gives eye contact to initiate a request or share enjoyment. According to Potter and Whittaker (2001) opportunities for spontaneous learning should be a key educational goal. Play-based intervention strategies provide teachers with more creative ways to consider how individual goals can be included in different activities to increase the generalization of specific skills.

The following section describes how the principles for establishing an Interactive Play approach in schools were applied to a special school where many of its pupils were diagnosed within the spectrum of autism. Before commencement of the project the school had established many of the structured approaches to teaching children with autism but there was a view amongst staff at that school that enhancing children's learning opportunities, and in particular their social communication, might be achieved through the introduction of an interactive approach using play.

The school project

The school is situated in a London borough that has a high proportion of its population from different ethnic backgrounds. The special school has provision for children aged four to sixteen years old with severe learning difficulties. It has separate primary and secondary departments and there are currently 110 children attending the school. At least 80 per cent of the pupils have a diagnosis of autism and this has considerably changed the way in which the curriculum has been delivered in recent years. The school population includes children from the Bengali, Punjabi and Arabic communities, and over 50 per cent of the pupils come from homes where English is not the first language. Pupils are taught in age-related Key Stage classes with a teacher and up to three teaching assistants. There is also a class for more able pupils with autism and Asperger's syndrome. In addition, the school is supported with a speech and language therapist, an occupational therapist, a music therapist and a clinical psychologist. It also has an outreach service that provides support for parents and children in other pre-school settings.

The project was run over five days, with a further two days for staff consultations. It was planned to provide:

- staff training on the principles and practice of Interactive Play for children with autism;
- a parent workshop;
- individual sessions with pupils;
- group session with pupils;
- staff consultation and feedback.

The training enabled staff at the school to formulate links between the developmental play needs of children and planning opportunities within the timetable for shared play experiences that would promote the development of communication and interaction to meet the pupils' personal, social and educational needs. The school is committed to involving the parents in all aspects of their children's education and a parent workshop enabled those parents who could attend to learn about interactive play and its relevance in their children's learning and development.

Each individual pupil and group was seen on two occasions. With the individual pupils, the first session provided an opportunity for staff to observe an adult–child interaction and the second session enabled a staff member to be observed interacting with the child while being offered verbal guidance to support the play and interaction. Staff were fully involved in the group sessions to maintain the ethos of a shared learning experience. Both the individual and group sessions were videoed and observed by up to three staff members.

Staff consultation took place subsequent to the interactive play sessions to give them an opportunity to discuss the planning and implementation of individual and group sessions of interactive play within the context of the classroom and the timetable. Having observed the interactive play sessions, staff needed to consider how to incorporate an interactive play approach to support the development of communication and social interaction, to identify links to pupils' IEPs and record and assess progress.

Results

The project design was not intended to be used in any way as formal research but to provide a model of training that would further staff knowledge through the practical application of an interactive approach based on clearly defined principles of children's development in relation to working with children with autism. Through the training, staff had been made aware of how to establish an empathetic connection with the child through the spontaneous exploration of objects and to recognize ways in which they could extend children's thinking and imaginative play by the creative responses they offered in the shared play experience.

Teachers identified six pupils for the one-to-one sessions, based on their needs for strategies to support the develop of communication, to extend an interest in exploring different objects and to reduce difficult behaviours that were a barrier to effective communication. Having completed a Sensory Happiness Profile (Longhorn 2002) on each child, materials, toys and objects were placed in the room for the children to explore and make a choice about what they wanted to play with. The interactive play sessions lasted forty-five minutes after which staff had an opportunity to discuss any significant aspects of the session that they had observed. Although the room was not unfamiliar to the children, the nature of what was happening in the room was different, so it was important that they were given time to familiarize themselves with the new experience. There was a noticeable difference in the children's responses during the second session, which indicated some understanding of the expectations and play that would engage them in interaction. Staff noted in the feedback that the pupils' participation and communication was particularly heightened owing to the focus on following the child's lead and the positive modelling of the play and interaction. Staff appreciated the opportunity to be guided in their sessions of interactive play with the child as this enabled them to develop more confidence to explore a different way of interacting with the child. Staff particularly noted during the planned sessions that the children were making more efforts to initiate communication, use more vocalizations or spoken language and develop more control over their interactions than in the more structured activities in the classroom.

Kahil was recommended by his teacher for an individual session. He was seven years old and in a class with five other pupils with whom he rarely initiated any contact. He was non-verbal and needed constant adult supervision and support to take part in any task or activity. He liked to explore a range of different objects at a sensory level but always in the same way and he never spent much time with one object or activity. The session was planned to enable Kahil to be supported in playing with his chosen activity and to extend his interest in sharing it with a partner. A sensory basket was placed in the playroom in which Kahil found a ball that lit up when it bounced against a surface. There were also some coloured feathers, shiny objects, wooden instruments and a large coloured ball that expanded when pulled apart. He showed immediate recognition that I was there to play with him and rolled the ball towards me. There was shared participation in the game as we rolled the ball to each other. He initiated bouncing the ball instead of rolling it and I responded by copying his actions. He took an interest in the feathers and we took turns to throw them up. When they touched his face he laughed and made lots of repeated sounds. He briefly explored the expanding ball and began jumping up and down as he watched it spin and collapse. We even laughed together when the small ball he was holding fell inside the large ball and he couldn't see it. Kahil initiated picking up the large ball to look inside for his favourite toy Kahil again explored the sensory basket and found the pot of bubbles, which he handed to me to blow for him. He remained in close proximity to me and spontaneously gave me frequent eye contact to ensure that I maintained blowing the bubbles so that he could catch them. Throughout our play time together, Kahil expressed a range of emotions that he was clearly able to regulate. He was very excited by the ball spinning and popping the bubbles with his tongue. He would occasionally withdraw from the activity and stand quietly before deciding what to play with next. He also realized that his smiles and laughter were being responded to by mine and on one occasion he came towards me for a hug.

Staff were able to recognize a range of social and communication skills that Kahil used to interact positively with me and share a play activity. There was also a realization that many of these skills are not always as noticeable when he is in the class with other pupils and the individual session had enabled the teacher to identify how these could be encouraged. Whilst there was no evidence on this occasion of using toys or objects imaginatively, Kahil used the small ball not just for the cause and effect light but also functionally by throwing, rolling, bouncing and kicking it.

A session with a more able group of pupils was designed to support social play skills, to develop an awareness of others through play and to help the teacher plan more creative ways for children to access the curriculum, particularly in the Literacy Hour. Staff noted that the sequence of planned social play activities enabled pupils to listen and cooperate with each other, share ideas and develop their own thinking about how to represent their own and others' ideas. At the end of the session pupils were given the opportunity to express their views on the different activities and to plan what they wanted to include in the next session. Having some responsibility over their own learning and shared experience was felt to support their involvement and motivation to relate to others in positive ways.

Another group included four nine-year-old boys who were not all from the same class. Although these boys were happy to interact with others in the classroom, their teachers felt that they had limited social play skills and did not understand how to engage with others in playful ways. A sequence of physical activities was planned to enable them to develop an awareness of one another by being in closer proximity, to take turns in playing a game and to support their own and another's enjoyment of the interaction. Seated on the floor, the session began with each child and staff member being introduced as cream was rubbed into their hands. This was aimed at reassuring the children that they would be nurtured during the session. One child moved away from the circle but made it possible for us to include him in the song. The children still seemed apprehensive about taking part and so a game of hide-and-seek was introduced; first, a staff member modelled by hiding under a blanket and a child chose to go and find her. On being uncovered the teacher appeared with much enthusiasm and excitement that delighted the boys. They took turns to be covered under the blanket and to be 'found'. As their excitement was raised so it was important that the next activity offered an opportunity for them to be more relaxed. Each child in turn was rocked in the blanket and then they helped to rock one another. The session ended with a song to say goodbye and to thank the children for taking part. Providing similar activities in the second session increased the extent to which two of the children used more spoken language to make choices and express their interest in the activities.

Staff consultations followed the sessions and were integral to the training process. The purposeful nature of interactive play was discussed in the context of meeting the child's educational targets and how the acquisition of skills for learning could be achieved through this approach. The Interactive Play Profile was introduced to record pupil's achievements, and staff undertook to complete this in conjunction with other assessments that the school was using. On completion of the project, staff completed a questionnaire designed to ascertain how the project had both influenced their understanding of Interactive Play and how it would influence their future planning and teaching of the pupils. The following are just some of the comments made by the staff:

- 'I thought that all children would develop play skills. I didn't realise that the more we model what the child is doing the more he responds to you.'
- 'I felt reassured that it was OK to play with a child on a one-to-one basis as part of a child's individual curriculum.'
- 'I was surprised by the reactions of the child when his actions were mirrored. I'm going to be more tuned in to the child and what they are trying to "say".'
- 'It has broadened my understanding of how to develop imaginative play and given me a lot of ideas for developing children's imagination.'
- 'I intend to use the children's creativity and imagination during literacy sessions to develop storytelling.'
- 'The most significant aspect of Interactive Play was observing how the child initiated the play and to see how the relationship was being formed in a relaxed learning environment.'

In summary, the staff felt that they had benefited from the training programme in a number of ways. In particular, they thought that their experience of the programme had:

- challenged assumptions of the nature of the autism;
- increased competence in planning individual sessions;
- confirmed the view of the role of play in children's learning;
- altered perceptions about interactive approaches to teaching;
- established a new quality in the adult–child relationship, which they hoped would foster more successful learning.

The effectiveness of the project was also reflected in the enthusiasm and interest that the staff developed as a result of feeling supported throughout the training. A final recommendation was to increase the recognition of the value of play in children's learning by incorporating this approach into a school play policy. This would ensure that parents and governors felt confident that children had access to a range of relevant teaching strategies that would be effective in increasing learning outcomes as well as skills for living. It also has implications for the staff in recognizing how the theoretical principles of play can be applied in practical terms using strategies that maintain their competency and enthusiasm for teaching.

School play policy

There is a danger that with so many different interventions for supporting children with special educational needs in the classroom

(1) they provide conflicting information that affects the smooth planning of learning experiences for children and (2) they reduce teachers' competency in understanding and working with children. On the other hand, play is universally recognized as having an impact on children's cognitive, social and emotional development. Teachers may therefore respond more positively to the implementation of an interactive approach that works alongside other more formal approaches to teaching and is based on the intuitive understanding of how children learn and develop children's social and communication skills through play. Early Years educators will undoubtedly regard play as having a significant influence on curriculum planning and delivery, but for children beyond the Early Years reference to play in school policies should remain a major consideration, whether or not they have a special educational need.

Because educators have not always emphasized the value of play when planning programmes for children with autism, school policy documents may not specifically acknowledge its purpose in children's learning, other than as a reference to play as a recreational activity. Equally, access to play may only be referenced in subject-based and school-wide policies because it has not been afforded the same discrete focus of professional debate and school development. To address this, staff will need to consider what is fundamental to good practice in terms of curriculum access and be committed to the view that 'all forms of play appear to be essential for the intellectual, imaginative and emotional development of the child and may be necessary steps to a further stage of development' (Brierley 1987: 110).

Like all policies, the school play policy will require a statement of principles that represent quality educational provision and in which there is acknowledgement of the role of play in children's social, cultural, emotional and intellectual well-being. It will need to provide a set of general aims on the use of play and how different approaches can support children's holistic development. In the play policy of a special school in Northern Ireland they write:

> Each class should strive to be a place where all the children's senses are engaged and stimulated and we must plan for the development of creativity, originality and expressiveness in an environment that supports discovery and exploration of materials, ideas and feelings. Children need help to extend their play skills and adults can contribute to the development of abstract thinking by adding resources, props, asking open-ended questions and creating exciting and age/ability appropriate challenges.

It is important that the policy acknowledges that children can learn through play in different ways and how this will have implications for curriculum planning and the management of the classroom and individual pupils. Making a distinction between structured play, interactive play and free play will also enable staff to identify how these can be planned and resourced in terms of staffing and equipment. The principles inherent in each of these strategies will underpin the planning and progression in children's play development and are described in the same school policy:

- Well-planned and well-resourced play activities will allow for progression in a child's thinking and understanding.
- Progression in play will reflect the observation and assessment of children's knowledge, skills and attitudes in order to provide developmentally appropriate experiences.
- Successful progression in play comes from a real understanding of the interests, needs and experiences of each child.

An effective policy will also show that recording and assessing play should undergo the same rigorous examination as other educational assessments, which represents a shift in acknowledging the value and status of play in children's development. When adults value play and are able to use play to plan and assess children's learning experiences, only then are the conditions set for developing children's potential. A significant factor in any policy on play will be that it represents children's entitlement to play within an educational context. It incorporates many aspects of learning through play that are common to all children, while at the same time respecting the diversity in children's different abilities, dispositions and needs.

Play would appear to have received less attention in the education of children with autism but it now seems that a new era is emerging that is allied to more child-focused interactive approaches to teaching and learning. Fundamentally it becomes the role of practitioners to ensure that the play experiences offered to children take place in environments that have a positive regard for their developmental needs and provide a sense of belonging, and that the ways in which they participate are accepted and valued. All children, regardless of their abilities, seek ways to understand and take part in their social world. They need first-hand experiences to enable them to express their unique ideas and personalities and also opportunities to actively communicate their interests. Play gives meaning and purpose to children's actions and it is through play that they can learn the significance of interacting in meaningful and enjoyable ways. It is not the practice of interactive play that is new but recognition of its value that is likely to affect its implementation and development in schools and other childcare settings. By adopting interactive play as an effective strategy for teaching communication and sociability it provides experiences that will enhance children's thinking and development. Children will then have the opportunity to discover positive ways in which they can become more competent in their learning and interations with others.

Bibliography

Abbott, L. (1994) '"Play is Ace!" Developing Play in Schools and Classrooms', in Moyles, J., ed., *The Excellence of Play*. Buckingham, UK: Open University Press.

Abbott, L. and Nutbrown, C. (eds) (2001) *Experiencing Reggio Emilia: Implications for Pre-school Provision*. Buckingham, UK: Open University Press.

Adolphs R., Sears, L. and Piven, J. (2001) 'Face processing in autism', *Journal of Cognitive Neuroscience*, 13: 232–40.

Ainsworth, M., Blehar, M. C., Waters, E. and Wall, S. (1978) *Patterns of Attachment*. Hillsdale, NJ: Erlbaum.

Aitken, K. J. and Trevarthen, C. (1997) 'Self/other organisation in human psychological development', *Developmental Psychopathology*, 9: 653–77.

Alvarez, A. (1992) *Live Company. Psychoanalytic Psychotherapy with Autistic, Borderline, Deprived and Abused Children*. London: Brunner-Routledge.

Alvarez, A. and Reid, S. (eds) (1999) *Autism and Personality: Findings from the Tavistock Autism Workshop*. London: Routledge.

Alvin, J. (1978) *Music Therapy for the Autistic Child*. Oxford: Oxford University Press.

Andersen-Wood, L. and Smith, B. R. (1997) *Working with Pragmatics. A Practical Guide to Promoting Communicative Confidence*. Bicester: Winslow.

Astington Wilde, J. (1994) *The Child's Discovery of the Mind*. London: Fontana Press.

Athey, C. (1990) *Extending Thought in Young Children: A Parent–Teacher Partnership*. London: Paul Chapman Publishers.

Axline, V. (1969) *Play Therapy*. New York: Ballantine Books.

Axline, V. (1982) 'Non-directive play therapy procedures and results', in Landreth, G., ed., *Play Therapy: Dynamics of the Process of Counselling Children*. Springfield, IL: Charles C. Thomas.

Ayres, A. J. (1979) *Sensory Integration and the Child*. Los Angeles, CA: Western Psychological Services.

Bägenholm, A. and Gillberg, C. (1991) 'Psychosocial effects on siblings of children with autism and mental retardation: a population-based study', *Journal of Mental Deficiency Research*, 35: 291–307.

Bailey, R. (2002) 'Playing social chess: children's play and social intelligence', *Early Years: An International Journal of Research and Development*, 22(2): 163–73.

Barnard, K. E. and Brazelton, T. B. (1990) *Touch: The Foundation of Experience*. Madison, WI: International Universities Press.

Barnes, M. (2004) *The Healing Path with Children: An Exploration for Parents and Professionals*. Fairwarp, UK: The Play Therapy Press.

Barnett, M. A. (1987) 'Empathy and related responses in children', in Eisenberg, N. and Strayer, J., eds, *Empathy and its Development*. Cambridge: Cambridge University Press.

Barton, L. (1997) 'Inclusive education: romantic, subversive or realistic?', *Journal of Inclusive Education*, 1(3): 231–42.

Beadle-Brown, J. and Whiten, A. (2004) 'Elicited imitation in adults and children with autism: Is there a deficit?', *Journal of Intellectual and Developmental Disability*, 29(2): 141–57.

Belsky, J (2002) 'Developmental origins of attachment styles', *Attachment and Human Development*, 4(2): 166–70.

Belton, T. (2001) 'Television and imagination: an investigation of the medium's influence on children's storymaking', *Media, Culture and Society*, 23: 799–820.

Bennett, N., Wood, L. and Rogers, S. (1997) *Teaching Through Play: Teachers Thinking and Classroom Practice*. Buckingham, UK: Open University Press.

Berggren, L. (2004) 'Thoughtful play… Victor D'Amico, artmaking as play', *IPA Newsletter* (Fall). www.ipausa.org.

Bernard-Opitz, V., Siow, I. and Tan, Y. K. (2004) 'Comparison of behavioural and natural play interventions for young children with autism', *Autism: The International Journal of Research and Practice*, 8(3): 319–33.

Beyer, J. and Gammeltoft, L. (2000) *Autism and Play*. London: Jessica Kingsley Publishers.

Bhattacharyya, A. (1997) 'Historical backdrop', in Dwivedi, K. N., ed., *The Therapeutic Use of Stories*. London: Routledge.

Blakemore-Brown, L. and Parr, M. (1996) 'Positive parenting', *Young Minds Magazine* 24: 24–5.

Blatchford, P., Battle, S. and Mays, J. (1982) *The First Transition: Home to Preschool*. Windsor: NFER/Nelson.

Boden, M. (1990) *The Creative Mind: Myths and Mechanisms*. London: Weidenfeld and Nicholson.

Bodrova, E. and Leong, D. (2003) 'The importance of being playful', *Educational Leadership*, 60(7): 50–3.

Bogdashina, O. (2003) *Sensory Perceptual Issues in Autism and Asperger Syndrome*. London: Jessica Kingsley Publishers.

Bornstein, M., Haynes, M., O'Reilly, A. and Painter, K. (1996) 'Solitary and collaborative pretense play in early childhood: sources of individual variation in the development of representational competence', *Child Development*, 67: 2910–29.

Bott, D. (2001) 'Towards a family-centred therapy. Post-modern developments in family therapy and the person-centred contribution', *Counselling Psychology Quarterly*, 14(2): 111–18.

Boucher J., Lewis, V. and Collis, G. (1998) 'Familiar face and voice matching and recognition in children with autism', *Journal of Psychology and Psychiatry*, 39: 171–81.

Bowlby, J. (1969) *Attachment and Loss*. London: Pimlico.

Bowlby, J. (1979) *The Making and Breaking of Affectional Bonds*. London: Tavistock Publications.

Bowlby, R. (2003) 'Attachment', video produced by R. Bowlby, London.

Brazelton, T. B., Koslowski, B. and Main, M. (1974) 'The origins of reciprocity: The early infant–mother interaction', in Bloom, M. and Rosenblum, L. A., eds, *The Effect of the Infant on its Caregiver*. New York: Wiley, pp. 49–76.

Brierley, J. (1987) *Give Me a Child Until He is Seven: Brain Studies in Early Childhood Education*. London: The Falmer Press.

Brisch, K.-H. (2004) *Treating Attachment Disorders: From Theory to Therapy*. New York and London: The Guilford Press.

Brody, G.H., Stoneham, Z., Davis, C. H. and Crapps, J. M. (1991) 'Observation of the role relations and behaviour between older children with mental retardation and their younger siblings', *American Journal on Mental Retardation*, 95: 527–36.

Brody, V. (1997) *The Dialogue of Touch. Developmental Play Therapy*. Northvale, NJ: Jason Aronson.

Brosnan, M., Scott, F., Fox, S. and Pye, J. (2004) 'Gestalt processing in autism: failure to process perceptual relationships and the implications for contextual understanding', *Journal of Child Psychology and Psychiatry*, 45(3): 459–69.

Brown-Macdonald, B. (2004) 'Bridging the gap between play therapy and cutting edge attachment theory', conference paper, Play Therapy and Child Psychotherapy World Congress.

Bruce, T. (1991) *Time to Play in Early Childhood Education*. London: Hodder and Stoughton.

Bruner, J. S. (1966) *Towards a Theory of Instruction*. Cambridge, MA: Harvard University Press.

Bruner, J. S. (1981) 'The social context of language acquisition', *Language and Communication*, 1: 155–78.

Bruner, J. S. (1983) *Child's Talk: Learning to Use Language*. New York: Norton.

Bruner, J. S. (1986) 'Play, thought and language prospects', *Quarterly Review of Education*, 16:77–83.

Bruner, J. S. (1990) *Acts of Meaning*. Cambridge, MA: Harvard University Press.

Bruner, J. S., Jolly, A. and Sylva, K. (1977) *Play: Its Role in Development and Evolution*. Harmondsworth: Penguin.

Burns, R. (1982) *Self-concept Development and Education*. London: Holt, Rinehart and Winston.

Burton, P. (2002) *Using Video Interactive Guidance (VIG) in a Learning Disabilities Team*. Advancing Health Care Practice. Foundation of Nursing Studies, Project Report.

Capps, I., Sigman, M. and Mundy, P. (1994) 'Attachment security in children with autism', *Development and Psychopathology*, 6: 249–61.

Carpenter, B. (ed.) (1997) *Families in Context: Emerging Trends in Family Support and Early Intervention*. London: David Fulton Publishers.

Carpenter, M., Nagel, K. and Tomasello, M. (1998) 'Social cognition, joint attention and communicative competence from 9 to 15 months of age'. Monographs of the Society for Research in Child Development, 63.

Carr, A. (2004) *Positive Psychology: The Science of Happiness and Human Strengths*. London: Brunner-Routledge.

Carroll, J. (1998) *Introduction to Therapeutic Play*. Oxford: Blackwell Science.

Carter, S. (1998) 'Neuroendocrine perspectives on social attachment and love', *Psychoneuroendocrenology*, 23(3): 779–818.

Case, C. and Dalley, T. (1992) *The Handbook of Art Therapy: An Introduction to Art Therapy in Theory and Practice*. London: Routledge.

Case, R. (1991) 'Stages in the development of the young child's first sense of self', *Developmental Review*, 11: 210–30.

Cattanach, A. (1997) *Children's Stories in Play Therapy*. London: Jessica Kingsley Publishers.

Chandler, S., Christie, P., Newson, E. and Prevezer, W. (2002) 'Developing a diagnostic and intervention package for 2–3-year-olds with autism: outcomes of the Frameworks for Communication approach', *Autism: the International Journal of Research and Practice*, 6(1): 47–70.

Chazan, S. (2002) *Profiles of Play: Assessing and Observing Structure and Process in Play Therapy*. London: Jessica Kingsley Publishers.

Christie, P., Newson, E., Newson, J. and Prevezer, W. (1992) 'An interactive approach to language, and communication for non-speaking children', in Lane, D.A. and Miller, A., eds, *Child and Adolescent Therapy: A Handbook*. Buckingham: Open University Press.

Clements, J. and Zarkowska, E. (2001) *Behavioural Concerns and Autistic Spectrum Disorders: Explanations and Strategies for Change*. London: Jessica Kingsley Publishers.

Cogher, L. (1999) 'The use of non-directive play in speech and language therapy', *Child Language Teaching and Therapy*, 15(1): 7–15.

Cohen, L. (2001) *Playful Parenting*. New York: Ballantine Books.

Collins, R. (1981) 'On the microfoundations of macrosociology', *American Journal of Sociology*, 86: 984–1014.

Coltman, P., Petyaeva, D. and Anghileri, J. (2002) 'Scaffolding learning through meaningful tasks and adult interaction', *Early Years*, 22(1): 39–49.

Cooper, P. (ed.) (1995) *Understanding and Supporting Children with Emotional and Behavioural Difficulties*. London: Jessica Kingsley Publishers.

Corke, M. (2002) *Approaches to Communication Through Music*. London: David Fulton Publishers.

Courchesne, E., Karnes, C. M., Davis, H. R., Ziccardi, R., Carper, R. A., Tigue, A. D., Chisum, H. J., Moses, P., Pierce, K., Lord, D., Lincoln, A. J., Pizzo, S., Schrieban, L., Haas, R. H., Akshoomoff, N. A. and Courchesne, R. Y. (2001) 'Unusual brain growth patterns in early life in patients with autistic disorder: an MRI study', *Neurology* 57(2): 245–54.

Craft, A. (2005) 'Changes in the landscape of creativity in education', in Wilson, A., ed., *Creativity in Primary Education*. Exeter: Learning Matters.

Csikszentmihalyi, M. (1990) *Flow: The Psychology of Optimal Experience*. New York: Harper Perennial.

Csikszentmihalyi, M. (1993) *The Evolving Self*. New York: Harper Collins.

Csikszentmihalyi, M. (1996) *Creativity: Flow and the Psychology of Discovery and Invention*. New York: Harper Perennial.

Dallos, R. (2006) *Attachment Narrative Therapy: Integrating Narrative, Systemic and Attachment Therapies*. Maidenhead: Open University Press.

Damiani, V. B. (1999) 'Responsibility and adjustment in siblings with disabilities: update and review', *Families in Society*, 80: 34–40.

Damon, W. and Hart, D. (1992) 'Self understanding and its role in social and moral development', in Bornstein, M. and Lamb, M., eds, *Developmental Psychology*. Hillsdale, NJ: Erlbaum.

Dau, E. (ed.) (1999) *Child's Play: Revisiting Play in Early Childhood Settings*. Sydney: Maclennan and Petty Pty.

Dawson, G. and Adams, A. H. (1984) 'Imitation and social responsiveness in autistic children', *Journal of Abnormal Child Psychology*, 12: 209–66.

Dawson, G. and Fischer, K. W. (eds) (1994) *Human Behaviour and the Developing Brain*. New York: The Guilford Press.

Dawson, G. and Osterling, J. (1997) 'Early intervention in autism', in Guralnick, M., ed., *The Effectiveness of Early Intervention*. Baltimore, MD: Brookes.

DeMyer, M., Barton, S., DeMyer, W., Norton, J. A., Allen, J. and Steele, R. (1973) 'Prognosis in autism: A follow up study', *Journal of Autism and Childhood Schizophrenia*, 3: 199–246.

Denham, S. (1998) *Emotional Development in Young Children*. New York: The Guilford Press.

Department for Education and Employment (DfEE) (2000) *Curriculum Guidance for the Foundation Stage*. London: QCA Publications.

Department for Education and Skills (DfES) (2003) *Excellence and Enjoyment: A Strategy for Primary Schools*. London: DfES Publications

Dissanayake, C. and Crossley, S. A. (1996) 'Proximity and social behaviours in autism: evidence for attachment', *Journal of Child Psychology and Psychiatry*, 37: 149–56.

Dixon, B. (1990) *Playing Them False: A Study of Children's Toys, Games and Puzzles*. Stoke-on-Trent: Trentham Books.

Donaldson, M. (1984) *Children's Minds*. London: Fontana.

Drewes, A. (2001) 'Play objects and play spaces', in Drewes, A., Carey, L. and Schaefer, C., eds, *School-based Play Therapy*. New York: Wiley and Sons.

Duffy, B. (1998) *Supporting Creativity and Imagination in the Early Years*. Buckingham, UK: Open University Press.

Dunham, P., Dunham, F., Hurshman, A. and Alexander, T. (1989) 'Social contingency effects on subsequent perceptual-cognitive tasks in young infants', *Child Development*, 60: 1468–96.

Dunn, J. (1993) *Young Children's Close Relationships: Beyond Attachment*. Newbury Park, CA: Sage Publications.

Dunn, J. and McGuire, S. (1992) 'Sibling and peer relationship in childhood', *Journal of Child Psychology and Psychiatry*, 33: 67–105.

Dyson, L. L. (1989) 'Adjustment of siblings of handicapped children: a comparison', *Journal of Paediatric Psychology*, 14: 215–29.

Edwards, B. (1999) *The New Drawing on the Right Side of the Brain*. New York: Penguin Putnam.

Eisenberg, N., Zhou, Q., Spinrad, T. L., Valiente, C., Fabes, R. A. and Liew, J. (2005) 'Relations amongst positive parenting, children's effortful control and externalising problems: A three-wave longitudinal study.' *Child Development*, 76(5): 1055–71.

Erikson, E. (1980) *Identity and the Life Cycle*, 2nd edn. New York: W.W. Norton.

Evans, K. and Dubowski, J. (2001) *Art Therapy with Children on the Autistic Spectrum*. London: Jessica Kingsley Publishers.

Eysenck, M. (2004) *Psychology: An International Perspective*. Hove: Psychology Press.

Farmer, M. (2002) 'Social interactionism in practice', in Griffiths, F., *Communication Counts: Speech and Language Difficulties in the Early Years*. London: David Fulton Publishers.

Feuerstein, R. S. (2000) 'Dynamic cognitive assessment and the instrumental enrichment program: origins and development', in Kozulin, A. and Rand, Y., eds, *Experience of Mediated Learning: An Impact on Feuerstein's Theory in Education and Psychology*. New York: Pergamon, pp. 147–65.

Feuerstein, R. S., Rand, Y., Hoffman, M. and Miller, R. (1980) *Instrumental Enrichment: An Intervention Program for Cognitive Modifiability*. Jerusalem: ICELP Press.

Feuerstein, R., Lein, P. and Tannenbaum, A. (eds) (1991) *Mediated Learning Experience*. London: Freund.

Field, T. (1993) 'Infant massage', *Zero to Three*, October/November.

Field, T., Lasko, D., Munday, P., Henteleff, T., Taplins, S. and Dowling, M. (1997) 'Autistic children's attentiveness and responsivity improved after touch therapy', *Journal of Autism and Developmental Disorders*, 27(3): 329–34.

Flavell, J. and Miller, P. (1998) 'Social cognition', in Kuhn, D. and Siegler, R., eds, *Handbook of Child Psychology: Cognition, Perception and Language*, Vol. 2, 5th edn. New York: Wiley, pp. 851–88.

Flavell, J., Green, F. and Flavell, E. (1993) 'Children's understanding of a stream of consciousness', *Child Development*, 64: 387–98.

Fogel, A. (1995) 'Relational narratives of the pre-linguistic self', in Rochat, P., ed., *The Self in Early Infancy: Theory and Research*. Amsterdam: Elsevier.

Fonagy, P. (2003) 'The development of psychopathology from infancy to adulthood: The mysterious unfolding of disturbance in time', *Infant Mental Health Journal*, 24(3): 212–39.

Fonagy, P., Steele, M., Steele, H., Moran, G. S. and Higgit, A. C. (1991) 'The capacity for understanding mental states: The reflective self in parent and child and its significance for security off attachment', *Infant Mental Health Journal*, 12: 201–18.

Fosha, D. (2001) 'The dyadic regulation of affect', *Psychotherapy in Practice*, 57(2): 227–42.

Foster, S. (1990) *The Communicative Competence of Young Children*. New York: Longman.

Franklin, M. (1994) 'Art, play and symbolisation in childhood and beyond: reconsidering connections', *Teachers College Record*, 95(4): 526–41.

Frith, U. (1989) *Autism: Explaining the Enigma*. Oxford: Blackwell.

Froebel, F. (1974) *The Education of Man*. Clifton, NJ: Kelley.

Gergen, K. (1994) *Realities and Relationships: Soundings in Social Construction*. Cambridge, MA: Harvard University Press.

Gerhardt, S. (2004) *Why Love Matters: How Affection Shapes a Baby's Brain*. Hove: Brunner-Routledge.

Gil, E. (1994) *Play in Family Therapy*. New York: The Guilford Press.

Gillberg, C. and Coleman, M. (1992) *The Biology of Autistic Syndromes*, 2nd edn. Clinics in Developmental Medicine, 126. London: MacKeith Press.

Girolametto, L., Verbey, M. and Tannock, R. (1994) 'Improving joint engagement in parent-child interaction: an intervention study', *Journal of Early Intervention*, 18(2):155–67.

Goldschmied, E. and Jackson, S. (1994) *People Under Three: Young Children in Day Care*. New York: Routledge.

Gopnik, A., Meltzoff, A. and Kuhl, P. (1999) *How Babies Think: The Science of Childhood*. London: Weidenfeld and Nicholson.

Grandin, T. (1992) 'Calming effects of deep touch pressure in patients with autistic disorder, college students and animals', *Journal of Child and Adolescent Psychopharmacology*, 1(2): 63–70.

Green, V. (ed.) (2003) *Emotional Development in Psychoanalysis, Attachment Theory and Neuroscience*. New York: Brunner-Routledge.

Greenspan, S. I. and Lieberman, A. F. (1994) 'Representational elaboration and differentiation: a clinical-quantitative approach to assessment of 2–4-year-olds', in Slade, A. and Palmer Wolf, D., eds, *Children at Play: Clinical and Developmental Approaches to Meaning and Representation*. New York: Oxford University Press.

Greenspan, S. I. and Wieder, S. (1998) *The Child with Special Needs: Encouraging Intellectual and Emotional Growth*. Reading, MA: Perseus Books.

Grelotti, D., Gauthier, I. and Shultz, R. (2002) 'Social interest and the development of cortical face specialisation: what autism teaches us about face processing', *Developmental Psychobiology*, 40(3): 213–25.

Grendlin, E. (1991) 'On emotion in therapy', in Safran, J. D. and Greenberg, L. S., eds, *Emotion, Psychotherapy and Change*. New York: The Guilford Press.

Griffiths, F. (2002) *Communication Counts: Speech and Language Difficulties in the Early Years*. London: David Fulton Publishers.

Hadley, E. (2002) 'Playful disruptions', *Early Years*, 22(1): 9–17.

Happé, F. (1999) 'Autism: Cognitive deficit or cognitive style?', *Trends in Cognitive Science,* 3: 216–22.

Harris, M. (1992) *Language Experience and Early Language Development: From Input to Uptake*. Hove: Lawrence Erlbaum.

Harter, S. (1998) 'The development of self-representations', in Eisenberg, N., ed., *Handbook of Child Psychology*, Vol. 3. Social, Emotional and Personality Development. New York: Wiley.

Hazler, R. and Barwick, N. (2001) *The Therapeutic Environment*. Buckingham, UK: Open University Press.

Heimann, M., Ullstadius, E., Dahlgren, S.-O. and Gillberg, C. (1992) 'Imitation in autism: A preliminary research note', *Behavioural Neurology*, 5: 219–27.

Herbert, E. and Carpenter, B. (1994) 'Fathers: the secondary partners: professional perceptions and a father's reflections', *Children and Society*, 8(1): 31–41.

Hobson, R. P. (1989) 'Beyond cognition: A theory of autism', in Dawson G., ed., *Autism: New Perspectives on Diagnosis, Nature and Treatment*. New York: The Guilford Press.

Hobson, R. P. (1993) *Autism and the Development of Mind*. Hove: Psychology Press.

Hobson, R. P. (2002) *A Cradle of Thought*. Oxford: Macmillan.

Hobson, R. P. (2004) 'Understanding the self and other', *Behavioral and Brain Sciences*, 27: 109–10.

Hobson, R. P., Ouston, J. and Lee, A. (1988) 'What's in a face? The case for autism', *British Journal of Psychology*, 79: 411–53.

Hollander, E., Novotny, S., Hanratty, M., Yaffe, R., DeCaria, C., Aronowitz, B. and Mosovich, S. (2003) 'Oxytocin infusion reduces repetitive behaviors in adults with autistic and Asperger's disorders', *Neuropsychopharmacology*, 28: 193–8.

Holmes, J. (2001) *The Search for The Secure Base*. London: Brunner-Routledge.

Hornby, G. (1995) *Working with Parents of Children with Special Needs*. London: Cassell.

Hughes, D. (1997) *Facilitating Developmental Attachment*. Northvale, NJ: Aronson.

Hughes, D. (1999) *Building the Bonds of Attachment*. New York: Guilford Press.

Hughes, D. (2003) 'Psychological interventions for the spectrum of attachment disorders and intrafamilial trauma', *Attachment and Human Development*, 5(3): 271–6.

Hughes, D. (2006) *Dyadic Developmental Psychotherapy. Conference Paper. Awakening Attachment in Troubled Children and Adults*. London: The Centre for Child Mental Health.

Hughes, F. P. (1991) *Children, Play and Development*. Boston, MA: Allyn and Bacon.

Hutt, C. (1979) 'Play in the under 5s: form, development and function', in Howells, J.G., ed., *Modern Perspectives in the Psychiatry of Infancy*. New York: Brunner/Marcel.

Insel, T. R. (1997) 'A neurobiological basis of social attachment', *Journal of American Psychiatry*, 154: 726–35.

Isaacs, S. (1966) *Intellectual Growth in Young Children*. London: Routledge and Kegan Paul.

Jackson, L. (2002) *Freaks, Geeks and Asperger Syndrome: A User Guide to Adolescence*. London: Jessica Kingsley Publishers.

James, B. (1994) *Handbook for Treatment of Attachment–Trauma Problems in Children*. New York: Lexington Books.

Jarrold, C. (2003) 'A review of research into pretend play in autism', *Autism: The International Journal of Research and Practice*, 7(4): 379–90.

Jarrold, C., Boucher, J. and Russell J. (1997) 'Language profiles in children with autism', *Autism: The International Journal of Research and Practice*, 1(1): 57–76.

Jennings, S. (1999) *Introduction to Developmental Play Therapy*. London: Jessica Kingsley Publishers.

Jennings, S. and Minde, Å. (1993) *Art Therapy and Dramatherapy*. London: Jessica Kingsley Publishers.

Jernberg, A. M. (1976) 'Theraplay Technique', in Shaefer, C.E., ed., *Therapeutic Uses of Children's Play*. New York: Jason Aronson.

Jernberg, A. M. and Booth, P. (2001) *Theraplay: Helping Parents and Children Build Better Relationships Through Attachment-Based Play*, 2nd edn. San Francisco: Jossey-Bass.

John-Steiner, V. (2000) *Creative Collaboration*. New York: Oxford University Press.

Jones, C. and Schwartz, I. (2004) 'Siblings, peers and adults: differential effects of models for children with autism', *Topics in Early Childhood Special Education*, 24(4): 187–98.

Jones, S. (1996) 'Imitation or exploration? Young infants' matching of adults' oral gestures', *Child Development*, 67: 1952–69.

Jontes, B. (2005) 'Developing a Child's Personal Artistic Identity', conference paper, Art in Early Childhood, Roehampton University, UK.

Jordan, R. (2001) *Autism with Severe Learning Difficulties*. London: Souvenir Press (Educational and Academic).

Jordan, R. (2003) 'Social play and autistic spectrum disorders', *Autism: The International Journal of Research and Practice*, 7(4): 347–60.

Jordan, R. and Libby, S. (2000) 'Developing and using play in the classroom', in Powell, S. and Jordan, R., eds, *Autism and Learning: A Guide to Good Practice*. London: David Fulton Publishers.

Jordan, R. and Powell, S. (1995) *Understanding and Teaching Children with Autism*. Chichester: John Wiley and Sons.

Jordan, R., Jones, G. and Murray D. (1998) *Educational Interventions for Children with Autism: A Literature Review of Recent and Current Research*. London: DfEE.

Jung, C. (1952) 'Synchronicity: An acausal connecting principle', in Jung C. G., Adhler, G. and Hull, R. F. C., *The Collected Works of Carl Gustav Jung*, Vol. 8. The Structure and Dynamics of the Psyche. Princeton, NJ: Princeton University Press.

Kalff, D. (1980) *Sandplay: A Psychotherapeutic Approach to the Psyche*. Santa Monica, CA: Sigo Press.

Kaminsky, L. and Dewey, D. (2001) 'Sibling relationships of children with autism', *Journal of Autism and Developmental Disorders*, 31: 399–411.

Kanner, L. (1943) 'Autistic disturbances of affective contact', *Nervous Child*, 2: 217–50.

Kaufman, B. (1994) *Son-Rise: The Miracle Continues*. Tiburon, CA: H. J. Kramer.

Keenan, T. (2002) *An Introduction to Child Development*. London: Sage Publications.

Kellie-Smith, G. (2003) 'Difficulty with learning or learning to be difficult?', in Archer, C. and Burnell, A., eds, *Trauma, Attachment and Family Permanence: Fear Can Stop You Loving*. London: Jessica Kingsley Publishers.

Kernberg, O. (1980) *Internal World and External Reality*. New York: Jason Aronson.

Koegel, R., Dyer, K. and Bell, L. (1987) 'The influence of child-preferred activities on autistic children's social behaviour', *Journal of Applied Behavioural Analysis*, 20: 243–52.

Kozulin, A. and Rand, Y. (eds) (2000) *Experience of Mediated Learning: An Impact of Feuerstein's Theory in Psychology and Education*. Oxford: Elsevier Science.

Laevers, F. (ed.) (1994) *Defining and Assessing Quality in Early Childhood Education*. Studia Paedogogica, Leuven: Leuven University Press.

Laevers, F. (1997) 'Assessing the quality of childcare provision: "Involvement" as criterion', *Researching Early Childhood*, 3: 151–65.

Lamb, M. E. (1977) 'Father–infant and mother–infant interaction in the first year of life', *Child Development*, 48:167–81.

Lamb, M. E. (1981) *The Role of the Father in Child Development*. New York: Wiley.

Landreth, G. (2001) *Innovations in Play Therapy: Issues, Process and Special Populations*. Philadelphia, PA: Brunner-Routledge.

Landreth, G. (2002) *Play Therapy: The Art of the Relationship*, 2nd edn. Philadelphia, PA: Brunner-Routledge.

Lantz, J., Nelson, J. and Loftin, R. (2004) 'Guiding children with autism in play: Applying the integrated play group model in school settings', *Teaching Exceptional Children*, 37(2), 8–14.

Laschinger, B. (2004) 'Attachment theory and The John Bowlby Memorial Lecturer: a short history', in White, K., ed., *Touch, Attachment and the Body*. London: Karnac.

Lawson, W. (2001) *Understanding and Working with the Spectrum of Autism: An Insider's View*. London: Jessica Kingsley Publishers.

Lawson, W. (2003) *Build Your Own Life: A Self-Help Guide to Asperger Syndrome*. London: Jessica Kingsley Publishers.

Lazarus, R. (1991) *Emotion and Adaptation*. New York: Oxford University Press.

LeDoux, J. (1996) *The Emotional Brain: The Mysterious Underpinnings of Emotional Life*. New York: Touchstone.

Le Goff, D. B. (2004) 'Use of Lego as a therapeutic medium for improving social competence', *Journal of Autism and Developmental Disorders*, 34(5): 557–71.

Lewis, V. (2003) 'Play and language in children with autism', *Autism: The International Journal of Research and Practice*, 7(4): 391–400.

Lewis, V. and Boucher, J. (1988) 'Spontaneous, instructed and elicited play in relatively able autistic children', *British Journal of Developmental Psychology*, 6: 325–9.

Libby, S., Powell, S., Messer, D. and Jordan, R. (1998) 'Spontaneous play in children with autism: A reappraisal', *Journal of Autism and Developmental Disorders*, 28(6): 487–97.

Lieberman, J. (1977) *Playfulness: Its Relationship to Imagination and Creativity*. New York: Academic Press.

Longhorn, F. (1988) *A Sensory Curriculum For Very Special People: A Practical Approach to Curriculum Planning*. London: Souvenir Press (Educational and Academic).

Longhorn, F. (1993) *Prerequisites To Learning for Very Special People*. Wootton: Catalyst Education Resources.

Longhorn, F. (2002) 'Assessing happiness for very special learners', *SLD Experience*, Summer, 33: 21–23.

Lowenfeld, M. (1979) *The World Technique*. London: George, Allen and Unwin.

McGee, J., Manalscino, J. F., Dobbs, D. and Menousek P. (1987) *Gentle Teaching: A Non-aversive Approach to Helping Persons with Mental Retardation*. New York: Human Sciences Press.

McHale, S. M. and Gamble, W. C. (1987) 'Sibling relationships and adjustment of children with disabled brothers and sisters', *Developmental Psychology*, 25: 421–29.

McHale, S. M. and Harris V. S. (1992) 'Children's experience with disabled and nondisabled siblings: links with personal adjustment and relationship evaluation', in Boer, F. and Dunn, J., eds, *Children's Relationships with Their Siblings: Developmental and Clinical Implications*. Hillsdale, NY: Lawrence Erlbaum Associates.

McMahon, L. (1992) *A Handbook of Play Therapy*. London: Routledge.

Mahoney, G. and Macdonald, J. (2004) *Responsive Teaching: Parent-mediated Developmental Intervention*. Case Western Reserve University, OH: ProEd .

Mahoney, G. and Perales, F. (2003) 'Using relationship-focused intervention to enhance the social-emotional functioning of young children with autism spectrum disorders', *Topics in Early Childhood Special Education*, 23(2): 77–89.

Mahoney, G. and Powell, A. (1988) 'Modifying parent–child interaction: Enhancing development of handicapped children', *Journal of Special Education*, 22: 82–96.

Mäkelä, J. (2003) 'What makes Theraplay® effective: Insights from developmental sciences', *The Theraplay® Institute Newsletter*, Fall/Winter.

Malaguzzi, L. (1993) 'For an education based on relationship', *Young Children*, 49(1): 9–12.

Mandler, J. M. (1996) 'Pre-verbal representation and language', in Bloom, P., Peterson, M., Nadel, L. and Garrett, M., eds, *Language and Space*. London: Bradford Books.

Maratos, O. (1998) 'Psychoanalysis and the management of pervasive developmental disorders, including autism', in Trevarthen, C., Aitken, K., Papoudi, D. and Robarts, J., eds, *Children with Autism: Diagnosis and Interventions to Meet their Needs*. London: Jessica Kingsley Publishers.

Marcus, D. and Nelson C. (2001) 'Neural bases and development of face recognition in autism', *CNS Spectrums: The International Journal of Neuropsychiatric Medicine*, 6(1): 36–59.

Marrone, M. (1998) *Attachment and Interaction*. London: Jessica Kingsley Publishers.

Meadows, S. (1993) *The Child as Thinker: The Development and Acquisition of Cognition in Childhood*. London: Routledge.

Meins, E., Fernyhough, C., Wainwright, R., Clark-Carter, D., Das Gupta, M., Fradley, E. and Tuckey, M. (2003) 'Pathways to understanding mind: construct validity and predictive validity of maternal mind-mindedness', *Child Development*, 4: 1194–211.

Meltzoff, A. N. and Gopnik, A. (1993) 'The role of imitation in understanding persons and developing a theory of mind', in Baron-Cohen, S., Tager-Flusberg, H. and Cohen, D.J., eds, *Understanding Others' Minds: Perspectives from Autism*. Oxford: Oxford University Press.

Ministry of Education (1996) *Te Whāriki Early Childhood Curriculum*. Wellington, NZ: Learning Media.

Minuchin, S. (1974) *Families and Family Therapy*. Cambridge, MA: Harvard University.

Modahl, C. (1992) 'Does oxytocin deficiency mediate social deficits in autism?', *Journal of Autism and Developmental Disorders*, 22(3): 449–51.

Modahl, C., Green, L., Fein, D., Morris, M., Waterhouse, L., Feinstein, C. and Levin, H. (1998) 'Plasma oxytocin levels in autistic children', *Biological Psychiatry*, 43(4): 270–7.

Moor, J. (2002) *Playing, Laughing and Learning with Children on the Autistic Spectrum*. London: Jessica Kingsley.

Moustakas, C. (1982) 'Emotional adjustment and the play therapy process', in Landreth, G., ed., *Play Therapy: Dynamics of the Process of Counselling Children*. Springfield, IL: Charles C. Thomas.

Moyles, J. (1989) *Just Playing? The Role and Status of Play in Early Childhood Education*. Buckingham, UK: Open University Press.

Moyles, J. (ed) (1994) *The Excellence of Play*. Buckingham, UK: Open University Press.

Mukaddes, N., Kaynak, N., Kinali, G., Besikci, H. and Isever, H. (2004) 'Psychoeducational treatment of children with autism and reactive attachment disorder', *Autism: The International Journal of Research and Practice*, 8(1): 101–9.

Mukhopadhyay, T. R. (2000) *Beyond the Silence: My Life, the World and Autism*. London: NAS Publications.

Nadel, J. and Pezé, A. (1993) 'Immediate imitation as a basis for primary communication in toddlers and autistic children', in Nadel, J. and Camioni, L., eds, *New Perspectives in Early Communicative Development*. London: Routledge.

Nadel, J., Guérini, C., Pezé, A. and Rivet, C. (1999) 'The evolving nature of imitation as a format for communication', in Nadel, J. and Butterworth, G., eds, *Imitation in Infancy*. Cambridge: Cambridge University Press.

Natiello, P. (2001) *The Person-Centred Approach: A Passionate Presence*. Ross-on-Wye: PCC Books.

National Advisory Committee on Creative and Cultural Education (1999) *All Our Futures: Creativity, Culture and Education*. London: DfEE Publications.

Neaum, S. and Tallack, J. (1997) *Good Practice in Implementing the Pre-school Curriculum*. London: Nelson Thornes.

Neisser, U. (1976) *Cognition and Reality: Principles and Implications of Cognitive Psychology*. New York: W. H. Freeman.

Newson, J. (1979) 'The growth of shared understandings between infant and caregiver', in Bullowa M., ed., *Before Speech*. Cambridge: Cambridge University Press.

Newson, J. and Newson E. (1979) *Toys and Playthings*. London: Allen and Unwin.

Newton, C. (1988) ' "Who knows me best?" Levels of participation in a child's world', *Educational Psychology in Practice*, 3(4): 35–9.

National Foundation for Educational Research (NFER) (2002) *Early Years Education: An International Perspective*. London: QCA Publications.

Nind, M. and Cochrane, S. (2003) 'Inclusive curricula? Pupils on the margins of special schools', in Nind, M., Sheehy, K. and Simmons, K., eds, *Inclusive Education: Learners and Learning Contexts*. London: David Fulton Publishers.

Nind, M. and Hewett, D. (1994) *Access to Communication*. London: David Fulton Publishers.

Nutbrown, C. (1999) *Threads of Thinking*, 2nd edn. London: Paul Chapman Publishing.

Oaklander, V. (1989) *Windows to Our Children: Gestalt Therapy Approach to Children and Adolescents*. New York: The Centre for Gestalt Development.

Ouvry, C. (1991) 'Access for pupils with profound and multiple learning difficulties', in Ashdown, R., Carpenter, B. and Bovair, K., eds, *The Curriculum Challenge: Access to the National Curriculum for Pupils with Learning Difficulties*. London: Falmer Press.

Ozonoff, S. (1995) 'Executive functions in autism', in Schopler, E. and Mesibov, G. B., eds, *Learning and Cognition in Autism*. New York: Plenum Press.

Panskepp, J. (1993) 'Commentary on the possible role of oxytocin in autism' (Letter to Editor), *Journal of Autism and Developmental Disorders*, 23(3): 567–9.

Panskepp, J. (1997) Interview with Professor Jaak Panskepp (www.autism.org) accessed 4 May 2006.

Panskepp, J. (1998) *Affective Neuroscience: The Foundations of Animal and Human Emotions*. Oxford: Oxford University Press.

Panskepp, J. (2001) 'The psychobiological consequences of infant emotions', *Infant Mental Health Journal*, 22(1/2): 133.

Pavlicevic, M. (1990) 'Dynamic interplay in clinical improvisation', *Journal of British Music Therapy*, 4(2): 5–9.

Pearmain, R. (2001) *The Heart of Listening: Attentional Qualities in Psychotherapy*. London: Continuum.

Pearson, J. (ed.) (1996) *Discovering the Self through Drama and Movement*. London: Jessica Kingsley Publishers.

Peeters, T. and Gillberg, C. (1999) *Autism: Medical and Educational Aspects*, 2nd edn. London: Whurr Publishers.

Pert, C. (1999) *Molecules of Emotion: The Science Behind Mind-Body Medicine*. London: Simon and Schuster UK.

Peter, M. (1994) *Drama for All*. London: David Fulton Publishers.

Peter, M. (2000) 'Developing drama for children with autism', *Good Autism Practice*, 1(1): 9–20.

Peter, M. (2003) 'Drama, Narrative and Early Learning', *British Journal of Special Education*, 30(1): 21–7.

Piaget, J. (1953) *The Origins of Intelligence in the Child*. London: Routledge and Kegan Paul.

Piaget, J. (1955) *The Language and Thought of the Child*. London: Routledge and Kegan Paul.

Piaget, J. (1962) *Play, Dreams and Imitation in Childhood*. London: Routledge and Kegan Paul.

Piaget, J. (1977) *The Grasp of Consciousness: Action and Concept in the Young Child*. London: Routledge and Kegan Paul.

Piers, M. W. and Landau, G. M. (1980) *The Gift of Play and Why Children Cannot Thrive Without It*. New York: Walker and Company.

Pinciotti, P. (1993) 'Creative drama and young children: The dramatic learning connection', *Arts Education Policy Review*, 94(6): 24–9.

Pinney, R. (1992) *Creative Listening*, 5th edn. London: Children's Hours Trust.

Potter, C. and Whittaker, C. (2001) *Enabling Communication in Children with Autism*. London: Jessica Kingsley Publishers.

Powell, S. and Jordan, R. (eds) (2001) *Autism and Learning: A Guide to Good Practice*. London: David Fulton Publishers.

Powell, T. H. and Gallagher, P. A. (1993) *Brothers and Sisters: a Special Part of Exceptional Families*, 2nd edn. Baltimore, MD: Paul Brookes Publishing Company.

Pretti-Frontczac, K. and Bricker, D. (2004) *An Activity-based Approach to Early Intervention*, 3rd edn. Baltimore, MD: Paul Brookes Publishing.

Prevezer, W. (1998) *Entering into Interaction*. Nottingham: Nottingham Regional Society for Adults and Children with Autism.

Prevezer, W. (2000) 'Music interaction and children with autism', in Powell S., ed., *Helping Children with Autism to Learn*. London: David Fulton Publishers.

Reed, P., Osborne, L. and Corness, M. (2004) The Effectiveness of Early Intervention Programmes for Autistic Spectrum Disorders: A Report for the South East Regional Special Educational Needs Partnership. Available on www.mugsy.org

Richer, J. and Coates, S. (2001) *Autism: The Search for Coherence*. London: Jessica Kingsley Publishers.

Richter, M. M. and Volmar, F. R. (1994) 'Reactive attachment disorder of infancy and early childhood', *Journal of American Academy of Child and Adolescent Psychiatry*, 33(3): 328–32.

Rinehart, N., Bradshaw, J., Moss, S., Brereton, A. and Tonge, B. (2000) 'Atypical interference of local detail of global processing in high functioning autism and Asperger's disorder', *Journal of Child Psychology and Psychiatry*, 41: 769–78.

Rivers, J. and Stoneham, Z. (2003) 'Sibling relationships when a child has autism: marital stress and support coping', *Journal of Autism and Developmental Disorders*, 33(4): 383–94.

Robinson, K. (2001) *Out of Our Minds: Learning to be Creative*. Chichester: Capstone.

Rogers, C. (1961) *On Becoming A Person*. New York: Houghton Mifflin.

Rogers, C. (1980) *A Way of Being*. New York: Houghton Mifflin.

Rogers, S. J. and Pennington, B.F. (1991) 'A theoretical approach to the deficits in infantile autism', *Development and Psychopathology*, 3: 137–62.

Rogers, S. J., Ozonoff, S. and Maslin-Cole, C. (1993) 'Developmental aspects of attachment behavior in young children with pervasive developmental disorders', *Journal of American Academy of Child and Adolescent Psychiatry*, 32: 1274–82.

Rowland, S. (1987) 'An interpretive model of teaching and learning', in Pollard A., ed. *Children and Their Primary Schools*. London: Falmer Press.

Russ, S. W. (1993) *Affect and Creativity: The Role of Affect and Play in the Creative Process*. Hillsdale, NJ: Lawrence Erlbaum Associates.

Russ, S. W. (2003) 'Play and creativity', *Scandinavian Journal of Educational Research*, 47: 291–303.

Rutter, M. (1983) 'Cognitive deficits in the pathogenesis of autism', *Journal of Child Psychology and Psychiatry*, 24: 513–31.

Rutter, M. (1997) 'Clinical implications of attachment concepts: retrospect and prospect', in Atkinson, L. and Zucker, K., eds, *Attachment and Psychopathology*. New York: The Guilford Press.

Ryan, R. M. and Deci, E. L. (2000) 'Self-determination theory and the facilitation of intrinsic motivation, social development and well-being', *American Psychologist*, 55: 68–78.

Sampson, E. E. (1993) *Celebrating the Other*. Boulder, CO: Westview Press.

Sanders, J. L. and Morgan, S. B. (1997) 'Family stress and adjustment as perceived by parents of children with autism or Down syndrome: Implications for intervention', *Child and Family Behavior Therapy*, 19: 305–11.

Sayeed, Z. and Guerin E. (2000) *Early Years Play: A Happy Medium for Assessment and Intervention*. London: David Fulton Publishers.

Schaefer, C. E. (ed.) (1993) *The Therapeutic Powers of Play*. New York: Jason Aronson.

Schaffer, R. (1996) *Social Development*. Oxford: Blackwell Publishers.

Schmidt Neven, R. (1996) *Emotional Milestones from Birth to Adulthood*. London: Jessica Kingsley Publishers.

Schopler, E. and Olley, J. G. (1982) 'Comprehensive educational services for autistic children: the TEACCH model', in Reynolds, C. R. and Gutkin, T. R., eds, *Handbook of School Psychology*. New York: Wiley, pp. 293–301.

Schore, A. (1994) *Affect Regulation and the Origin of the Self: The Neurobiology of Emotional Development*. Hillsdale, NJ: Lawrence Erlbaum Associates.

Schore, A. (1997) 'Early organisation of the nonlinear right brain and development of a predisposition to psychiatric disorders', *Development and Psychopathology*, 9: 595–631.

Schore, A. (2001) 'The effects of early relational trauma on right brain development, affect regulation and infant mental health', *Infant Mental Health Journal*, 22: 201–69.

Schore, A. (2003) 'The development of the right brain', in Green, V., ed., *Emotional Development in Psychoanalysis, Attachment Theory and Neuroscience*. New York: Brunner-Routledge.

Schreibmann, L. (2000) 'Intensive behavioural/psychoeducational treatments for autism: Research needs and future directions', *Journal of Autism and Pervasive Developmental Disorders*, 30: 373–8.

Seach, D. (2005) 'Discovering the self through play and creativity', Conference Paper. Art in Early Childhood. Roehampton University.

Shapiro, T., Sherman, M., Calamari, G. and Koch, D. (1987) 'Attachment in autism and other developmental disorders', *Journal of American Academy of Child and Adolescent Psychiatry*, 26: 480–4.

Sherborne, V. (2001) *Developmental Movement for Children*, 2nd edn. London: Worth Publishing.

Sherratt, D. (2001) 'Play, performance, symbols and affect', in Richer, J. and Coates, S., eds, *Autism: the Search for Coherence*. London: Jessica Kingsley Publishers.

Sherratt, D. (2002) 'Developing pretend play in children with autism: An intervention study', *Autism: The International Journal of Research and Practice*, 6(2): 169–81.

Sherratt, D. and Donald, G. (2004) 'Connectedness: developing a shared construction of affect and cognition in children with autism', *British Journal of Special Education*, 31(1): 10–15.

Sherratt, D. and Peter, M. (2002) *Developing Play and Drama in Children with Autistic Spectrum Disorders*. London: David Fulton Publishers.

Siegel, D. (1995) 'Memory, trauma and psychotherapy: A cognitive science view', *Journal of Psychotherapy Practice and Research*, 4: 93–122.

Siegel, D. (1999) *The Developing Mind: How Relationships and the Brain Interact to Shape Who We Are*. New York: The Guilford Press.

Sigman, M. D., Yirmiya, N. and Capps, L. (1995) 'Social and cognitive understanding in high-functioning children with autism', in Schopler E. and Mesibov G. B., eds, *Learning and Cognition in Autism*. New York: Plenum Press, pp. 159–76.

Singer, D. G. and Singer J. L. (1990) *The House of Make Believe*. Cambridge, MA: Harvard University Press.

Singer, J. A. and Salovey, P. (1993) *The Remembered Self: Emotion and Memory in Personality*. New York: Free Press.

Smilansky, S. and Sheftya, L. (1990) *Facilitating Play: A Medium for Promoting Cognitive, Socioemotional and Academic Development in Young Children*. Gaithersburg, MD: Psychological and Educational Publications.

Smith, I. M. and Bryson, S. E. (1994) 'Imitation and action in autism: A critical review', *Psychological Bulletin*, 116(2): 259–73.

Sroufe, A. (1989) 'Relationships, self and individual adaptation', in Sameroff, A. and Emde, R., eds, *Relationship Disturbances in Early Childhood*. New York: Basic Books, pp. 77–94.

Sroufe, A. (1996) *Emotional Development: The Organisation of Emotional Life in the Early Years*. New York: Cambridge University Press.

Stahmer, A. C. (1995) 'Teaching symbolic play skills to children using pivotal response training', *Journal of Autism and Developmental Disorders*, 25(2): 123–41.

Steele, H. and Steele, M. (1998) 'Attachment and psychoanalysis: Time for a reunion', *Social Development*, 7(11): 92–119.

Steele, H., Steele, M. and Fonagy, P. (1996) 'Association among attachment classifications between mother, fathers and their infants: evidence for a relationship-specific perspective', *Child Development*, 67: 541–55.

Stern, D. (1985) 'Affect attunement', in Call, J. D., Galenson, E. and Tyson, R. L., eds, *Frontiers of Infant Psychiatry*, Vol. 2. New York: Basic Books.

Stern, D. (2003) *The Interpersonal World of the Infant. A View from Psychoanalysis and Developmental Psychology*. London: Karnac.

Stewart, C. (2001) *The Symbolic Impetus: How Creative Fantasy Motivates Development*. London: Free Association Books.

Stone, W. L., Lemanek, K. L., Fischel, P. T., Fernández, M. C. and Altemeier, W. A. (1990) 'Play and imitation skills in the diagnosis of autism in young children', *Paediatrics*, 86(2): 267–72.

Stoneham, Z. (2001) 'Supporting positive relationships during childhood', *Mental Retardation and Developmental Disabilities Research Reviews*, 7: 134–42.

Sunderland, M. (2006) *The Science of Parenting: Practical Guidance on Sleep, Crying, Play and Building Emotional Wellbeing for Life*. London: Dorling Kindersley.

Sussman, F. (1999) *More Than Words: Helping Parents Promote Communication and Social Skills in Children with Autism Spectrum Disorder*. Toronto: The Hanen Center.

Sutton-Smith, B. (1966) 'Piaget on Play: A critique', *Psychological Review*, 12: 285–98.

Sutton-Smith, B. (1986) *Toys as Culture*. New York: Gardner Press.

Sutton-Smith, B. (1994) 'Does play prepare for the future?', in Goldstein J. H., ed., *Toys Play and Child Development*. Cambridge: Cambridge University Press.

Sutton-Smith, B. (1997) *The Ambiguity of Play*. Cambridge, MA: Harvard University Press.

Sylva, K., Roy, C. and Painter, M. (1980) *Childwatching at Playgroup and Nursery*. London: Grant Macintyre.

Tannock, R., Girolametto, L. and Siegel, L. (1992) 'Language intervention with children who have developmental delays: Effects of an early intervention approach', *American Journal on Mental Retardation*, 93: 154–65.

Thomas, N. J. T. (1997) 'A stimulus to the imagination. A review of questioning consciousness: The interplay of imagery, cognition and emotion in the human brain by Ralph D. Ellis', *Psyche*, 3(4): on-line http://psyche.cs.monash.edu.au/v3/psyche-3-04-thomas.html

Thompson, R. A. (1991) 'Emotional regulation and emotional development', *Educational Psychology Review*, 3: 69–307.

Thomson, M. (1997) *On Art and Therapy*. London: Free Association Books

Tomasello, M. and Farrar, M. J. (1986) 'Joint attention and early language', *Child Development*, 57: 1454–63.

Trevarthen, C. (1989) 'Development of early social interactions and the effective regulation of brain growth', in von Euler, C., Forssberg, H. and Lagercrantz, H., eds, *Neurobiology of Infant Behaviour*. Wenner–Gren Center International Symposium Series, Vol. 55. Basingstoke: Macmillan, pp. 191–216.

Trevarthen, C. (1993) 'The function of emotions in early infant communication and development', in Nadel, J. and Camaioni, L., eds, *New Perspectives in Early Communicative Development*. London: Routledge, pp. 48–81.

Trevarthen, C. (1995) 'The child's need to learn a culture', *Children and Society*, 9(1): 5–19.

Trevarthen, C. (2004) 'Intimate contact from birth', in White, K., ed., *Touch, Attachment and the Body*. London: Karnac.

Trevarthen, C. and Aitken, K. (2001) 'Infant intersubjectivity: Research, theory and clinical applications', *Journal of Child Psychology and Psychiatry*, 42(1): 3–38.

Trevarthen, C., Aitken, K., Papoudi, D. and Robarts, J. (1998) *Children with Autism: Diagnosis and Interventions to Meet their Needs*. London: Jessica Kingsley Publishers.

Tronick, E. Z. (1998) 'Dyadically expanded states of consciousness and the process of therapeutic change', *Infant Mental Health Journal*, 19: 290–9.

Tucker, D. M. and Derryberry, D. (1992) 'Motivated attention: Anxiety and the frontal executive functions', *Neuropsychiatry, Neurophysiology and Behavioural Neurology*, 5: 233–52.

Tustin, F. (1981) *Autistic States in Children*. London: Routledge and Kegan Paul.

Uvas-Moberg, K. (1998) 'Oxytocin may mediate the benefits of positive social interaction and emotions', *Psychoneuroendocrinology*, 23(8): 819–35.

van Berckelaer-Onnes, I. A. (2003) 'Promoting early play', *Autism: The International Journal of Research and Practice*, 7(4): 415–23.

Van Dyk, A. and Wiedis, D. (2001) 'Sandplay and assessment techniques with pre-school-age children', in Drewes, A., Carey, L. and Schaefer C., eds, *School Based Play Therapy*. New York: Wiley and Sons.

Vanier, J. (1973) *Tears of Silence*. London: Darton, Longman and Todd.

Verté, S., Roeyers, H. and Buysse, A. (2003) 'Behavioural problems, social competence and self-concept in siblings of children with autism', *Child: Care, Health and Development* 29(3): 193–205.

Vygotsky, L. (1978) *Mind in Society*. Cambridge, MA: Harvard University Press.

Waddell, M. (1998) *Inside Lives: Psychoanalysis and the Growth of Personality*. London: Duckworth.

Walden, T. (1996) 'Social responsivity: judging signals of children with and without developmental delays', *Child Development*, 67: 2074–85.

Walters, C. (2004) 'Developmental factors in puppet play with children and families', Conference Paper, Play Therapy and Child Psychotherapy, World Congress, Chichester, UK.

Warren, B. (ed.) (1993) *Using the Creative Arts in Therapy*. London: Routledge.

Waterhouse, L., Fein, D. and Modahl, C. (1996) 'Neurofunctional mechanisms in autism', *Psychological Review*, 103: 457–89.

Webster, A. (1987) 'Enabling language acquisition: the developmental evidence', *British Psychological Society: division of Educational and Child Psychology Newsletter*, 27: 25–31.

Webster, A., Feiler, A. and Webster, V. (2003) 'Early intensive family intervention and evidence of effectiveness: Lessons from the South West Autism Programme', *Early Child Development and Care. Special Autism Issue*, 173(4): 383–98.

Webster, A., Feiler, A., Webster, V. and Lovell, C. (2004) 'Parental perspectives on early intensive intervention for children diagnosed with autistic spectrum disorder', *Journal of Early Childhood Research*, 2(1): 25–49.

Weinrib, E. L. (2004) *The Sandplay Therapy Process: Images of the Self*. Cloverdale, CA: Temenos Press.

Wells, G. (1986) *The Meaning Makers: Children Learning Language and Using Language to Learn*. Oxford: Heinemann Educational Publishers.

Wentworth, C. (2001) 'Creative Arts Therapy: Neural Systems Integration', *The World of Children*, 4: 49–74.

West, J. (1992) *Child-centred Play Therapy*. London: Arnold.

Wethered, A. (1993) *Movement and Drama in Therapy*. London: Jessica Kingsley Publishers.

Whitaker, P. (2004) 'Fostering communication and shared play between mainstream peers and children with autism: approaches, outcomes and experience', *British Journal of Special Education*, 31(4): 215–22.

Wieder, S. and Greenspan, S. I. (2003) 'Climbing the symbolic ladder in the DIR model through floor time/interactive play', *Autism: The International Journal of Research and Practice*, 7(4): 425–35.

Williams, D. (1988) *Autism: An Inside-Out Approach*. London: Jessica Kingsley Publishers.

Williams, D. (1992) *Nobody Nowhere*. London: Transworld Publishers.

Williams, D. (1998) *Autism and Sensing: The Unlost Instinct.* London: Jessica Kingsley Publishers.

Williams, E., Reddy, V. and Costall, A. (2001) 'Taking a closer look at functional play in children with autism', *Journal of Autism and Developmental Disorders*, 31(1): 67–77.

Wilson, K., Kendrick, P. and Ryan, V. (1992) *Play Therapy: A Non-directive Approach for Children and Adolescents.* London: Baillière Tindall.

Wimpory, D. C., Chadwick, P. and Nash, S. (1995) 'Brief report: Musical interaction therapy for children with autism: an evaluative case study with two year follow-up', *Journal of Autism and Developmental Disorders*, 25: 541–52.

Wing, L. (1986) *Early Childhood Autism*, 2nd edn. Oxford: Pergamon Press.

Wing, L. (1996) *The Autistic Spectrum: A Guide for Parents and Professionals.* London: Constable.

Winnicott, D. W. (1971) *Playing and Reality.* London: Tavistock Publications.

Wolfberg, P. (1999) *Play and Imagination in Children with Autism.* New York: Teachers College Press.

Wolfberg, P. and Schuler, A. (1993) 'Fostering peer interaction, imagination, play and spontaneous language in children with autism', *Child Language Teaching and Therapy Journal*, 15(1): 41–52.

Wood, B. S. (1981) *Children and Communication: Verbal and Nonverbal Language Development.* Upper Saddle River, NJ: Prentice-Hall.

Wood, E. and Attfield, J. (1996) *Play, Learning and the Early Childhood Curriculum.* London: Paul Chapman Publishing.

Woody, R. (2004) 'Modern family interventions', *American Journal of Family Therapy*, 32: 353–7.

Yirmiya, N. and Sigman, M. (2001) 'Attachment in children with autism', in Richer, J. and Coates, S., eds, *Autism: the Search for Coherence.* London: Jessica Kingsley Publishers.

Yoder, P. J., Kaiser, A. P. and Alpert, C. L. (1991) 'An exploratory study of the interaction between language teaching methods and child characteristics', *Journal of Speech and Hearing Research*, 34: 155–67.

Index